David Elleray began refereeing in 1968, aged thirteen. He progressed through amateur and semi-professional leagues to become a Football League referee in 1986. He was on the original panel of Premier League referees and became a FIFA Referee in 1992. He refereed the 1992 Charity Shield, the 1994 FA Cup Final and the 2001 Worthington Cup Final, officiating at Wembley fourteen times and in over seventy international matches. Highlights include the 1995 World Club Championship in Tokyo, the 1996 Mandela Inauguration Trophy (South Africa v Brazil), Euro '96 and the 1998 UEFA Super Cup Final. He is a member of the FA Council and the FA Referees' Committee, and also a UEFA referee instructor and observer. His duties as a House Master at Harrow School, where he is also Director of Boarding, meant he was not able to referee in the 1998 World Cup Finals in France. He is Honorary President of the Referees' Association of England.

*Also by David Elleray*

Referee!

# THE MAN
# IN THE
# MIDDLE

## DAVID ELLERAY

TIME WARNER
BOOKS

TIME WARNER BOOKS

First published in Great Britain in August 2004 by Time Warner Books
This paperback edition published in August 2005 by Time Warner Books

A CIP catalogue record for this book
is available from the British Library.

ISBN 0 7515 3580 X

Typeset in Sabon by M Rules
Printed and bound in Great Britain by
Clays Ltd, St Ives plc

The author gratefully acknowledges permission
to quote from: *Keane: The Autobiography*
by Roy Keane with Eamon Dunphy (Michael Joseph, 2002)
Copyright © Keanepeak Ltd, 2002

Time Warner Books
An imprint of
Time Warner Book Group UK
Brettenham House
Lancaster Place
London WC2E 7EN

www.twbg.co.uk

To
*Daniel, Douglas and Nicholas*

# Acknowledgements

Synthesising careers in refereeing and at Harrow School has only been possible because of the support of many people.

My refereeing was nurtured by Duncan Jackson and Alan Gausden, and developed under the guidance of two great men, Ken Ridden and John Goggins. I was privileged to share the good and the tough times with staunch friends, notably Peter Jones, Steve Lodge and Martin Bodenham. In my latter years the inspiration of Daniel Bennett was immeasurable as was the love and support of the Keen family.

Throughout my time at Harrow I was fortunate that the Governors and four Head Masters (and Nick Bomford in particular) allowed me more time away than I had any right to expect. I learnt the skills of Housemastering from David Sumner and George Attenborough and have been wonderfully assisted as House Master of Druries by exceptional matrons and tutors, while the interest and tolerance of the Druries boys and parents have sustained me and kept my feet on the ground.

I acknowledge the sacrifices my parents made for me when I was young. My grandmother has been a beacon of light in my life, as have my godchildren, especially Holly, Anna, Emma and Lucy Mrowiec and Katie Bieneman. Their parents, Mel, Vivien, Peter and Lynnette, along with Peter Hunter have been a constant source of encouragement and support.

This book would not have been completed without the professional dedication of John Saddler, Tom Bromley and Richard Collins, or the kindness of the Wojewodzki and Duffy families who let me use their homes to write undisturbed.

I would also like to pay tribute to the several thousand colleagues with whom I have officiated and the players, managers and fans who, with Harrow colleagues, pupils and parents, have helped make my life so colourful and happy.

David Elleray
April 2004

# Contents

# List of Illustrations

Sending off the Brazilian captain, Dunga. (*Pressefoto Rauchensteiner*)

The COSAFA Cup Final, Namibia. (*David Elleray*)

Black tights in the icy waste of Kiev. (*David Elleray*)

Dean Holdsworth thinks the decision is a stinker. (*Action Images/Tony O'Brien*)

Sent tumbling by Nicky Butt. (*Action Images*)

Waving a broken corner flag. (*Cleva*)

In disguise at the 1999 FA Cup Final. (*David Elleray*)

Chatting with David Beckham. (*Sporting Pictures/Robin Hume*)

Chatting with Robbie Savage. (*Action Images/Andrew Budd*)

Showing Roy Keane the red card. (*Action Images/Tony O'Brien*)

Sending off Wayne Rooney. (*Action Images/Brandon Malone*)

The line-up before the final match. (*David Elleray*)

Asking Dave Babski's advice. (*Ross Kinnard/Getty Images*)

Sending off Matthew Upson. (*Action Images/John Sibley*)

A word of thanks from Bobby Robson. (*David Elleray*)

Front jacket image: *Action Images*

Back jacket image courtesy of the author

# *Prologue*

I don't think I have ever felt as proud as I did at 2.57 p.m. on Saturday 14 May 1994. I had just shaken hands with Dennis Wise of Chelsea and Steve Bruce of Manchester United, captains of the respective teams. The coin, an old 10p piece I always used, had spun into the air and fallen as heads so that Manchester United chose which end to defend. The photographs had been taken, I had shaken hands with my two linesmen, Paul Rejer and Graham Barber, and the reserve referee, Gerald Ashby, had wished me good luck for the final time.

I looked round the pitch and took in the noise as it grew to the crescendo which greets the kickoff. It was already even louder than the roar which had drowned out the final bar of the National Anthem. I drank in the atmosphere and knew that the moment I had dreamed of for twenty-six years had come. I tried to clear my mind of the maelstrom of thoughts and images which had assailed me from the moment I had joined the teams in the tunnel. Images of cold, wet afternoons on Dover's recreation grounds merged with those of the marble halls of Highbury and the magnificence of the Bernabéu Stadium. I thought of my proud parents and my friends who were somewhere in the stands and I recalled briefly all those who had helped me reach this summit. I also thought how lucky I was to be standing there about to do something that tens of thousands of referees throughout the world would give anything to be able to do. I was filled with emotion and yet remarkably calm. The National Anthem had been the most difficult. It is impossible not to feel your spine tingle as the music plays and the crowd sings. I could easily have started to cry and yet my preparation for the game was so intense that I also felt as if I was standing apart from it all looking in. I was ready for my lifelong dream to become reality but, before we started, I had one more thing to do.

As 3.00 p.m. approached I knew that the television commentators would be confirming the team line-ups and the likely playing formations. Finally, they would briefly focus on the referee and, just at the time when I thought I would be in shot, in those few seconds before I blew the first whistle, I reached up with my left hand and tugged my left ear lobe. A nervous gesture? No. The boys of Druries, back at Harrow, had asked me to wave to them 'so we know you are thinking of us, sir!' I had told them I could not wave but we had agreed on a sign and this was it.

I blew the plastic, pealess Fox 40 whistle and the 1994 FA Cup Final started. It began with a crash as after eighty seconds Erland Johnsen clattered into Ryan Giggs with such a fierce tackle that, momentarily, I thought of sending him off. There was no great player reaction and I contented myself with the second fastest yellow card in a Cup Final. He was joined in my book by Steve Bruce in the eighteenth minute as Chelsea increasingly dominated the half. In the twenty-fifth minute, while the Manchester United defence was going through a slow and clumsy spell, Gary Pallister cleared the ball straight to Gavin Peacock who, twenty yards out, let the ball drop and fired it against the Manchester United crossbar. By half-time it was still goalless but from my point of view the game had gone almost perfectly.

Manchester United steadily fought their way back into the

game and in the sixty-first minute Ryan Giggs attacked down the left, shimmied towards the penalty area and knocked a perfect pass through Steve Clarke's legs to Denis Irwin. Eddie Newton upended him spectacularly and it was one of the easiest penalty decisions of my career. No one complained and Cantona side-footed the ball past Dimitri Kharine's left hand to make it 1-0.

Six minutes later a crossfield ball from Mark Hughes was picked up by Andrei Kanchelskis and as he ran towards and then into the Chelsea penalty area he was challenged by Frank Sinclair and went to ground. Without thinking what I was doing, I blew the whistle. Was it a foul? Had it been inside or outside the penalty area? My dream was about to turn into a nightmare as, in a split second, I was faced with making a decision, in front of a TV audience of several hundred million, which would haunt me for the rest of my career.

# Chapter One

# *The Early Years*

*'He could give a lesson to many of his elders.'*
CLUB SECRETARY

I had always liked football but became hooked as an eleven-year-old in 1966 when the World Cup captured my attention. England's semi-final against Portugal was unbelievably exciting as Nobby Stiles neutralised the great Eusebio and Bobby Charlton scored twice to secure a remarkable victory. The Final remains one of the most nerve-wracking experiences of my life. When England were 2-1 up I could hardly cope with the tension and during extra time it became too much to bear. England were leading 3-2 and I fled into the next room, unable to watch. Suddenly, my father shouted, 'They've scored again!' Believing Germany had equalised once more I burst into tears, not realising that I was, at that very moment, missing Kenneth Wolstenholme's famous 'Some people are on the pitch, they think it's all over . . . it is now!'

When I went to Dover Grammar School for Boys a few months later I was very disappointed to discover that I was not a particularly competent footballer. I managed to get into the second teams as a right half, but I did not have the coordination to progress to the first team and I was spectacularly unable to head the ball. It was immensely frustrating but as I hated doing anything if I could not do it well I looked for other sporting avenues. I enjoyed rugby but my spindly frame did not really equip me for anything other than scrum half. My best sports were tennis and badminton. While I gained some satisfaction from staying after school and playing badminton or tennis for hours, I was nonetheless drawn to the team games and had a great admiration for those senior boys who were the football sporting heroes. I can still remember one, Graham Oxenham, who, with great ceremony, was awarded his Kent Schools FA badge in morning assembly. There was a lustre about him and the others who wore that Kent badge and, as a twelve-year-old, I was in awe of these sporting 'gods' who seemed to be six and half feet tall. I needed somehow to be like them and I wanted to wear a Kent Schools football badge on my blazer more than anything else.

So when I am asked why I started refereeing the answer, fundamentally, is that it was because I was never going to make it as a player and it offered a way of maintaining an active involvement. Supporting Dover, my local Southern League club, was not enough. Looking back, I wonder if it was the controversy of that third England goal in the 1966 World Cup Final that started it all. I can still remember that moment as clearly as if it was yesterday. Geoff Hurst shoots, the ball hits the bar and bounces down and out, and Roger Hunt turns and celebrates. There is confusion and then the camera pans onto the Swiss referee, Godfrey Dienst, going over to consult the mustachioed Russian linesman, Tofik Bakhramov, with a white belt holding up his shorts. After a moment of confusion he nods and points to the centre circle and the goal is awarded. It was the greatest drama imaginable. Did the sight of the referee and linesmen being on centre stage with the fate of the World Cup in their hands plant something in my mind?

Whatever it was that lit the spark, almost eighteen months later, on 20 January 1968, I refereed my first match aged thirteen years and four months. It was between two third-year house teams from the grammar school. A family friend, Duncan Jackson, who had taught me at primary school, was a Southern League linesman and had given me my first kit; although I was extremely nervous, I at least looked and felt the part. I greatly enjoyed the experience and there was something satisfying about being in control and enforcing discipline. I have always responded well to a disciplined environment and that made me a strict referee and, in later years, a strict schoolmaster. More significantly, I like to be in charge. Whether refereeing attracted me because I was in control or whether it brought out an innate desire for control I will never know. All I can say is that I have never been a very good No. 2 and, in any situation, no matter how hard I try, I always end up taking charge.

I found refereeing very fulfilling and the money meant I did not have to do a paper round to supplement my pocket money. I refereed matches at school and then I became a linesman on the local Youth and Men's Leagues. My first experience of refereeing a men's match came in March 1968 when, aged thirteen and a half, I refereed Customs v British Rail in the Dover and District Wednesday Football League. I have few memories of that match. I had started keeping a record of all my matches so I know that the score was 0-3 at half-time and 0-5 at the end. I did not 'book' anyone nor did I award any penalties. Thinking back on my time as a young teenager refereeing in and around Dover, I cannot recall ever being frightened, intimidated or badly treated by any player or spectator. This is in stark contrast to the abuse and violence that some referees now endure on the local parks. If ever a player started being difficult or argumentative the other players sorted him out. I think they were grateful to have a neutral referee and I was told that people admired me for being brave enough to referee at such a young age.

I loved what I was doing and began to earn a reasonable reputation on the local school and adult football circuit. When I refereed a schoolboy county trial I had already got further than I ever would have done as a player so everything after that was a bonus. I was even awarded that longed-for Kent Schools FA badge in recognition of my refereeing of the game. I have always been an ambitious person so, at this early stage, I set my sights on refereeing the 1998 or 2002 World Cup Final. I was determined to be England's No. 1 referee and from then on I never doubted that I would get there. Refereeing seemed to be my destiny and it increasingly absorbed my thoughts and began to take over large parts of my life. It was a strange thing for a teenager to want to do but I was happy refereeing whenever I could.

I usually did four matches each weekend: a school game on Saturday morning and a men's Dover and District League match in the afternoon. On Sunday morning I refereed in the Hythe and District League and the East Kent Youth League in the afternoon. The local leagues were short of referees so they appointed me to games but I then received the only ban of my refereeing career when the Kent County FA wrote saying I was unqualified and too young to referee. I was mortified. The letter arrived the day after I had sent off a school friend, Nick Headon, who later became the first drummer of the punk group The Clash. However, the stubbornness of youth and my passion for football meant that I had no intention of giving up.

A few weeks later a KCFA official, D. F. Rawlings, asked me to visit him to take the referee's exam. I passed with a mark of 98 per cent thanks mainly to a local referee, Alan Gausden, who coached me for the exam and was my first mentor. I received a letter from the KCFA saying that I was now a qualified referee but could not handle any games until I was 16. I am not easily defeated and I soon found a solution. When each month's fixtures were sent to the clubs the League secretary would leave a game each week without an allocated referee. I would go to this game and offer my services, so for two years I officiated as an 'outlaw' referee.

I was mad keen on everything to do with football. I remember risking getting into trouble at school whenever a draw was being made for the FA Cup. I put my transistor radio in my trouser pocket and ran the earpiece and wire up under my blazer, along the sleeve into my left ear. I then sat with my head propped on my arm, my hand hiding the earpiece and wire as I listened with great excitement. Even in those days I did not support a major team; I knew I wanted to be a top referee and had to remain completely neutral. Anyway, there were no big teams near Dover so I had no natural allegiance, although I did develop a soft spot for Brighton as my father often took me to watch them when I stayed with my grandparents.

I absorbed all I could about refereeing and I loved watching *Match of the Day* on Saturday evenings. Ideally, my parents would be out so I could watch it on my own. On those occasions I would dress up in my referee's kit and pretend I was officiating. I put my fingers over the top of my whistle so that when I blew it no sound came out. Once this caused me great embarrassment as in my excitement I forgot to cover the whistle and I blew it so loudly that my sister came downstairs and complained about the noise. She was always looking for opportunities to tease me so, when she saw me in my full regalia, she had tons of ammunition and she never let me forget it.

My devotion to refereeing was so great that I no longer indulged in the usual schoolboy activities at weekends. I would get as much of my homework as possible done on a Friday night before meticulously packing my kit in a small, brown suitcase. I made a wooden box for my whistles and watches and I very carefully ironed my kit so that I was as smart as possible. My first kit was heavy black cotton with button-on collar and cuffs. I changed all the white buttons so that, elegantly, I thought, there was a black button in the middle of the white starched cuffs. I also put my black and white Kent County FA referee's badge on a red background to add a bit of colour. In those days it was fashionable among some Football League referees to have a white handkerchief poking out of the breast pocket, so I did the same.

Most Saturday afternoons I would return home after a game and listen to the Football League results. I started to keep scrapbooks of press cuttings about the top referees and each one had his own page. I also kept detailed records for each referee, noting down their matches, the scores and the disciplinary action they took. I arranged for the Football League to send me the monthly appointments booklet and did all I could to find out who refereed a game when the appointed referee was unavailable through injury or illness. I bombarded the Football League with so many requests for information that they eventually wrote telling me that the volume of my enquiries was excessive and they could no longer assist me. On Saturday evenings I would sort out my kit, make sure my records were up to date and then go out with my friends or my girl-friend. I suspect I was seen as something of a novelty or perhaps an oddity but I was so intensely focused on my refereeing that I was not really aware of what my friends thought. I just knew that it was something I wanted to do for as long as possible and after every game I started working out how I could become a better referee.

I was getting so much enjoyment out of refereeing that I wanted to learn all I could about the game. I was worried that not playing meant I did not understand the game from the players' angle and that this might hold me back. I decided to try to find out what the players thought and I wrote to Leeds United, the top team at that time, asking them if I could spend a couple of days with them. I had a nice letter back from Don Revie suggesting I contact some southern clubs; although I did, none bothered to reply. As well as avidly watching *Match of the Day* I loved going to big matches. I remember being taken to watch a game at Chelsea and at the end of the match the crush of the crowd was so great that I was lifted off my feet and carried along for several hundred yards without touching the ground. Upton Park was a regular haunt for my father and me as he always believed that, no matter what the result, 'you always see a good game at West Ham'. I well remember a magnificent match between West Ham and Manchester United which, if my memory serves, was 3-2 to the Hammers. West Ham boasted players like Bobby Moore, Geoff Hurst and Martin Peters while the United team included George Best, Bobby Charlton, Denis Law and Nobby Stiles. I also remember the referee almost falling into the crowd as he tried to get between two squabbling players. I was obsessed with football but I was also greatly enjoying my school work and the general atmosphere at school.

I liked administration and at sixteen I became the fixtures and appointments secretary for the Dover Men's Saturday League. It seems strange, now, looking back to those days in the late 1960s when as a fifteen- to sixteen-year-old I was refereeing and running men's football without any abuse or trouble.

At the end of my second season I had my first taste of international football when I refereed a friendly between Tilmanstone Colliery Welfare FC and Monchy Athletic FC from a mining community near Amiens in France. *The Dover Express*[1] had a photograph of me with the two captains before the game and part of the caption read 'There were smiles an hour and a half later as the captains turned to congratulate the fifteen-year-old referee, David Elleray, on his handling of the game.' 'He could give a lesson to many of his elders,' said Tilmanstone Secretary Bob Cooper. The excitement of doing an 'international match' was enormous and I bored my friends for the rest of the weekend, telling them how well I had handled the game and that I had even understood some of what the Monchy players were saying, thanks to my French lessons at school. Refereeing men's football was very good for my future man-management of players as I knew that adults would not accept me being bossy or officious. One technique I deliberately developed was to fold my arms whenever I reprimanded a player to make sure I did not wag my finger at him. This stayed with me throughout my career and became one of my distinctive trademarks.

There was no doubt that refereeing had taken a grip of me and my thirst for all things refereeing was by now insatiable. I became a cricket umpire and a qualified basketball referee, refereeing inter-house and inter-school matches when I was not needed for football. I studied the referees on the Football League so well that to this day I can still recite, in alphabetical order, the Football League Referees' lists for the late 1960s and early 1970s. My role model was Norman Burtenshaw from Great Yarmouth who was an exceptionally fit and strict referee. I think it was his strictness which attracted me most: when he was in charge of a game there was no doubt that everything would be firmly controlled. He worked very hard at his fitness and always looked immaculately turned out. I enjoyed the controversial Clive Thomas and admired Jack Taylor's man-management of the game.

When you first started refereeing you were a Class Three referee. You then moved up through Class Two and Class One and thereafter your progress was through the senior amateur leagues into the semi-professional leagues and, it was to be hoped, to the top leagues. The levels have different names these days but the system is essentially still the same. Although I had become officially registered as a referee when I was sixteen, I was classified as a 'Youth Referee' until I was eighteen.

Promotion through the lower ranks can be a matter of luck. I refereed sixty matches a season but was assessed on only three. The KCFA chose which three and a former referee would turn up, unannounced, at the game. He would often try to mix undetected with the few spectators so that the referee did not know he was being assessed; this sometimes led to comical circumstances with assessors lurking behind trees or pulling hats down across their faces so they could hardly see the game at all. Of course, such measures rarely worked as we all knew who the assessors were and referees are pretty good at spotting the man with the notebook. If you had a good assessor he would come and chat at the end of the game and give you some advice but often they just scurried off. You did not receive a report and you had no idea whether or not you were doing well. At the end of each game the clubs were required to mark the referee and send this mark to the League, and towards the end of the season the KCFA Referees' Committee looked at the assessments and the club marks. When I first started refereeing the mark was out of four but that was felt to be too limited a range and it was changed to ten. I always came top of the marks league table on the Dover and District League, not because I was the best referee but because the clubs had to send the marks to me as League Secretary and they obviously felt they could not give me a low score.

While refereeing was the most important thing in my life I also loved school, where there were several inspirational masters and a few who were quite the reverse. Without realising it at the time I found myself studying the masters as they went about their tasks. I admired those who were strict and fair, but had little time for those who were nice one day and awful the next. Ken Ruffell was my Geography teacher; he made the subject come alive and was responsible for my love of geography. His arthritis meant that the notes he wrote on the board were difficult to read and when he returned one piece of work he had written something illegible at the end of it. I asked him what it said and he replied, 'I can't read this.' 'Nor can I, sir, that's why I've asked you what it says.' With a broad grin he said, 'You idiot, it says *I can't read this*, but obviously my handwriting is as bad as yours!'

Dover Grammar taught me a great deal about how to get the best out of schoolboys. The disciplined routine gave us security and we were encouraged to try to do our best. My first Head Master was Michael Hinton who, it was rumoured, had a glass eye and was known as 'Cyclops'. He was such a frightening man that when I did an excellent piece of work and was sent to show it to him I was so scared that I never went. What I did realise was that punishments were a great deterrent. I was inclined to be somewhat mischievous but I knew where the boundaries were and never crossed them.

When people debate the rights and wrongs of corporal punishment they often quote the punishment books that show the same boys coming back time and again to be punished. What those books do not show are the thousands of boys like me for whom the cane was a genuine deterrent. My schooldays taught me that there will always be some people who will break rules and others who never will. In the middle are the majority who might, depending on the severity of the repercussions if they are caught. It is this 'middle group' who should be the school teacher's battleground and we should do all we can to stop as many of them as possible from smoking, drinking, bullying, cheating or whatever by having clear rules and clear punishments.

I passed my O levels well and chose Geography, History and French as my A levels. I was confident of the first two, as they were my favourite subjects, and did French because I thought it would help me when I became an international referee. I was appointed a school prefect for my last year. I could think of nothing better than becoming a full-time referee but I had three more realistic careers in mind: teacher, barrister or doctor. Teaching gradually emerged as my first choice and I chose Geography as my university subject even though I enjoyed History rather more. I just felt that Geography would be more interesting to teach.

Towards the end of the Summer Term in 1972 Ken Ruffell asked me if I had considered applying for Oxford or Cambridge. 'Which one should I apply for?' I asked. 'Well, they always say Oxford and Cambridge, so as Oxford comes first it must be the best, so apply there!' Oxford was largely dominated by the public schools but they were keen to take more state school pupils and one of their strategies was to encourage applicants to take the Oxford and Cambridge Entrance examinations in the Autumn Term before A levels, something of a radical change as most applicants took them after A level in what was known as the seventh term. More significantly, if pupils did very well in the entrance exams they would not be set specific A level grades to take up their place.

I would be the first boy at Dover Grammar to try this new entry route and the Head Master told me I could have a go provided I did not get too depressed when I failed. The idea was that it would indicate whether it was worth having a proper attempt after A levels. I took two Geography papers and one General Paper in which there was a gift of a question asking candidates to write about their favourite pastime or hobby. I must have spent most of the three hours in a critical self-analysis about my refereeing and my character. It was probably the first time I had really analysed the psychology of why I enjoyed refereeing. At one point I said the reason I enjoyed the showmanship of refereeing was probably because it was in my genes as my father's parents, and indeed my father, had been on the stage. Granddad was a ventriloquist and Grandma his glamorous assistant in the days of 'variety' before television, when the musical hall was a major source of entertainment. My grandparents knew Laurel and Hardy well and my love of acting certainly came from them. Throughout my school career I was involved in school plays, ultimately playing the part of the Virgin Mary in *The Redemption*, an adaptation of the York Miracle plays. Later in my career I particularly enjoyed refereeing abroad where referees are allowed, indeed encouraged, to be flamboyant in their signalling and their reaction to players.

When I went for my interview at Oxford I was so daunted by the architecture and the grandness of the city that I walked up and down outside Hertford College for a good fifteen minutes before I summoned up the courage to go in. I spent two days intimidated by everything I saw and everyone I met. I had interviews at five colleges and by the end of it all I was absolutely exhausted. I was also exhilarated and desperate to get a place. I knew that I had no chance but the place had overpowered and inspired me and I was determined to try again the following year.

The day the results were announced I was officiating in a Kent v Middlesex Schools match at the Feltham Arena, only a few miles from Harrow. All day I became more and more convinced that there would be a telegram of acceptance waiting for me when I got home. This feeling grew by the hour, but finding out whether or not I had been successful was delayed as thick fog on the M2 meant that I got home several hours late. When I walked into the house I was taken aback that there were none of the hugs or words of congratulations that I had expected. I wandered disconsolately into the sitting room and there on the mantelpiece was a telegram. It read simply *Place. Congratulations. Hertford.* My success left me with a philosophy which I try to pass on to others, especially boys at Harrow and young referees: you should never underestimate yourself. If there is the slightest chance of success, have a go. 'Don't decide you are not good enough when you might be. Let someone else make that decision' is my philosophy. I also believe that it is better to try and not succeed than not try and then spend the rest of your life wondering if you might have succeeded.

My entry to Oxford left me with a great sense of inferiority. I felt that I had got in by a fluke, through an essay on refereeing and because the college was trying to broaden its entry base. The whole of my first term at Oxford was dominated by this inferiority and insecurity to such an extent that I almost had a nervous break-down. By Christmas I had only made three friends and the baying laugh of the public school types, who seemed so confident and assured, did nothing to help my morale. In the end it was make or break and it was a conversation with a fellow student who seemed so confident with work, sport and women which opened my eyes. Here he was, superficially the most together person in college and yet he was more wracked with self-doubt than I had ever been.

My time at Oxford was full of personal discovery and challenge. I overcame my intellectual inferiority complex by working extremely hard and in the university examinations at the end of the first year I gained a 'first class' pass, one of four from

Hertford College which was regarded as probably the best Geography college at that time. Interestingly, one of the others to achieve a 'first' was Barnaby Lenon of Keble College, whom I saw as one of my rivals. Little did I know that twenty-four years later he and I would be rivals for the Headmastership of Harrow. Hertford's reputation was based in part on a dynamic pair of young Geography tutors: Andrew Goudie and John Patten. Both were destined for success – Goudie became Professor of Geography at Oxford and John Patten went into politics, rising to Education Secretary under John Major before quitting the Commons and taking a seat in the House of Lords. I was awarded a scholarship which I celebrated at a sherry party followed by a pub crawl – I have never been so ill in my life but I felt that I had successfully conquered my feelings of academic inferiority and I was ready to take on new challenges.

I felt inspired and full of confidence, threw myself into everything and within a term I had been elected College President. As well as local football, I also refereed inter-college football matches and organised the inter-college football and this administration brought me into regular contact with Professor Sir Harold Thompson, an outstanding Oxford chemist and probably the last dictatorial FA Chairman. Whenever I saw him he had two or three pairs of glasses perched on his nose and he called everyone by their surname. I remembered this when he sacked Sir Alf Ramsey and the press made a great play of the fact that Thompson addressed the heroic England manager as 'Ramsey' whenever he spoke to him. That was the way people of Thompson's generation operated and I was reminded of it when I was appointed to Harrow. The first letter I received after my appointment from the Head Master started 'Dear Elleray'. I was offended as prior to my appointment I had been addressed as 'Dear Mr Elleray'. But more of Harrow later.

That Easter I refereed at the English Schools FA (ESFA) U19 football festival at Skegness with the Kent Schools party. This was the start of many happy years out on the Lincolnshire playing fields refereeing some of the best schoolboy footballers in England. My first match was on the Coronation playing fields (we quickly nicknamed them 'Consternation playing fields') on a cold day where the harsh easterly wind blew rain and snow almost horizontally into our faces. Suffolk beat Middlesex 'C' 3-0 and, unbeknown to me at the time, one of the Suffolk players was Mel Mrowiec, whom I would meet a couple of years later at Oxford, and who would become one of my closest friends and a Harrow colleague. I would also become godfather to his four daughters, Holly, Anna, Emma and Lucy.

I received a letter on 2 May 1974 telling me that I had been promoted and I was now a Class Two referee. I had taken my first step up the refereeing ladder and I was thrilled as I had not yet reached the required age of twenty. I was now faced with a problem of how to get promotion to Class One as in Kent referees were not allowed to apply and had to be 'spotted' by someone or recommended. This was too risky for my liking so I withdrew my registration with Kent and applied to be a full member of the Oxfordshire FA so that I could then apply to them for the next promotion.

That summer brought a great football–work clash as I had my end of year Geography examinations and there were also the World Cup finals in Germany. I got up early to get as much work as possible done before the matches kicked off and I was glued to the students' television in the very room that had caused me so much upset in my first term, when I had watched England eliminated by Poland in that remarkable game at Wembley.

Towards the end of the tournament one of my refereeing idols, Jack Taylor, was appointed to referee the Final between West Germany and Holland. He famously awarded Holland a penalty before a German player had touched the ball but I remember the match for two other refereeing reasons. Taylor did his usual pre-match check just before kickoff and noticed that there were no corner flags. It was incredible that such a simple mistake could be made and reminded me that even on the biggest game you must go through all your routines and rituals. The second interesting point, later revealed in Taylor's autobiography, was the communication system he devised with his linesmen, neither of whom could speak much English. If they wanted him to book or send off a player they had to write the player's number on a small piece of red or yellow card and put beside it G for Germany or H for Holland and discreetly call Jack over and show him the card. I remembered this and used something similar when I refereed in Brazil some twenty-five years later.

The main significance of Taylor's appointment was that it further convinced me that I was destined to referee the World Cup Final. George Reader of England had refereed what was effectively the Final in 1950 and with Taylor doing the 1974 Final I was sure that the next time an English referee would do the Final would be in another twenty-four years – 1998. I intended to be that referee.

My Saturdays were spent on buses and trains taking me to towns and villages around Oxford as I had also become a linesman on the Hellenic League. This had been an exciting step as this was 'senior amateur' football played across much of Oxfordshire, Gloucestershire and beyond. Matches were played on proper grounds with dressing rooms and a small stand and the pitch was fenced off from the crowd. One match I lined was at Moreton-in-Marsh and it took me three bus journeys and a train ride to get there. I set off at 10.30 in the morning and got home at about 8.00 p.m. I loved it, though, as I was experiencing something more than local parks football.

I applied for promotion to Class One at the start of season 1975/6 and I was assessed on three matches, gaining marks of 9.0, 8.0 and 7.5. You needed to average above 7.5, so with an average of 8.16, I was promoted. This was the highest classification you could achieve and, in theory, you were capable of refereeing any match in the country. In reality, you had simply proved yourself to be a senior amateur referee and the progress was now through the leagues. I was still a linesman on the Hellenic League and my next step would be promotion to the Hellenic League referees' list and, as soon as possible after that, a place as a linesman on one of the semi-professional leagues like the Isthmian League. The system is such that you referee at one level while lining at the next league above to give you experience of that higher level of football. If your refereeing marks are good enough then, at the end of a season, you might be promoted from the linesmen's list to the referees' list. You then hope to become a linesman on the next league up.

My first season as a Class One was somewhat frustrating as I did not get promotion to the referees' list of the Hellenic League so the quality of games I was refereeing did not change. However, I re-registered with Kent and received my first ever appointment in the FA Cup, as a linesman for Margate v Sittingbourne in the preliminary round, the first set of matches in the competition. The game was played on 4 September 1976, a day after my twenty-second birthday, and resulted in a 2-2 draw so I lined the replay three days later when Margate won 1-0 at Sittingbourne. I had begun the journey which, almost eighteen years later, culminated in the Cup Final.

That school mastering was my vocation had been confirmed when I undertook work experience at a primary school after my O levels, so as I neared the end of my degree I had to decide exactly what to do. I had been extremely busy as JCR President, refereeing and running the inter-college football, so I knew it was unlikely that I would get another 'first'. Knowing that I wanted to teach I had felt it would be better for me to develop broader interests than confine myself to the library to gain another first. The exams went well and I just missed being called for a *viva voce* to get a first class degree. I had a place at the Oxford Department of Education to do my teacher training certificate but I had also applied to undertake a doctoral thesis in Historical Geography. I was interviewed and rejected by Cambridge but won a scholarship to stay at Oxford. I was wracked with doubt about research so I decided I would postpone it and do my teaching certificate. By this time I had been elected by the graduates as MCR President which guaranteed me a fourth year living in college.

With the teacher training year underway I needed to begin to make decisions about my future. I remember sitting in the college bar late one night joking with a friend about our futures. I had seen a Geography post at Harrow School and he had seen a lecturer's position for Law at Manchester University. We spent a jolly fifteen minutes fooling around pretending we had both got the jobs and would be visiting each other. We agreed that, as a joke, we would both apply and the irony was that we were both successful. I also applied to Tonbridge as I longed to return to my native Kent.

I had decided that if I did not get a good teaching position I would take up my scholarship and study for my Ph.D. Why did I apply to a top boarding public school when I was the product of a state school? I decided that there were three elements to teaching: academic, sport and pastoral care. I knew that I would have greater opportunities in the latter two at a boarding school. Just as important, I had very happy memories of my time at Dover Grammar and felt at home in the school environment.

It was in mid-November that I sent off my applications and the first to respond was Tonbridge. I was invited for interview on a Monday morning in early December but could not travel down until the evening because, as MCR President, I had to read a lesson at the college carol service. I arrived late at night and the next morning sat down to breakfast with the Head Master, Christopher Everett. He had come late into the education system having been in the Foreign Office, serving, most notably, in Washington during the Kennedy era in the early sixties when Lord Harlech was British ambassador.

A simple, state-educated young man from an ordinary background, I felt completely out of my depth as I was offered kippers and the morning paper at breakfast. I tried to strike up a conversation with the Head but it soon became clear that this was not on the menu. The whole morning was a grilling experience with Everett asking me why Geography should be taught in schools and the Head of department giving me A level Geography papers and asking me to explain what answers the questions were looking for. I was drained as I left and convinced that I had failed, although I had greatly enjoyed the day, not least lunch in one of the boarding houses.

I returned to Oxford somewhat subdued and a few days later I headed off to London for my Harrow interview; it was also the day of the Oxford v Cambridge soccer varsity match at Wembley. The Harrow experience could not have been more different. Michael Hoban, the Head Master, chatted amiably as he ran through my C.V. When he came to the football he turned and pointed out of his study window at the rugby fields which were just visible through the trees. 'We have just levelled and drained some pitches for soccer and we now need someone to get the sport going,' he remarked. I was then collected by the Head of the Geography department, Edward Gould, who, within fifty yards of the Head's study, told me the job was mine.

# Chapter Two

# *Moving up the Ladder*

'Linesman, linesman . . . you're going to die.'
MILLWALL SUPPORTER

I arrived at Harrow in autumn 1977 ready for anything but somewhat in awe of the history and magnificence of the buildings. My emotions were similar to those on that day when I had hesitated at the porter's lodge of Hertford College, unsure as to whether or not I had any right to become a member of Oxford University.

Masters at Harrow are known as 'beaks' and wear a suit and gown to teach. Gould had briefed me very well and had made it clear that he would not interfere 'unless there is a riot or your results are dreadful'. As with my refereeing I was determined to make a strong start. One of the punishments at Harrow is called 'double', the School's unique form of lines. Two hundred double is two hundred lines which have to be copied neatly from a text book with at least forty letters per line. One hundred double takes about forty-five minutes. My first lesson was a Fifth Form division and early on one boy, James Cogswill, decided that this new beak was good for a ragging. I decided to make a stand and set him 150 double. Gould had advised that, except for technical offences such as forgetting a book, I should never set less than one hundred. There were apocryphal stories of a poorly briefed Master setting a boy five double and then being persuaded to be lenient and reducing it to two double!

The division seemed rather surprised by my sternness and I had a relatively easy remaining twenty minutes. The rest of the day passed without incident but by the end of it I had a thumping headache. There is something rather intimidating about twenty pairs of adolescent eyes watching your every movement, waiting to pounce at the slightest sign of weakness or hesitation. The next day I had Cogswill's division again and he arrived at the start and announced, somewhat apologetically, that he had lost the double chit I had given him. I suspected that I was being set up, so I gave him a chit for two hundred double, adding fifty for 'losing' the original.

I was a non-resident House Tutor in Bradbys boarding House and I was very lucky to be working with Alan Sankey who was a House Master of the old school. It gave me the chance to see the dying embers of aspects of public school life which were the stuff of Tom Brown and other fiction. Looking back now it is remarkable what went on in the late seventies and what was accepted; it would give today's litigious parents a field day and 'human rights' were rarely given a moment's thought.

Alan had a fantastic sense of what was right and wrong and possessed the most magical 'feel' for school life. He did not have a proactive bone in his body but his reaction to almost everything was spot on and fair. There was no side to him and the boys held him in great respect. Given such traditional views it was no surprise that he was the last House Master at Harrow to use the cane. He beat boys who were caught smoking and I also remember him beating two boys who threw an apple out of a window which hit the windscreen of a passing car. The indignant Indian driver demanded summary justice for what he termed a 'racist' attack. The justice was certainly summary but as one of the boys was himself Indian it is extremely unlikely that the incident was anything other than a moment of schoolboy silliness.

Fagging was still an accepted part of Harrow life and I remember one new boy, Tim Hinton, rushing up to the Head of House's room after Prep to make him a cup of tea and to sweep his floor. If the senior boy was responsible and kind it gave the fag a real sense of belonging; he also had an 'older brother' figure who looked after and guided him. It clearly did Hinton no harm as he eventually became Head of School. Some seniors abused their position and the fags had a dreadful time, being sent on the most ridiculous errands. Like all systems, however, it is the people not the system who are often at fault when it goes wrong.

My major challenge was to re-establish football in the School. Many words at Harrow have an 'er' suffix; for example, exercise is 'eccer' and the boys' blue uniform jacket is a 'bluer'. Association Football was known in Victorian times as 'soccer' as distinct from rugby football, which was 'rugger'. Harrow also has a third field sport, Harrow Football, known as 'footer'; it is one of the ancient school games from which rugby and soccer developed and is played in January and February when the fields are muddy. There are eleven players on each side and they play with a large leather ball which becomes very difficult to kick as it gets heavier as the game progresses. Players are allowed to barge each other as they try to score by getting the ball between two rugby posts known as the 'base'. Many aspects of modern football can be seen in 'footer': ten yards in football and rugby comes from Harrow Football. When the ball has been kicked in the air a player can catch it and shout 'yards' if he wants a free kick at the 'base'. The umpire puts his stick on the ground where the ball was caught, the player runs up to the stick and then takes three big paces and the two-man defensive wall stands where he lands on his third stride, roughly ten yards from the stick. There are throw-ins from the side and no rugby-style tackling is allowed. I greatly enjoyed umpiring Harrow Football as it took me back to the very origins of the game and many of the Laws.

I was blissfully unaware of the controversy that the re-introduction of soccer, after a half-century gap, would generate. Harrow, a rugby-playing school, has a great soccer heritage: Charles Alcock, the man who founded the FA Cup and really got football off the ground in this country, was an Old Harrovian. My arrival at Harrow had been heralded as the rebirth of soccer, which had been an outlawed sport for many years because of the dominance of rugby. In fact, the Master I replaced in the Geography department, Charles Laborde, had been an England rugby trialist and it was rumoured that he would beat any boy found with a round ball. He was not alone in despising the sport and I soon discovered that some rugby people have an almost pathological hatred of soccer. I faced opposition from the 'rugger buggers' and those who thought that soccer would be the death knell of the ancient game of 'footer'.

Encouraged by the Head Master, who was keen to see the new playing fields used for soccer, I set about organising trials and fixtures. However, there were forces conspiring against me in the background. I was given permission to play matches on Wednesday afternoons with only senior boys but my plans were scuppered by the Masters in charge of the School's cadet force and Harrow Football. Both were keen rugby beaks and feared soccer would ultimately threaten rugby's pre-eminence in the School. Welcome to the world of academic intrigue!

There was also an element of snobbery at work as soccer was seen by some as a 'common' game played by 'Kevins', the Harrow boys' pejorative name for local boys. I felt completely let down. I had to cancel all the fixtures and start again with permission to play only on Sundays in the Spring Term. Clearly Michael Hoban felt guilty about the way I had been treated as he phoned me on Christmas Eve, at the end of my first term, apologising for what had happened and urging me to battle on. Thus encouraged, I continued to arrange matches and our first game was against an Old Harrovian team almost exactly fifty years after the last School match had been played at Harrow. The afternoon had a surreal start when four large black limousines parked beside the pitch. I was going through a warm-up routine with the players when one asked to be excused. 'You can't leave the warm up,' I declared. 'I must,' he replied, 'I have to check that my godfather is OK.' 'I'm sorry, but your godfather can wait until after the game to see you.' 'Sir, I am sorry but I have to go because my godfather expects to see me.' 'Well, if he's that important you'd better go. Who is he, by the way?' 'King Hussein of Jordan, sir.' The king watched the entire match. At one point the ball was kicked towards his car. He got out to return it but his bodyguards pounced on the ball quickly, almost as if they thought it was primed to explode.

I organised a number of matches against other rugby-playing schools as the traditional soccer-playing schools such as Eton, Repton and Charterhouse would at this stage be too strong for us. However, an incident at our first away match at Wellington College threatened to destroy the sport. After the game my opposite number was driving me back to the Masters' Common Room when we came across the Harrow 1st XI chanting football songs on their way to the dressing room. To my horror one of them gestured towards the driver and shouted, 'You're gonna get your f*****g heads kicked in!' I asked my colleague to stop the car and as I got out there followed a Chaplinesque scene as boys dived into the nearest bushes leaving the poor culprit on his own. His faced drained and I thought he was going to pass out. I simply said in my iciest voice, 'I'll see you later.'

On the coach home I told the boys that they were not to mention the incident to anyone because soccer's opponents would use it as evidence that the game was bringing the worst elements of behaviour into School. The boy himself was mortified. He was already fed up because as Head of House he had to see the House Master at 10.30 every night to report that all the boys were in bed. This curtailed his regular midweek London jaunts, which were not to nightclubs, but, along with a friend from another House, to The Den. At the time Millwall had a pretty bad reputation for hooliganism and it seemed extraordinary that two Harrovians were regularly bunking out of School to watch games featuring a club with allegedly the worst thugs in English football.

I greatly enjoyed coaching the 1st XI but I was hampered by my inability to demonstrate the moves or skills I wanted the boys to perfect. I was more of a motivator than a coach and, I suspect, my manner was more like Ferguson or Wenger than Houllier or Robson. I got irritated by mistakes and also got cross if marginal refereeing decisions went against my team. I hated losing and really had to force myself to be gracious in defeat. I wanted the boys to enjoy the matches but Harrovians are difficult to coach as they have a great dislike of practising for anything, be it sport, plays, concerts or whatever. However, they always believe it will come good on the day and they certainly have a tremendous capacity to perform when it matters.

I was twenty-three and desperate to move up the refereeing ladder. I was running the line on the Isthmian League and the early rounds of the FA competitions and when I lined for Barnet v Carshalton in the FA Trophy I remember being quite thrilled when I flagged for offside for a goal by Jimmy Greaves to be disallowed. He was making something of a footballing comeback at Barnet after various troubles and was the first big name I had encountered. However, my refereeing was confined to school matches and local leagues as I was unable to get into the promotion system. I needed to be on a Feeder league, and refereeing well, to become an Isthmian referee.

I regularly refereed in the Euroman international tournament in Liège in Belgium and was excited at being involved in football between teams with different attitudes and approaches. I was fascinated by the fact that continental teams had better ball control than the English players and also how they were much more patient in their build-up and preferred to keep possession by playing the ball backwards rather than hoof it upfield and hope that something would develop. I was very proud at the end of one tournament to be awarded the Trophie de Jean Chevalier as 'Referee of the Tournament' ahead of referees such as Joel Quinou of France, who later officiated in several World Cup semi-finals. It was a glimmer of light in what had been a very frustrating first season in Middlesex.

In summer 1978 my luck changed and I started refereeing on a Feeder league, the Hellenic, and began moving up the promotion ladder. I loved refereeing but found lining frustrating as I was not in control. I saw lining solely as a means of getting experience so I was very excited to line to Clive White of Harrow, then one of the top FIFA referees in Europe. This was a time when being in the presence of a Football League linesman, let alone a FIFA referee, was a red-letter day. I was in awe of those officials who had reached the highest level and I hung on their every word and watched them like a hawk during the game to pick up useful points for my refereeing. I did not model myself on anyone in particular but I did watch for things which would improve my refereeing.

At the English Schools Skegness Festival one year I had a wonderful day where George Courtney, who became an outstanding international referee, lined to me in the morning and I lined to him in the afternoon. George was to become one of my role models and it was his air of calm and assurance which I sought to incorporate into my game. My commitment to refereeing was total; for instance, I refereed North Yorkshire v Hertfordshire at Skegness on the Friday afternoon and then drove back to Harrow to referee on the Hellenic League on the Saturday afternoon. I then returned to Skegness, refereed Durham v Greater Manchester on the Sunday morning, and then drove home again in time for the start of term next morning.

Over the next few seasons my refereeing career took off and I began to make a mark. A feature of my two careers over the next twenty years or so was that as one reached a plateau the other progressed so I was fortunate that my ambitions were satiated either by my refereeing or my schoolmastering. I was well established in the Hellenic League but one club, Northwood FC, did not like me at all. They gave me very low marks which threatened my chances of promotion but then suddenly started marking me 10/10 on every game. When I asked why the Secretary said, 'We think you are useless but the League won't get rid of you so all we can do is give you top marks and hope you'll be promoted to another league!' His and my wish came true at the end of season 1979/80 when I was promoted to referee on the Isthmian League.

One aspect of my refereeing that increasingly intrigued me was the great dichotomy between the way I officiated and my reaction to controversy. I will not duck an issue or take the easy way out but I hate being criticised, not because I think I am right, but because I find it hurtful. Logically, therefore, I should have been a diplomatic referee who avoided confrontation and controversy unless it was unavoidable, but the reverse was true. Although I loathe arguments and trouble, I cannot stand by and ignore things which I think are wrong. As a referee you need to develop a thick skin and become inured to criticism and abuse, but that required a somewhat special coping strategy: I appeared to ignore it but it actually hit home. Strangely, I was always able to cope with what I saw as unfair criticism although it would irritate me, but the criticism when I was wrong was the hardest to bear because I knew it was justified.

At the end of season 1981/2 I missed refereeing the Isthmian League Cup Final by 0.01 of a mark. I was fourth in the Isthmian League merit order, above all the Football League linesmen, so I was utterly shattered when five referees were promoted and I was not one of them. My records for that season end with the words 'completely disillusioned' written after the last game. Apparently, referees had to do two seasons on a Contributory league before they could be promoted. I was getting pretty fed up with being held back because I was young but I was determined to make it impossible for them not to promote me next time, and a season later I was again fourth in the Isthmian League merit order. One day I went downstairs to collect my post and there was a letter from the Football League. It was a fantastic moment and I could not wait to telephone my parents and tell them that I was now a linesman on the best league in the world.

My first game was Southend v Walsall and I was delighted that the referee was Mike Taylor whom I knew from my refereeing days in Dover. I have a dread of getting things wrong and I was so determined not to be late that I set off straight after breakfast, having packed and repacked my kit several times. Match officials had to be at the ground ninety minutes before kickoff but I arrived in Southend at around 10.30 a.m. and spent the next couple of hours pacing round the town centre trying to calm my nerves.

I changed in a daze and before I knew it I was out in the middle shaking hands with the captains. It was then time to go to my end of the field and check the goal nets. My legs were like jelly and I was convinced that they would give way before I reached the goal. Although we check the nets as part of the pre-match pitch inspection there is always a danger that they might become unhooked or develop a hole during the kickaround, so it was the linesmen's responsibility to double-check them quickly before kickoff. The players had changed ends and they were all now waiting for me to finish my inspection. I was being punctilious and clearly irritated the referee who gestured for me to get into position.

The match started quietly and I was relieved that I did not have too many decisions to make and those that came my way were easy and, more importantly, I got them right. Then, in the eighteenth minute, Steve Philips of Southend hit a brilliant volley and, as the ball hit the stanchion, the side netting billowed inwards creating the optical illusion that he had scored. I was at that end and knew that the ball had not gone into the net. The referee, ignoring standard practice, awarded a goal without first checking that everything was all right. I knew that I had moved up to a new level of football but it seemed remarkable that goals were being allowed when the ball had not gone into the net. I took up the standard position for a goal kick, level with the six-yard line. Everyone was cheering until Ron Green, the Walsall goalkeeper, put the ball down for a goal kick. The referee looked puzzled and came and said 'What's the problem?' 'The ball did not go in the net so it's a goal kick,' I replied. He looked pretty unconvinced but the Walsall defenders were now protesting and he gave the goal kick. A chant of 'Kill the linesman' went up around the ground and I began to wonder what I had let myself in for; but when I got back to the halfway line the Walsall manager told me I was right and as I got no abuse from the Southend bench I felt reassured.

At half-time I had a huge row with the referee who was probably cross with himself for having given the goal without checking with me first. 'Why didn't you flag straight away? 'I would have done but you gave the goal without looking at me, so what could I do?' It began to get unpleasant and the other linesman intervened and Taylor disappeared into the lavatory for about five minutes. He scarcely spoke to me for the rest of the day. It was a thoroughly miserable first match and my spirits sank even lower when he announced that his next game was Aldershot v Reading the coming Wednesday. I was due to be linesman for that match as well.

By now I had moved into Bradbys as the resident House Tutor and saw boarding House life much more closely. Harrow was beginning to modernise but I still heard the cry of 'boy, boy, boy' as a senior boy summoned a fag to do some petty task for him. The seniors were very approachable and as they were allowed several cans of beer a week I was often invited to 'pop in for a drink after Prep, sir'. The part of the House where the boys live is known as 'the boys' side' while the House Master lives on 'the private side'. The senior boys still had a lot of authority over the other boys and were in a large measure responsible for discipline during prep and for enforcing bedtimes. When I arrived at Harrow I had expected the boys to live in long, stark dormitories but all the Houses have study bedrooms. Two or three boys shared a study bedroom for their first few years but once they were in the Sixth Form they have their own room. Sometimes room-mates get on well but at other times it is dreadful. I remember two boys being made to share and they hung a large, black curtain down the middle of the room and neither ventured into the other's area. However, by half-term the curtain had been removed and they became good friends.

Early in the term I had a major confrontation with a South African boy. He had behaved badly at House lunch and I summoned him to the study and gave him a hundred 'double'. He looked at me with utter contempt and announced, 'If you think giving me double will get my respect you are very much mistaken.' 'I don't particularly care whether you respect me or not but you'll now do two hundred double,' I replied. Several days later he came and asked to talk the matter over as in South Africa it had never occurred to him that he should not respect a master and he was unsettled by my attitude. I explained that I would not demand respect but would hope to earn it. This was new to him but he seemed to accept what I was saying. As we concluded the conversation I asked him what I should have done to gain his respect because I felt the amount of double I had set was quite a major punishment by Harrow standards. 'You should have beaten me, sir!' This explained a lot about him and it was no great surprise when, sometime later, I found him making junior miscreants run round the house squash court until they were totally exhausted while he cracked a bull whip at their feet!

My refereeing was now making great demands on my time and increasingly beginning to impinge on my teaching, especially on Saturdays as there were five lessons followed by School sports fixtures. I arranged with the Head of Geography that other Masters would cover for me if I was away and I tried to keep Saturday absences to a minimum. The Head Master was very supportive and generously said that the progress I was making in football reflected well on the School. Had I not had this support I could not have made the move to professional football and my career would have been stifled. I asked the football authorities to appoint me to more games in the School holidays than in term time and this juggling act became an increasingly important time-management issue for the rest of my career.

I greatly enjoyed Harrow. I coached cricket, tennis and rugby as well as soccer and when I became resident House Tutor at Moretons I learned a great deal from the House Master, David Sumner, who had wonderful values and attitudes but, by his own admission, was a little out of date. I remember being called to his study one evening and finding him almost apoplectic with rage. 'Look, one of the cleaners found this magazine in a junior boy's room. It's . . . bestial!' He thrust it at me and I was expecting some awful Swedish publication only to find it was an old copy of *Knave*. 'David, this is, I'm afraid, very much at the soft end of pornography today.' I told him. 'Well, in that case I'm delighted I've got someone like you to deal with it then!' he replied with a grin. 'I told you I was out of date!!' Five terms later, George Attenborough took over and quickly established a reputation as one of Harrow's best ever House Masters. He was hugely popular with boys and parents. Whenever there was a problem he would invite me down to the study to discuss it. Knowing that he would light his pipe or a cigar as soon as I arrived I would always put on my oldest jumper as I knew I would reek of smoke by the end of the conversation. I would take the 'hang 'em and flog 'em' stance while George was, by inclination, a bit of a softie. We would have a good debate until we met somewhere in the middle. George always dealt very fairly with the boys and, more importantly, never held a grudge or gave a boy the impression that he could not redeem himself. He would condemn the 'crime' but not portray it as a character defect and once the punishment was over the slate was wiped clean. He was a model of correctness and he taught me a great deal about when to wade in and when to turn a blind eye, although he said it was important to let the boys know later on that he had turned a blind eye! I learned so much from George and when I became a House Master I tried very hard to emulate his attitudes and philosophies.

I was thrilled when, in 1985, I was appointed Head of Geography. Running the department would increase my work-load greatly but I was ambitious and delighted to have a chance to begin moving up the Harrow hierarchy. I was also appointed Chairman of the Independent Schools Geography Committee and charged with undertaking a nationwide survey of schools' opinions; I then had to produce a new syllabus for the Geography exam which formed part of the Common Entrance examinations which boys and girls had to pass in order to move to senior public schools. I was also put onto the University of Cambridge GCE Examination Board. My life was getting busy and I had to ensure that the two halves complemented each other and did not overwhelm me.

My lining was also becoming exciting and I was gaining valuable experience of big crowds and top teams. My first Division One match was Ipswich v Southampton on 21 February 1984 and the referee, Dave Axcell, made it a very special occasion for me. As usual, I had arrived very early but so had he and he gave me a full guided tour of the ground and the facilities. The club offi-cials were also very kind and ever since I have always had a soft spot for Ipswich Town FC who remain one of the nicest clubs in senior football. I had my first experience of officiating with a top club seven months later when I was linesman at Luton in the First Division when Liverpool were the visitors. I was in awe of Liverpool, then one of the best clubs in Europe, and when Joe Fagan and David Pleat came into the referees' dressing room to exchange team sheets I became a stuttering wreck, or so it seemed to me at the time. Soon after I went to Watford for a taste of European football, as linesman for England's U16 UEFA quarter-final against France. I did not do especially well and at one point flagged for offside from a throw-in. I think this confirmed in the mind of the FA Referees Officer, Reg Paine, that I was not a top linesman.

Running the line meant that you were very close to the crowd, especially at some of the smaller grounds. You could often hear everything that was said and it was surprising how apparently meek and mild people became snarling and abusive once the game started. One day I was running the line at Crystal Palace when I gave a throw-in against the home team and amongst the usual derisory comments I heard, 'You got that one wrong, sir!' I turned round, something linesmen are strictly forbidden to do, and spotted two Harrovians who smiled and then turned bright red with embarrassment. 'I'll see you two later,' I said sternly and then smiled. A few of the spectators caught on but I had my revenge the next day when it transpired that the boys did not have permission to be at the match and for a few hours I let them think that I would report them to the Head Master. I let them off, not least because it was the only time that I was called 'sir' by an unhappy spectator, although I was often called things soundly somewhat similar. I was given a clear demonstration of the relative value of players and officials in the minds of spectators when I was linesman at The Valley for an FA Cup tie between Charlton and Spurs. Midway through the second half Glenn Hoddle came over to take a corner kick for Spurs and as I stood back to give him room to take the kick a number of 50p pieces were thrown at him. About ten minutes later I gave a contentious free kick against the home team and I too was pelted with coins, except they were 10p and 2p pieces!

On match days I had a light breakfast and then very little else apart from several cups of tea (ideally Earl Grey) and possibly a Mars bar. I once lined at Peterborough on a very cold winter's day and just before the kickoff the referee, Trelford Mills from Barnsley, offered me some whisky saying 'Eee, get that inside thee, lad, it'll warm thee up!' I took a larger swig than intended and by the time the game started I was feeling the effects of drinking on an empty stomach. Whenever I moved my head from looking down the touchline to looking across the field for offside my eyes seemed to take several seconds to catch up. Fortunately, I got to half-time without any mishaps and very firmly declined the offer of another swig.

Lining at Millwall was a testing experience and some might have welcomed a stiffener before a game there. The Den was a cold, intimidating place although the staff were extremely friendly. I had heard many horror stories, the most notorious being when one of my refereeing heroes, Norman Burtenshaw, was knocked over by the fans at the end of a match and there had been the threat of a national referees strike in protest at the assault. There had also been an incident when a linesman had had a manhole cover dropped on him after a game. I lined there when Millwall played Wimbledon in the FA Cup in 1985 and it was one of the most harrowing experiences of my career. I had been warned about the crowd on the open side opposite the main stand but I was not prepared for an afternoon of non-stop abuse. Whenever I gave a decision against Millwall I was roundly abused, spat at and had tea thrown at me. Fortunately, I had been advised to wear an old kit and I was grateful for the protective fences whose future was under review after the appalling deaths and injuries at Heysel earlier in the year.

The spookiest part of it was one fan in particular who spent most of the game walking up and down behind me not screaming abuse but quietly saying, 'Linesman, linesman, look at me. I want you to recognise my face so the next time you see it you will know it's the moment you are going to die.' He later changed this to 'Linesman, I'm going home to acid bath your wife.' I was horrified that so much abuse could take place without the police or stewards intervening. After the game, I recounted it all to the other officials who just smiled knowingly and said I had done the best thing by ignoring it. I wish I'd had a small tape recorder and kept it running and then sent it to the FA. On the way home I reflected on whether fences were needed because fans behaved badly, or whether being caged in encouraged poor behaviour. On balance, given the violence that was also regularly perpetrated outside the grounds, I felt that the fences were probably necessary although they were a terrible indictment of the state of the game and society.

This experience further strengthened my resolve to become a Football League referee as I really did not enjoy lining. In fact, I hated it. I felt isolated and vulnerable. I particularly loathed the admittedly occasional referee who ignored me for most of the game and then pointed at me as if to say 'it's his fault' if something went wrong. I resolved that I would never treat my linesmen like that and I always worked hard to make my colleagues feel important and genuinely part of the team.

To become a Football League referee I had to get onto the Panel List of referees where my potential would be assessed on matches in the Gola League and the Football Combination. How well or badly I did as a Football League linesman did not matter; it all depended on my Isthmian League club marks so getting a good response from players and the clubs was vital. The main problem was that being strict meant I was getting poor club marks. I analysed my performances and decided that while players and managers generally accept referees being strict on physical offences, they get irritated if they are fussy over non-physical matters. If you were quick to book for a passing comment or not retreating ten yards at a free kick but then did not deal with the bad fouls you quickly lost respect. I resolved that as far as possible my first booking in a game would be for a foul and I would try to man-manage the non-physical offences. This quickly brought about an improvement and my rapport with the players steadily got better. As there is generally an inverse correlation between the number of bookings and the mark, my marks began to improve.

In many ways it was an unfair system which favoured those referees who did not apply the Laws of the Game but refereed to please the clubs. It would have been much better if there had been independent assessors who would judge you on your overall performance as clubs tended just to look at the result, disciplinary action and controversial decision given against them. The absence of assessors meant I had to work out for myself what had gone wrong and what I could do to prevent a repetition. It was at this stage of my career that I developed a highly tuned self-analysis procedure which began during the game and continued on my journey home. My focus was not so much so on what I had done well but what I could have done better. Working on weak areas was much more important to me than feeling good about things that had gone well.

At the end of season 1983/4 I refereed the Middlesex Charity Cup Final at Wembley – not the famous stadium but Wembley FC. The match was delayed when a small briefcase was found propped against a spectator barrier and, as this was a time of IRA activity in London, there were fears that it might be a bomb. I got bored with the delay and bravely (or foolishly) picked it up and put it in the furthest corner of the car park. The Bomb Squad were called but the game proceeded without any trouble although I was harangued by the Secretary of the away team afterwards for moving his briefcase! The following day I received a letter telling me that I had been promoted to referee on the Panel leagues and I was thus just one step away from reaching the Football League.

My first Panel match, Dagenham v Maidstone, was much tougher than any Isthmian League game I had refereed. The players were fitter and much more professional and I struggled to keep up with play as I was sticking too rigidly to the diagonal system of running from the corner of one penalty area to the other. I needed to be nearer to the play so I became more flexible in my patrol path and this had some success. At half-time one of the linesmen observed that I seemed to stop on the edge of the penalty area as if it was a shark-infested pit and that I should continue into the area on some occasions to be closer to play, especially if there was the likelihood of a confrontation. I was grateful for the advice.

I had a succession of difficult matches but worked very hard at all aspects of my refereeing and learned a great deal. The hardest was Maidstone v Weymouth, in which I booked seven players; I had never worked so hard in a game. I had rarely had so many bookings so I was greatly concerned that I had not got the measure of the game. However, when the assessor's report came through it was glowing and what had been, in my mind, a make-or-break performance gave me the confidence that I could referee at that level and, perhaps, even higher. I was particularly thankful that my future was no longer determined by club marks. I was assessed on every game and a few days after each game I would receive a two-sided report which would comment on all aspects of my refereeing, notably match control, fitness and positioning, use of the advantage, application of the Laws and cooperation with the linesmen.

Gola League matches were usually tougher than the Football Combination games which were often used by the Football League clubs to test young players or to give match practice to senior players coming back from injury. There seemed to be an unwritten agreement that neither side would be too physical so that players would not miss out on a chance of getting back into the first team through injury. Some matches were tough, especially the local derbies, and in November I booked four players when Spurs played West Ham; one of the culprits was Paul Ince of West Ham with whom I would have many future battles. I often saw teams on a regular basis and once refereed at Millwall three times in six days. One game was abandoned after twelve minutes because of a downpour which left the pitch flooded and the players joked that Arsenal were 3-0 up only because they were playing with the tide. I returned three days later and had to send a player off for 'foul and abusive language' when he swore at me so loudly that it echoed round the almost empty Den. I was quite tolerant of what might be called 'industrial language' as many players routinely swore in their normal conversation and I did not believe that I should be the upholder of outdated Victorian values as far as language was concerned. I only dismissed a player if I thought his intention was to be abusive so it was not so much the words he used but the tone and facial expression which I judged.

In April 1986 I was invited by the Football League for interview in Blackpool. I was grilled by Graham Kelly (Football League Secretary), Jack Wiseman and Ken Ridden from the FA, and John Goggins (Football League Referees Officer). I was only thirty-one and one of the early questions was whether I was too young and inexperienced to take the next step. I said I been refereeing for over eighteen years and had officiated in more than a thousand matches so I was sure I was ready. In fact, I was desperate to take the next step. They then said that George Courtney had just been taken ill and could not referee Everton v Manchester United that evening; would I be prepared to do the game? I agreed and was downcast when they said they were not serious but were merely testing my self-confidence. At the end of the interview I was told that the result would be posted in about a week's time.

It seemed to take an age for the letter to arrive and when it did I was just about to go off to referee a reserve match at Fulham. I had not been expecting any post that day so it was a shock to find the envelope at the bottom of the stairs with a Lytham St Annes postmark. Memories of opening and reading school and university results letters flooded back. I was so nervous that for about five minutes I just looked at the unopened letter. Would my dream come true? If it did, I would be the youngest Football League referee in the country and the first one young enough still to be on the list in the twenty-first century. If it did not, I would be cast into the depths of depression, not least because the Isthmian League were threatening to demote me for not doing enough games. That really would have been the end of my hopes of becoming a top referee. I eventually summoned the courage to open the envelope and got no further than the opening words, 'We are pleased to inform you that . . .'

I was on.

# Chapter Three

# *Making My Name*

*'We may be useless but we don't cheat.'*
DAVID ELLERAY

The thrill of becoming a Football League referee at the age of thirty-one grew as the summer passed and I felt exhilarated rather than daunted by the challenges that lay ahead. I started on Friday 12 September 1986 at Colchester United. The visitors to Layer Road were Torquay United and Peter Clayton, a close refereeing colleague, drove me to the match so that I could focus on the game and not worry about negotiating the Friday evening rush-hour traffic. I was pensive but when I reached the ground I became professional and focused.

I was outwardly calm when I walked onto the field but deep inside I was unbelievably nervous. As we were about to kick off I noticed the home team goalie making an illegal mark with his studs in the middle of the six-yard line as a reference point for the centre of the goal. Should I begin my Football League career with a yellow card before the game had even started? I did not want to begin with a pedantic technical booking and ignored it, although I am still troubled that my first Football League decision was to duck an issue. Ironically, that was something that I was rarely accused of over the next seventeen years.

The game seemed so fast and furious that I did not have time to draw breath. I went through the ninety minutes on a pure adrenalin rush. Colchester were too strong for Torquay and took a commanding 2-0 half-time lead and added a third in the second half. I remember very little; it all passed in a flash. My predominant memory is of the bright floodlights and hectic end-to-end football. I felt like someone trying to swim rather unsuccessfully against a very strong current. I had some say in what was going on but I was not sure I was in full control. There was no controversy and the highlight of the game was an excellent hat trick from the young Colchester midfielder, Tony English. I was assessed on every game and I was delighted when my assessment arrived a few days later and it was very complimentary. I was sent a copy of the local newspaper which commented on several players being booked by 'fussy referee Mr Elleray who is in his first season on the League list'.[2]

I had refereed the game strictly by the book, as was my style at that stage in my career. I was well known on the Isthmian League but I was unknown on the Football League and felt I had to be strong otherwise the players would take advantage of my perceived youth and inexperience. New referees usually take more disciplinary action than the more established officials, because they lack the confidence to 'take a chance' and the players sometimes try their luck with a new official. It is exactly the same at Harrow and every other school in the country. A new teacher takes time to become established and the pupils will try to see what they can get away with. Established teachers already have a reputation ('Don't mess with Elleray, he can be a real bastard') and so there are fewer problems and less disciplinary action is taken. Of course, there are always exceptions and some referees remained rigidly strict throughout their careers while others, like Peter Jones and Keith Hackett, had a natural ability for man-management and a people-based philosophy which quickly led to fewer problems and greater respect. I was keen to make a name for myself as a no-nonsense referee as quickly as I could.

My next match, Peterborough v Crewe, produced my first Football League sending off – Mark Nightingale of the home team. I had booked him for hauling down Gary Blissett in the twenty-seventh minute and when he clattered into a challenge five minutes from the end I had no option but to dismiss him. My strict stance continued with four yellow cards, all for fouls, as Southend beat Rochdale 5-3 and I then went to Molineux for Wolves v Tranmere, incredibly in a Fourth Division match. The first booking was the Tranmere goalkeeper, O'Rourke, who came out of his penalty area to handle the ball (deliberate handball to stop an attack was not a sending-off offence then). Ten minutes later an extraordinary incident occurred. Wolves were attacking and lobbed the ball over Tranmere defender Ronnie Moore, who jumped up, caught it and put it down on the ground for the inevitable free kick and booking. I blew the whistle and Moore started walking towards me. However, a Wolves player saw a chance to catch the Tranmere defence napping and quickly took the free kick. What was I to do? The player had to be booked but if I stopped play Wolves would suffer. They had already had a good attack stopped illegally and now their forward was breaking clear with a chance to score. I had a split second to make a crucial decision. I decided that the spirit of the Laws allowed me to let play continue, which I did. Unfortunately, the attack did not lead to a goal and it was about a minute before the ball next went out of play whereupon I booked Moore for the handball, although the press reported it as being for dissent.

I was still refereeing Isthmian League matches which I found difficult. I was on a real high refereeing on the Football League and sometimes wondered what I was doing officiating in front of a few hundred fans at Haringey or Berkhamsted. These thoughts angered me as they were a dangerous sign of confidence crossing the line into arrogance and I had to be very careful that I did not take it out on the players. Occasionally, a player would dispute a decision and I felt like saying 'Who are you to argue with a Football League referee?' I never said it, of course, and, after a while I regained my mental equilibrium by reminding myself regularly that I was no better than the players and they had the right to a game which was fairly and enthusiastically refereed. I had an extremely tough Isthmian League cup match between Oxford City and Tilbury United which was watched by Dennis Hedges, the Oxford-based Football League referee. He still tells people that after this game he knew that I would get to the top as a referee, although few other people thought the same by the end of the match. It was an entertaining game which Tilbury won 2-3 after extra time and I showed the yellow card ten times, with three players being sent off. The first dismissal came for the home team in the seventy-ninth minute and in extra time Tilbury had players sent off, in the 110th and 115th minutes. Afterwards, the Oxford City Secretary came to pay us. Instead of the usual niceties he simply threw the money on the floor and said, 'If you've any conscience you'll leave it there.'

After a quiet game at Swindon (two yellow cards) and a more lively one at Northampton (four yellow cards, two of them in the fourth minute) in early November I was appointed to my first Second Division match, Reading v Barnsley. One of the linesmen was Ray Pearce whose brother, Stuart, had recently moved from Wealdstone to Nottingham Forest on a path that would take him to the England team and make him one of the country's sporting heroes. The ground was packed and after a few minutes I realised that I had, again, moved up a level. The quality of play was better than anything I had seen in my Third and Fourth Division matches and the players were more aggressive and combative. Midway through the first half Bob Hazell of Reading had a skirmish with Darren Foreman of Barnsley after Hazell had fouled him on the Barnsley left wing. I pulled both players to one side and told them to calm down and not do anything silly. The free kick was knocked towards the Reading penalty area and as it was cleared upfield I noticed Foreman lying flat on his face. I stopped play and called the trainer on to treat the blood streaming from his nose.

Ray Pearce had seen nothing; I was convinced that Hazell had hit Foreman but what could I do? I decided to try a bit of kidology so I called Hazell over and said, 'What did you do that for?' 'It was the only way to shut him up!' came the reply. With that, I sent Hazell off. Technically, a referee can only book or send a player off for something he or one of his linesmen has seen but I have always believed in refereeing within the spirit of the Laws. Hazell was guilty of violent conduct and if he admitted it then that was all the evidence I needed. By the end of the game I had also sent off Paul Futcher of Barnsley for violent conduct after he lost his composure and elbowed Trevor Senior in the face. He had been goaded all afternoon by the home fans because his brother Ron had allegedly elbowed the Reading captain, Martin Hicks, a fortnight earlier. The game ended scoreless not least because, on a flag from the linesman, I disallowed a goal by Barnsley's Dobbin for offside three minutes from time. When Hazell was quoted in the newspapers the next day as saying, 'I deserved to be sent off', I felt thoroughly vindicated.

My strictness next came to the fore at Selhurst Park on a crisp, sunny Boxing Day morning when Crystal Palace (the Eagles) played Brighton and Hove Albion (the Seagulls). There was a noon kickoff to try to prevent crowd trouble as matches between these two teams had a history of on- and off-field violence, as reflected by one reporter who wrote afterwards, 'the referee thought by acting very early he would nip trouble in the bud in a fixture where we have seen some diabolical incidents.'[3] The early exchanges were fiery but a sixth-minute booking for Brian Sparrow of Palace settled things down. There was the occasional booking as the players battled for supremacy but the game exploded in the eightieth minute when Palace's Ian Wright stopped Brighton taking a quick free kick and was pushed by Brighton's Dale Jasper. I booked Wright for his offence but as Jasper had already been booked I had no alternative but to send him off. A further yellow card, for Gavin Nebbeling of Palace, left me with a tally of one red and six yellows. Afterwards, Alan Mullery, the Brighton manager, claimed I had been overstrict, 'He booked everyone – but my missus could have tackled harder!'[4] The *Brighton Evening Argus* reported the next day that 'Mr Elleray tried to make an impression on the game. He did that by the finish, so much so that the 10,365 crowd had run out of seasonal goodwill, and were calling for his blood.'[5] I may have been strict but there had been none of the nastiness of previous matches, although I got no credit from anyone except the assessor. As I reread my press cuttings from these early Football League matches I realise that I was steadily making a name for myself, even if that was not the prime intention. What I was trying to do was referee correctly but, lacking the confidence of a more experienced official, I was booking offences which, later in my career, I would successfully manage.

The third of January 1987 was a great day as it was my First Division debut. Sheffield Wednesday made the relatively short journey down the M1 to receive a 6-1 thrashing at the hands of Leicester City at Filbert Street. It was a hugely enjoyable experience, despite a bad case of pre-match nerves partly brought on when I found out that England manager Bobby Robson was at the game. Why the presence of the England manager made me nervous I cannot imagine; he was hardly likely to give me a second glance! The pre-match nerves had also come from genuine concern at moving up to a new level. Throughout my career I was always working to take the next step up the ladder but when it arrived there was always some self-doubt as to whether I was good enough to perform at the higher level. Until you have tried something you never know if you will be able to cope and the bigger stadium, larger crowd and greater media focus, plus the prospect of refereeing 'famous' players, had all preyed on my mind as I drove to the match. Fortunately, the players wanted to get on with the game without any interference from me and I had only one booking, Lee Chapman of Wednesday, for reacting aggressively in the thirtieth minute. Mirroring my first Football League match, there was a hat-trick for the home team, this time from record signing Steve Moran.

Although I was now a Football League referee, I continued to make myself unavailable in the last fortnight of term and the first week of the School holidays because I knew that I would be mentally and physically tired. I could probably cope with the physical tiredness but the long Harrow terms took it out of me mentally and there was no point refereeing a game if I was not 100 per cent. We are constantly told that if we have an injury we should not officiate but there is little focus on the mental aspects of refereeing. If someone is going through a stressful time at home or at work, they are not really in the right frame of mind to referee. Refereeing can be a great antidote to stress but it is unfair on yourself and, more importantly, on those playing and watching if you are not at your best. I was ruthless about not doing games when I was mentally tired. As well as owing it to the players and fans, there was no point refereeing poorly and getting a bad mark which would cloud the season's performance and possibly stop me progressing further up the ladder.

Referees run about seven to eight miles in a match and need a combination of stamina to keep going for ninety minutes and also the ability to sprint from one end of the field to the other for a quick break. Before each season starts referees have fitness tests and in those days we were required to do the Cooper Test, which consisted of sprints and a twelve-minute run where we had to cover at least 2400m. That distance has since been raised to 2700m. The combination of the long run and the sprints was supposed to be a good test of the different demands made on a referee during a game but these days greater credence is given to multistage tests like the 'bleep test'. I have always been lucky that I have a high level of natural fitness and I hardly did any training during the season as the regularity of matches and coaching sport most afternoons kept me in good shape. It was not until I passed the age of forty that I had to start training and it was an aspect of refereeing which I hated.

A new experience for me was the regular Football League meetings. The newly promoted referees attended a meeting in the Midlands where I was delighted to learn that I was in the top ten in the merit order of all Football League referees. The thirteen new referees included really good friends like Roger Wiseman and Kelvin Morton, and we had a pleasant meal on the Saturday night before the formal sessions next morning. When we assembled after breakfast two of our colleagues were missing. One arrived ten minutes late and the other did not appear until much later. They looked much the worse for wear as they had been drinking until the early hours of the morning and had overslept. Their hangovers were clearly evident and they created a very bad impression. Unsurprisingly, one was removed from the list after only a couple of seasons while the other never hit the heights. Even today, some of the country's top referees are putting their fitness and, indeed, their careers at risk by overdrinking.

Midway through my second season I was the guinea pig in a new assessment scheme. At this time there was no contact between referees and assessors before or after the match and assessors had only recently started signing their reports. John Goggins asked me to meet the assessor, Leo Callaghan, before the Newport v Middlesbrough match. I had a great admiration for the small, white-haired man, having watched him years before immaculately control a stormy Millwall v Hull game largely through the strength of his personality. I was somewhat daunted at the prospect of meeting him not least because Goggins said he was the most cantankerous assessor on the list! We met in a hotel lobby and had a wonderful hour-long chat about refereeing. He was a fund of knowledge and experience but was also keen to hear about refereeing in the 1980s as he felt out of touch with the modern referee.

The game went very well, not least because I was really motivated to do well in front of, and for, Callaghan. Torrential rain made conditions something of a lottery and Middlesbrough snatched a 0-1 victory with a last-minute goal from Tony Mowbray. I had three yellow cards all for fouls. I met Callaghan back at the hotel and he was highly complimentary about my fitness and management of the game. 'I'm glad you are strict, but not fussy,' he told me. He deemed the experiment a great success and several days later Goggins phoned me to say, 'You must be a miracle worker, David! We were sure that Callaghan would kill it stone dead but it's quite the reverse. It looks like it'll become a regular part of the pre-match routine fairly soon.' We discussed various modifications. I felt the assessor should meet all three officials at the ground about ninety minutes before kickoff with the debrief in the dressing room afterwards. This system was introduced selectively later that season and then a full version continued almost unchanged until 2003/4.

One aspect I was working hard on was my relationship with the players. I was routinely likened to a schoolmaster and his pupils and the tabloid media enjoyed suggesting that I treated players like naughty schoolboys. If I had a match where there were a large number of bookings they often said I took names as if I was ticking off the school register. Of course, there are many similarities between refereeing and teaching as both involve a high degree of man-management allied to application of rules and disciplining those who offend. The players were obviously aware of my teaching background and I remember a Southend player after I had issued several yellow cards saying to me, 'I bet you're a tough bastard with the strap at school!' At Harrow, I like the challenge of the cheeky rogues who have character but dislike those who are mean or bullies. I felt the same about the players. The 'fun' players were a challenge but I had no time for the cynical, dirty players who would do anything to win and did not mind harming opponents or the game itself. In both teaching and refereeing you need to identify the 'opinion former' within the group. In the classroom it is the boy who most of the others follow. If you make him behave properly and get him on your side, most of the rest will follow. On the field it is the player who backchats too much or constantly fouls. If you are lucky you have a player, sometimes the captain, who will help you manage the others.

Whenever I booked or sent a player off I had to write a report and send it to the FA within forty-eight hours, giving the offender's name and club and details of the incident. (The word 'booked' does not appear in the Laws – the official term is 'cautioned'.) The offences were put into one of the official categories and for most bookings it was 'ungentlemanly conduct'. Unsurprisingly, when I booked Nigel Stevenson of Swansea for pulling an opponent's hair I classified it as ungentlemanly conduct! The phrase was a nice throwback to the Victorian origins of football and it was a shame that political correctness in the 1990s led to it being changed to 'unsporting behaviour'. Fouls were deemed 'ungentlemanly', as was retaliation, while the other categories included dissent, entering or leaving the field of play without the referee's permission and persisting in misconduct. The sending off offences were persisting in misconduct after having been booked, using foul or abusive language, violent conduct and serious foul play. Serious foul play occurred if a player acted violently when making a challenge for the ball, such as an over-the-top tackle or illegal use of the arm, whereas violent conduct occurred away from the ball, if a player retaliated and kicked, punched or butted a player, for example.

It was nine bookings, a failure to dismiss and a policeman which caused me to hit the national press headlines for the first time when I refereed a stormy Second Division promotion battle between Portsmouth and Leeds United. The main talking point was Supt Bob Dawes confronting me on the pitch at half-time alleging that Leeds' Ian Baird, who once played for Portsmouth's arch rivals Southampton, had made a V sign to the home fans in the twentieth minute. The police wanted me to go to the Leeds dressing room and warn Baird that if he gestured to the crowd he would be arrested and that he might be arrested at the end of the game for the first-half incident. I was not really prepared to be the messenger boy but Supt Dawes insisted so I had a quiet word with Baird as we went out and, as expected, he protested his innocence.

The newspapers were full of the story next day and linked it to the nine bookings and an incident when Neil Aspin of Leeds punched his physio, Alan Sutton. I was criticised for not sending Aspin off for violent conduct but I could understand his reaction as Sutton had unintentionally hurt him as he tried to ascertain the extent of the injury. It led to the rather extraordinary sight of the Portsmouth physio treating his opposite number on the touchline. A consistent thread was now running through reports about my refereeing and this time they said 'nine bookings was more a testament to referee David Elleray's straight-down-the-line performance than anything else'.[6]

Over the next few seasons I steadily established myself on the Football League and I had a series of matches and incidents which brought my name increasingly to people's attention. Although I did not appreciate it at the time, being involved in controversy, while unpleasant, had the benefit of making my name known amongst the players, managers and fans. People are much happier dealing with a known quantity and once you become recognised life somehow becomes much easier. As I progressed through the lower leagues I had discovered that unless you had had a real stinker first time round, clubs and players always treated you with more respect if you had refereed them before. Throughout my career I found that once players started calling me 'David' rather than 'referee' they were more accepting of the run-of-the-mill decisions and I got on with them better.

I received a strange invitation after I 'sent off' a Swindon substitute at the end of a rousing match at Ipswich. As the offence had taken place after the final whistle I could only report John Kelly for committing a sending-off offence. A minute or two later Lou Macari, the Swindon manager, asked me to speak to his team to explain why Kelly had been sent off. I wondered if I was being set up but Macari made his players sit down and listen to what I had to say. I briefly explained that use of the word 'cheat' on its own could have been enough to have a player sent off but when I added the adjectives that Kelly had also used the sympathy seemed to be on my side. It had been a very worthwhile exercise and it is a pity it does not happen more often.

I still had a lot to learn and when I walked out to referee Arsenal v West Ham in late September 1987 I had the biggest case of stage fright of my life. I think reality suddenly hit me as I stood in the centre circle at Highbury, about to take charge of some of the best players in the Football League under the gaze of more than 40,000 people, the largest crowd I had ever refereed in front of. My legs felt like jelly and then went so heavy that I did not think I could walk, let alone run. The feeling was akin to one of those nightmares you have in which you are being chased and when you try to run away your legs won't move. It was an incredibly frightening experience and I was convinced that when I blew the whistle to start I would find myself rooted to the spot. It took me about fifteen minutes to get back to normal.

My next two Division One games gave the press something to write about. In the first I sent off Lee Chapman in Sheffield Wednesday's 3-0 defeat at Nottingham Forest. He went for telling me to 'f**k off' after I had penalised him for a foul. I was very quick to show him the red card and afterwards wondered if I had been trigger-happy. There was some press debate about someone being sent off for what many would regard as industrial language. The underlying implication was that, as I taught at Harrow, I was out of touch with the realties of the football world but I felt that Chapman had been deliberately abusive. Law XII required referees to dismiss a player for 'foul or abusive language' but no particular words were specified. Referees use their own judgement and the tone of the voice and the look on the face are as significant as exactly what is said.

The boys at Harrow loved it and on the following Monday morning they had pinned on my form room door all the press cuttings from the *Sun* and the *News of the World* under a heading 'Des does some sending off' with the critical bits highlighted (for some obscure reason my Harrow nickname is 'Des'). They even highlighted a piece which reported that forty soccer fans had been arrested after they ran riot in a city centre and labelled it 'And look at what trouble he caused'. There was not a lot of geography done that morning.

The comments gnawed away at me and brought to mind something Clive White had once said: 'You'll never make it as a top referee as you have too posh an accent.' While being at Harrow gave me an enhanced status with officials and administrators, I had to be careful not to alienate myself from the players by appearing to be a toff who was not on their level. I was not going to lower my standards and start swearing, not least because I would not be very convincing if I did, but I needed to turn being at Harrow to my advantage. Referees who are 'characters' have a greater chance of establishing a good rapport and reputation with the players. I decided I had to become more approachable and try to introduce more humour into my game. I would also be very careful never to appear overofficious or dictatorial. Beyond that, there was not much I could do although I resolved to try not to be too sensitive to verbal comments from players.

When I returned to Fratton Park in November for their match against the defending champions, Everton, Portsmouth had gained promotion and I was hoping for a quieter afternoon than on my previous visit. The crowd were voluble from the start and both teams became increasingly frustrated as neither side was able to score. I always get concerned when after half an hour or more no one has scored as the players and crowd tend to get irritated and often turn their frustration on the referee. I managed to maintain fairly good control until the closing minutes when Portsmouth, losing 0-1, lost their heads. Kevin Dillon, who I always found a very difficult player (he would never listen when you tried to reason with him), argued vehemently against one of my decisions and as I had already booked him I had no option but to send him off. This brought the crowd to fever pitch. Their hostility transmitted itself to the players and within three minute Mick Kennedy elbowed Peter Reid in the face and I sent him off too.

The crowd were incandescent that two Portsmouth players had been sent off and I had to decide where to be when I blew the final whistle. Should I blow it close to the tunnel and sprint off the field, risking being caught up among angry managers, trainers and substitutes, or should I be in the centre circle and let the players leave first but risk being attacked by the spectators? At the end of the game linesmen are expected to go to the referee as quickly as possible so that they leave as a team. This gives some degree of security in numbers and also means that there are three pairs of eyes and ears should anything unpleasant occur. I decided it would be undignified to rush off so blew with the majority of the players between the tunnel and me. The stewards and police escorted us off to a cacophony of boos and abuse, and I was grateful for their vigilance as several objects were thrown. We stayed in the dressing room for a long time to allow the crowd to disperse but there were still a few die-hards around when we eventually went to our cars and we were pleased that we had the police with us.

Unsurprisingly, the Portsmouth manager Alan Ball, repeated his complaint about referees being heartless and the *Sun* was full of negative quotes from Ball who said, 'Referees have been the bane of my life since I was seventeen'[7] and Dillon who said 'David Elleray was too young and inexperienced for the game'.[8] It was the worst day of the season, and several newspapers ran headlines saying 'It's War', going on to claim that 'Soccer broke into almost open war between clubs and referees yesterday, when NINE players were sent off'.[9] At least there was some variation on the 'taking names like a teacher's register' press comments as the *Liverpool Echo* reported that Dillon was 'unlucky to walk, falling victim to the overfussy David Elleray, whose notebook at the end of the day resembled an electoral roll'.[10]

However, if ever a match helped me make my name it was in February 1989 when top-of-the table Millwall entertained title favourites Arsenal at The Den for the first time in the First Division. Several weeks before the game I was asked to take part in a programme for Granada TV's *Out of Order* series. The intention was to look at the treatment of referees by comparing my game at Millwall with a local league game in Bristol. The unique feature of the programme was that both referees would wear microphones so that everyone could hear the sort of things players say to referees. The FA had always refused permission as they were afraid of what the microphone might reveal. There were lengthy discussions and I said that I was happy to take part as the focus of the programme was going to be on the need to tackle the abuse and violence meted out to local parks referees. The Football League gave their blessing and both clubs were contacted and agreed to take part. I waited and waited for the FA to make a decision but they would not do so. I telephoned them three times the day before the game but they did not return my calls and, in the end, they took a supine stance of not saying yes or no. This was typical of the FA who at this stage had shown themselves to be lacking strength of purpose on many issues, not least tackling the scourge of hooliganism.

I was not too worried about what the players might say as everyone in football knows that players swear. You only have to lip-read on *Match of the Day* or listen when you watch a football match at any level to be aware of the bad language. I was more concerned that in the heat of a very tense match I might say something I would regret. A tough match was anticipated and Arsenal were certainly not relishing visiting the small ground with its hostile and intimidating atmosphere. There was a huge police presence and the match was being beamed live to much of Scandinavia where football was enjoying a winter break. The sound engineers came and fitted the microphone as discreetly as they could to my referee's shirt and I wore a small belt round my waist which held the battery. As I went out for the start several Millwall players gave me a knowing look and one said, 'You'll never have a quieter afternoon than today, David!'

The match started in a crescendo of noise and the exchanges were firm but fair. By the end of the game I had booked two Arsenal players, Michael Thomas for a foul in the fiftieth minute and David Rocastle in the fifty-fifth minute for sustained dissent, which included calling a decision 'crap'. There had only been one major incident when, in the second half, during a scrabble in the Millwall goalmouth the home keeper pulled the ball back from the line and Arsenal thought they had scored. Neither I nor my linesman was sure that the whole of the ball had crossed the line so play continued. There were so many protests from Arsenal that to calm things down I whistled loudly and awarded a free kick to Millwall. I then moved up towards the halfway line for the next phase of play and as Tony Adams ran past me he said 'You cheat!' I gave a great long blast on my whistle and called Adams over. In the few moments before he reached me I had to decide whether or not to send him off. My instincts told me to manage the situation so I said, 'Once we've made a decision we will not change it. I'm not having you call me a cheat.' Adams replied, 'I'm frustrated', to which I responded, 'OK, you're frustrated but there is a variation of words you can use and cheat is not one of them.' Adams then said, 'The linesman should make those decisions', and I ended the exchange with, 'We may be useless but we don't cheat – all right?' He laughed like a drain and the incident was forgotten. Arsenal emerged 2-1 winners and everyone seemed happy as there were lots of handshakes and pleasantries from the players. In fact, as we left the field one Arsenal player, Lee Dixon, put his arm round my shoulder and said, 'Well done, David. You had a great game.'

I had largely forgotten about the microphone as my focus

and concentration were so intense that I blocked almost everything else out. Indeed, in some games I hardly noticed whether it was raining, such was the extent of my concentration. Moving through the leagues I became increasingly adept at blocking out crowd noise and clearing my mind of incidents so that if I made a mistake I did not let it prey on my mind.

There had been an amusing moment at half-time enjoyed by those who think referees are robots rather than human beings when the sound engineer announced, 'David, I've just come to change your batteries.' In my post-match TV interview I said I genuinely felt that it had been a typical First Division game and one in which, apart from the Rocastle dissent, I had enjoyed a good rapport with the players and they had given us very little trouble. However, the papers were full of headlines like 'Livewire Referee Shock' and 'Referees Bug Swearing Players'. The papers also reported that there was a growing belief that match officials should be wired for sound to provide evidence at disciplinary hearings in what would be football's next step into the age of technology.

I went up to Manchester a few weeks later to view the programme with John Goggins, and we were delighted with the interesting contrast between the local game and the Millwall match. They showed Rocastle's dissent but also one or two lighter exchanges with the players. The only debate was whether to remove Adams' 'cheat' comment. I felt there was a danger that players everywhere would believe that calling a referee a 'cheat' was acceptable as what is seen on television is very quickly replicated on the local parks. Goggins was keen that it stayed in and said, 'If we keep it in then it will show the PFA and others that referees like you, who are less established, can referee sensibly and do not automatically reach for the book every time someone says something. It will also be good to see you using humour as a way to deal with a heated exchange.' I was persuaded.

When the programme was televised I was confidently looking

forward to a really interesting programme which might help referreeing at all levels, but as soon as it started there was something wrong. The local game had gone and Tommy Docherty was now presenting. The theme was still abuse of referees but the new angle was that it was no surprise local referees got a tough time when a top team like Arsenal treated referees so badly. All they showed were the players arguing with decisions. David O'Leary was seen haranguing a linesman and the David Rocastle dissent was shown in full. What aggrieved me most was the bleeps that they had put in to cover up obscenities. This gave the impression that the players were swearing more than they had. They even twisted an amusing incident after the game when George Graham, the Arsenal manager, came for a moan but retreated hurriedly when he saw the cameras and lights. Docherty commented, 'George Graham would have been better off trying to discipline his players than have a go at the referee.'

I was unaware that the newspapers had highlighted the programme that morning. The *Daily Mail* had a headline of 'Arsenal Stars In TV Shame' and the report said, 'In a five minute television film, three of Arsenal's most respected internationals are seen haranguing referee David Elleray at Millwall. Elleray, the first referee to be given a microphone, is labelled a "cheat" and one decision dismissed as "crap".'[11]

Arsenal went on the defensive saying that they had not given their permission for me to wear a microphone. In reality, the club had agreed but the message had obviously not got through to the players: unlike them, the Millwall players were angelic all afternoon. The 'cheat' debate raged in the press and at referees' meetings up and down the country. Opinion was divided. Mike Foster, assistant secretary of the Football League, put the exchanges into some context when he rightly said, 'If a referee was to take action against every player who swore, there would be very few left on the pitch.'[12] Some saw it as an indictment of the national game and called for retrospective punishment of Adams but in the end the only person who was criticised was me. The FA did not approve of the way I had treated the players and I have to admit that whenever I watch the programme I cringe at my aggressiveness and the way I talked down to the players. I come across as a stroppy, pedantic schoolmaster telling the players to 'Come here!' or 'Go away!'

The microphone had also picked up me saying 'Stand up!' in a real schoolmasterly way to Tony Adams after the 'cheat' comment. Players sometimes bend down to fiddle with their boots or pull up their socks when the referee starts to talk to them. This is designed to demonstrate a lack of respect and I always insisted that the player stood up. In extreme circumstance I would take a step back and gesture for the player to stand up before I continued to talk. Such actions by referees are often misinterpreted as arrogant but few people would tolerate speaking to someone who deliberately looked away or bent down in open defiance. However, the tone of my voice was not conducive to treating players respectfully and this was not the only example exposed by the programme. There was one moment when I was booking Thomas and another Arsenal player came up to make his point and I waved him away with a dismissive gesture as I said, rather pompously, 'Go away, I don't want you, go away!' The boys at Harrow quickly picked this up and for weeks afterwards I would hear them repeating these words behind my back and waving their arms in the same dismissive manner.

# Chapter Four

# *Getting to the Top*

*'David Elleray, the man who put the "off" into official, sprang back into his familiar groove.'*

THE OBSERVER[3]

By the summer of 1989 I was firmly established at Harrow and on the Football League. My sights were now on the next step up in each career. I was desperate to become one of Harrow's eleven House Masters and even more determined to be a FIFA referee. As with all professions, the further up the pyramid you go the fewer places are available, but I was not content with being one of the top eighty referees in the country. I wanted to be one of the ten FIFA badge holders and ultimately England's best.

I trained very hard while holidaying in Hong Kong but I was somewhat distracted by developments at Harrow. Sir Alan Outram was due to retire as House Master of Druries in August 1991 and his successor would be appointed soon. Apparently, I was on the short list to succeed him. The first week of term passed without any indication of the Head Master's thoughts and every time the phone rang or I received a letter in the

School's internal mail my heart missed a beat and I was pleased that I had my refereeing to take my mind off things.

On Saturday 9 September I refereed Bournemouth v Newcastle in the Second Division. It was a challenging game with Dean Court filled to the gunnels. My mind was clearly distracted by the events at Harrow and I did not referee especially well. I drove back unhappy with my performance and thinking the worst about my chances of getting Druries. I had a miserable weekend. On the Monday I taught two evening lessons and then went into London for a referees' meeting. I got back at about 10.30 and, as I opened the front door, I almost trod on a small white envelope with the Head Master's distinctive italic writing on it. This was it. As with the Football League letter I sat at the bottom of the stairs and my hands shook. I turned the letter over and over and my blood ran hot and cold wondering what it said. I carefully opened it and read:

> Dear David,
> I would like you to succeed Alan Outram as House
> Master of Druries in September 1991. Please let me know
> if you accept and, if you do, who should succeed you as
> Head of Geography.
> > Yours ever
> > Ian Beer

I was elated and for the next few minutes I just sat there reading the words over and over again. I read them so many times that I can still visualise the exact wording of the letter. The appointment was announced the following afternoon and that evening I was on supper duty in the School Dining Hall. As I wandered round I walked into the Druries area and the whole House stood up, applauded and cheered. I was really touched but soon brought down to earth when I moved into the Moretons area next door where I was subjected to good-natured booing and hissing.

This was one of the happiest times of my life and certainly the best piece of Harrow news I ever received. From the start of my Harrow career I had felt an affinity with boarding House life and knew that it was an onerous but immensely privileged position to be in. Being a House Master gives you the opportunity to touch the lives of so many youngsters and help them find their way through adolescence and into manhood. Adolescence, I believe, is the most crucial stage of development because the teenage rebellion sees them reject all previous values and opinions and, as they assert themselves as adult individuals, they take on new attitudes and values. The House Master is in the unique position of being able to influence those values and my role would be to imbue the boys with the values of honesty, kindness to others and a determination to do their best at everything.

Boosted by this news, I felt more and more comfortable with my refereeing and I sensed a growing acceptance from the players and clubs. I now wanted to gain as much experience as possible and try to establish myself as the best referee in the country. I developed strategies to cope with the press and the criticism; instead of rushing to read what every paper had written, I contented myself with the broadsheet reports which focused on the game in a less sensational way.

However, my confidence was tested to the very limit when I refereed a First Division match at White Hart Lane between Spurs and Luton. I was looking forward to the game as I got on well with both teams. The match started fiercely with a heavy first minute challenge and after eleven minutes I booked Luton's Darron McDonough for bodychecking Gary Lineker. The tension rose or, as one paper put it, 'the atmosphere became polluted'[14]. Two minutes later Spurs' Steve Sedgley clattered into Iain Dowie who reacted aggressively and I had to use all my powers of persuasion to calm them down before I could book them. I gave them one of those long lectures which rile the crowd but create time for tempers to cool. The ploy failed and ninety seconds later Spurs' Nayim steamed into a tackle and was booked. The game was on the brink of spiralling out of control. I steeled myself and for the next few minutes penalised every sign of foul play. I was trying to bring the game under control by being exceptionally intolerant and strict. I did all I could to present a calm façade so that, even if I was panicking like mad underneath, I gave the impression that I was in complete control of myself. The crowd did not like the incessant whistling but I had a large measure of success and the play became less frenetic.

Unfortunately it did not last. I penalised Nayim and he refused to retreat ten yards from the free kick and let loose a volley of invective and a series of obscene gestures. I had no alternative but to show him the red card which I did from a distance as I sensed he was on the verge of losing total control. He was ushered from the field and the temperature rose again. I was in for a difficult sixteen minutes until half-time. I was doing my best to calm the players down and some were responding when, out of the blue, Pat Van Den Hauwe of Spurs launched himself into a two-footed tackle which was one of the worst I have ever seen on a football field. He took off in the direction of Dowie leading with both feet, travelling through the air at waist height, in an assault out of a Bruce Lee film. Mercifully, he hardly made contact otherwise Dowie could have been seriously injured. I quickly reached for the red card, hoping to avoid a mass confrontation. Everyone was very angry, the Luton players with Van Den Hauwe and the Spurs players at me for sending him off. The crowd went berserk and I was subjected to a barrage of abuse for the next eight minutes, quelled only temporarily when I booked Marvin Johnson of Luton just before half-time. I did not have to indicate how much additional time there was so I played virtually none as everyone needed to get off and calm down. As I went up the tunnel Paul Gascoigne confronted me with a volley of abuse before he was dragged away.

I reached the dressing room and slumped on the bench with my head in my hands. 'What am I going to do?' I thought. I had first to decide what to do about Gazza. I would have every justification in sending him off for foul and abusive language as referees have the power to book or dismiss players for offences committed at half-time. However, I could not find the courage to dismiss him; in fact, I was having real difficulty even contemplating going out for the second half. The storm of abuse as I left the field had really got to me and for the only time in my refereeing career I was afraid of going back out. My confidence was severely shaken and I seriously considered handing over to one of the linesmen. I spent five minutes in mental turmoil. It was a watershed in my career because if I could not find the strength to complete the game I would be finished. Could I throw away everything that I had achieved and forsake all the opportunities which lay in front of me? Yes, I could because I was not sure I could find it in me to go out and face forty-five minutes of more abuse and venom. I felt completely broken.

Then, before I really knew what was happening, one of the linesmen rang the bell for the players to go out and I was walking down the tunnel and back into the cauldron. The crowd greeted me with a torrent of abuse but I somehow found an inner calmness and knew that I would be all right. The game quietened down and the players started to play football. The private battles were more subdued but just as I thought everything was fine Ceri Hughes of Luton committed a very bad tackle on Gary Lineker and I had no alternative but to show the red card for the third time. It turned out to be the only disciplinary action I took in that half and the game finished quietly with Tottenham winning 2-1 and 27,000 people going home wondering who on earth this David Elleray was. The assessor was Brian Daniels, a marvellous, straight-talking former military policeman and in his post-match debrief he simply said, 'Great. If they behave like that you're right to sort them out. Anyway, it makes sending the reports cheaper 'cos you did so many they can go by bloody parcel post!'

I don't think anyone knew how close I had come to surrendering. It was a seminal moment for me. I had faced down my own particular demons and found the mental resolve to see the task through. I never again felt so low during a match. Somehow, I knew that never again would I contemplate running away from a situation and that gave me great strength, not least in some challenging moments on and off the field in the next thirteen years.

Needless to say, there were lurid headlines and graphic descriptions of events. Van Den Hauwe's tackle attracted some of the most extreme comments. One paper said it gave 'a new horrific meaning to the over-the-top tackle'[15] while another described it as 'elephantine'. Generally, the press were quite supportive of the action I had taken and I am sure that that was in part because I had been prepared to speak to them afterwards, something which referees were largely discouraged from doing. The most interesting article was in the *Guardian* where David Lacey wrote, 'The match survived as a spectacle because Elleray did not hesitate to reduce the numbers to nineteen through a strict but necessary application of the laws.'[16] It was a perceptive insight into the game and the role of referees. I am sure that this article and the generally favourable press coverage marked something of a turning point in my career as my style of strict refereeing was increasingly seen as being acceptable, if not vital, as the professional game struggled with ugliness on and off the field. The link with my being at Harrow was irresistible for some, and one predictable headline was 'Master canes the bad boys'[17].

I began getting more exposure on television and also with the big teams, particularly Manchester United, who would feature in some of my best and worst refereeing experiences. On Boxing Day 1989 I travelled to Villa Park for one of the biggest games of my career to date. It was the first of the thirty-six times I refereed Manchester United; for some reason most were away games. Aston Villa were riding high in the League but United were in the middle of a barren spell and were slipping towards the relegation zone. Villa Park was already quite busy when I arrived some three hours before kickoff and it was no surprise when the police delayed the start. After a twenty-five-minute delay we kicked off in front of Villa's largest crowd since their Championship winning days in 1981. As I blew the whistle to summon the captains I could still hear the police helicopter hovering above the ground telling those still queuing that the ground was full.

The first half posed few problems which was probably a good thing as I was almost transfixed by the huge crowd and the array of talent on show which included David Platt, Brian McClair, Mark Hughes and Paul Ince. Manchester United sorely missed the injured Bryan Robson and crumbled in the second half, conceding three goals in fifteen minutes, with Platt creating two and scoring one. Villa moved into third place and the papers the next day commented that Alex Ferguson's position would be under increasing threat if his team's ineptness persisted into the New Year. The game had been my first 'big match' test and I was pleased that I had not been distracted by the noisy crowd or famous players. As I drove home I had a warm glow inside knowing that I had been on the same pitch as some of England's best players and, while not an equal, I had been there in my own right and had been up to the occasion. It had been a wonderful experience being in the midst of the great glamour which surrounds Manchester United. I was on a real high because I had not felt intimidated and the match had been uncontroversial.

My first visit to Old Trafford came when I was reserve referee for their Rumbelows Cup semi-final with Leeds United. I was in awe of the stadium. The referees' dressing room was the best I had seen and I was impressed that, in addition to the bath towels, we each had a Manchester United dressing gown hanging on a peg. The following season I got my first chance to referee there. I was staying with friends and at about 8.30 a.m. I got a call asking me to get to Old Trafford immediately as there were concerns about the pitch. Although it was only 9.30 when I arrived there were already several hundred fans milling around outside. Manchester United's pitch was not at its best and I trudged out onto an almost flooded surface. As I stood in the centre circle with water coming over my shoes it was clear that there was little prospect of playing. The club said it would be very helpful if I could make a decision before 11.00 as that was the time when the local police would be reporting for duty and when the catering operation swung into full action.

I was just about to call it off when Alex Ferguson appeared at the end of the players' tunnel, which in those days was on the halfway line. He shouted, 'David, what's this nonsense about the game being in doubt? The pitch looks fine.' 'Come out here, Alex, and see for yourself!' I retorted. Looking thunderous he started marching onto the pitch. He was not wearing Wellingtons and after about ten yards he stopped and declared, 'Well, what are you waiting for? We can't play on this!' His face then broke into a broad grin and he chatted to us for a while and arranged for the linesmen and me to have an early lunch in one of the club dining areas. This was the first of many occasions when I was able to enjoy his company away from the tension of the match. He was charming, knowledgeable and very understanding about the pressures on referees. He also admitted that he knew he seemed a different person during and after matches but I got the impression that, at least on some occasions, his 'rage' was staged. The newspapers could not avoid a sly dig at my 'hard man' image and the *Observer* commented, 'David Elleray, Judge Jeffreys with a red card and whistle . . . only uttered his catchphrase "Off" once yesterday . . . (to) leave the pitch devoid of players, something even he has failed to achieve in a competitive game – yet.'[18]

I saw another example of Ferguson's soft side when I went there for an FA Cup replay with Southampton. I arrived early and as I reached the dressing room with Bill Davis, who ran the Harrow Combined Cadet Force and who was a great Manchester United fan, we bumped into Alex Ferguson. I introduced Bill and explained why he was with me and the next thing I knew Ferguson had taken him off. Bill did not reappear for forty minutes as Ferguson personally gave him a conducted tour of the dressing rooms and the main parts of Old Trafford. It spoke volumes for Ferguson's kindness that he could do that a few hours before a major match but he was in a very different mood at the end of the game.

Old Trafford was full to capacity and a cracking match ensued. I was determined to stamp on any signs of the nastiness that had punctuated the first match. Ferguson had surprised everyone by dropping his top striker, Mark Hughes, for the relatively unknown eighteen-year-old Ryan Giggs. The talking point of the match came in extra time when a Bryan Robson header was cleared off the line and the Manchester United fans and players claimed that it was a goal. I was in the standard position for a corner kick, about sixteen yards out from the goal line, and could not see if the whole of the ball had crossed the line and the linesman, who was standing behind the corner flag, did not flag. TV evidence was not totally conclusive but the balance of probability suggested that I should have given a goal. The game went to penalties which the FA had introduced to tackle the fixture congestion problem. As I blew the final whistle an enraged Ferguson stormed onto the pitch haranguing me about the 'goal' and also claiming that I had played eighty seconds short. This was one of Alex's early run-ins with referees over the amount of additional time allowed.

Technically, when the penalties were being taken the only people allowed on the field were the twenty-two players but Ferguson was in such a rage that we decided it was not worth risking a major confrontation by sending him to the touchline so he was allowed to stay on the pitch to watch. When Ryan Giggs came forward to take his kick Southampton were leading 4-2 and he had to score to keep United in the FA Cup. Tim Flowers pulled off a fine save and United were out, the first time a First Division team had been eliminated from the FA Cup on penalties.

Seven weeks later I had a glimpse of the United of the future when I refereed the FA Youth Cup semi-final between Spurs and Manchester United. Playing for United that day were Gary Neville, David Beckham, Nicky Butt and Robbie Savage. Manchester United won 2-1 and proceeded to the final which they also won, to lift their first but by no means last major piece of silverware for Alex Ferguson.

Referees usually start the season strictly, especially if there are Law changes, and then ease off as the season progresses. My senior refereeing career followed a similar pattern and I started off strictly but became more relaxed as the years passed. In the early 1990s I was still towards the stricter end of the scale. I opened season 1991/2 at Highfield Road where Coventry were due to play Manchester City. It was baking hot in Coventry and as I wandered around the pitch I thought the goals looked rather small. We called the groundsman who measured both crossbars and found that they were about six inches too low. I told him to sort the problem out and spoke to the Coventry Secretary who said they had played two pre-season friendlies and no one had complained. They said nothing could be done so I said that I would have to call the match off. That seemed to do the trick and within thirty minutes the goals were regulation size.

Manchester City won 1-0 but only after I had issued what were probably the first four yellow cards of the season. After ninety seconds Andy Pearce (Coventry) flattened Niall Quinn with a bad, late tackle and within seconds Andy Hill (Manchester City) deliberately pulled back Kevin Gallacher. Three minutes into the season and two yellow cards. The niggling continued and two minutes later Gallacher was fouled by Keith Curle, Man City's £2.5 million close-season signing from Wimbledon, and reacted aggressively, leaving me with no option but to book them both. What a start to the season's hostilities! I was not totally surprised because no matter how much pre-season training the players do they need time to adjust to the pace of the first competitive game of the season and understandably some tackles are fractionally mistimed. The searing heat did not help tempers either and I was pleased that I was supported by both managers afterwards. Coventry's Terry Butcher said, 'Both sides were lucky to finish with eleven men. I thought the referee handled it very well',[19] while Man City player-manager Peter Reid said, 'I would like to pay tribute to the referee. He took strong action in the opening minutes when he booked four players and that was exactly what the game needed. He calmed down a potentially explosive situation.'[20]

Ten days later I was at Selhurst Park for Crystal Palace and Wimbledon. The two clubs were by now sharing a ground – you cannot get a more 'local derby' than that. The match was later dubbed, quite wrongly, the 'Battle of Selhurst Park'. The early exchanges were pretty fair and there was no malice or hostility. Ian Wright of Palace lost his cool and was booked for dissent but all was quiet until the thirtieth minute when Nigel Martyn, the Palace goalkeeper, raced out of his penalty area and flattened Robbie Earle with a dreadful tackle and I sent him off for serious foul play. The crowd were unhappy and Steve Coppell, the Palace manager, was so irate that I had to go across to the dugout and calm him down.

All proceeded quietly until just before half-time when a goal-bound shot from Palace's Mark Bright was handled on the line by Terry Phelan and I had no option but to send him off. It was the sort of sending off that no one disputes but people feel is harsh as the 'offence' is not violent or unpleasant. Indeed, I shrugged my shoulders as I raised the red card and Terry smiled weakly and trudged off. However, while not violent or aggressive in one sense it is one of the worst offences as it strikes at the heart of the whole purpose of football – scoring goals. Stopping a certain goal illegally can change the outcome of a match and a penalty is not always full recompense as it might be missed or saved. Moreover, the penalty is the 'team' punishment and the red card is the 'player' punishment. If I had my way, I would award a 'penalty goal' and then there would be no need to send the player off or the risk of the penalty not being scored.

So much had happened that I had to add on nine minutes at the end of the half. There was a strange atmosphere at half-time. The statistics – three goals, one penalty, one yellow and two red cards – suggested a fearsome local encounter but this was not the case. The second half continued just as strangely. I was greatly helped by booking Wimbledon's Roger Joseph who committed a rash challenge after twenty-five seconds of the second half and the yellow card reminded everyone to be careful. Midway through the half Vaughan Ryan of Wimbledon committed a series of fouls resulting in him being booked in the seventy-seventh minute and sent off five minutes later. So for the second time in eight months I had issued three red cards in a First Division match. It had certainly been a local derby to remember but the three dismissals belied a contest which had generally been played in an excellent spirit. Indeed, the players embraced warmly afterwards.

For the second match running I was supported by both managers. Wimbledon boss Ray Harford said, 'I think he had a good game. He kept control and had to send the players off. I certainly didn't agree with the crowd abusing him. He was only doing his job.'[21] Steve Coppell, always a very thoughtful manager, felt that the stricter guidelines given the referee at the start of the season were to blame as he rightly predicted that I would attract a lot of criticism: 'David Elleray will get dog's abuse in the papers but he's only doing what the FA are telling him to do.'[22] He went on to comment about the danger of referees becoming 'robots' and losing their flexibility to use 'common sense'. He said 'Shades of grey are no longer part of the game. There are not many opportunities for referees to say "Well, I'll use my noddle". The FA are doling out robot referees which no one wants.' It was very pleasing to have had such public support from four highly respected managers; it gave me confidence that what I was doing was right and I was steadily earning the respect of those actively involved in the game, regardless of what the press might be saying. David Lacey again supported me, commenting 'Elleray's strictures managed to produce a passably entertaining game. Not that Elleray is one of Coppell's refereeing androids . . . he is his own man with his own distinct style of controlling games – a personality amongst referees.'[23]

For days afterwards the debate about the strict refereeing, which

had been prompted by Italia '90 being littered with foul challenges, raged. I found myself thrust into the centre of the
controversy and felt confident enough to speak out about the
choice football faced. I believed that football could not have it
both ways. Referees had been criticised for being inconsistent,
with players and managers claiming they did not know where they
stood as the same foul would be a booking one week but not the
next. The authorities had decided it was easier for the players if the
referees were consistent. Referees were operating with a higher
degree of consistency but were being called robots. The added
problem was a small group of lenient referees who were not following the agreed line. We dubbed them the 'alternative' referees;
their inconsistency made it more difficult for players and managers adjusting to the new, stricter interpretations.

Problems generated by changing football's disciplinary regime
resounded with me at Harrow as I prepared to take on Druries.
Boys are remarkably conservative and do not like change, so
every new House Master faces difficulties as he attempts to
stamp his imprimatur on the House. Having always wanted to
be a House Master, the two-year lead-in gave me time to prepare, but it was also very frustrating as I wanted to get on with
the job as quickly as possible. Patience is not my greatest virtue.
In mid-July 1991 I got the keys to what would be my home for
at least the next twelve years, the standard period of tenure.
Druries has a wonderful west-facing garden and I spent several
very pleasant early evenings with a glass of wine reading through
the boys' files. Alan Outram had been an immaculately firm
and fair House Master and I was taking over a well-run House.
I decided early on that the best way to get the boys on my side
was to entertain them a great deal and show as much interest as
possible in what they were doing and achieving. I felt that the
House was a sleeping giant and gave a great deal of thought to
what I would say to the boys on my first night as House Master.
     At last it was the first day of term. The new boys arrived at

about 5.00 p.m. and the rest came back in dribs and drabs. Some parents dropped in to wish me well or to give me their son's pocket money or his passport. Amid the routine of these visits I had a meeting with one mother which brought home to me the enormity of being House Master to sixty-three boys. I will always remember her opening words: 'You don't know me but my three sons are in Druries. Their father is dying of a brain tumour and we are all going to need your help.' The boys knew the gravity of the situation and she was keen that I should do all I could to support them and allow them to get on with their lives, but also have time and contact with their dying father. The conversation had a profound effect on me and the rest of the term was overshadowed by the father's decline and eventual death.

Just before 9.00 p.m. the bell rang and the boys assembled in the hall, known as the 'call-over room' from the 'call-over' (roll call) which precedes breakfast and follows supper. There was a firm knock on my study door and Matthew Raynham, Head of House and Head of School, invited me through. Inside I felt as if I was about to walk out to referee the Cup Final and I steeled myself for what I knew would be, for me at least, a key moment in my House Mastership.

The Head of House read out each boy's name and they each answered, 'Here, sir!' in time-honoured fashion. I had a few routine notices and then it was time to give them my vision for Druries. I made it a rallying cry based on tradition and expectation. I reminded them that Druries was the first of the large boarding Houses to be established, as evidenced by its proximity to the Old Schools, site of the original school building. I mentioned eminent Old Drurieans, like Lord Byron and Lord Palmerston, and I then told them that Druries, in the words of the House song, is 'oldest and best', and my aim was to work with them to ensure that it remained so. The message seemed to go down well and there were cheers and applause as I left the room, or at least that is how I like to remember it!

I had strong views about how a House should be run, having

learned so much as a resident tutor for George Attenborough and David Sumner. Druries had been most efficiently run so I resolved to observe things before I started making changes. I was glad I did because, in the end, I did not materially change many of the routines as they worked well and the boys were content. Too much change causes insecurity, an emotion strong enough in many adolescents anyway. I was pleased not to be refereeing too much as I needed to focus on the House. The boys accepted me remarkably well.

I worked hard to motivate the boys but towards the end of the term I was aware of some tension. I had a visit from Raynham and his deputy who told me they thought I was on the boys' side far too much and that I should leave them to run things. While I could understand their feelings I was determined that the House would not lapse into a boy-run oligarchy. I said I would go round the House whenever I wanted as I was ultimately responsible to the Governors for the running of the House and, while I would never do anything to undermine morale, I had to make sure discipline was kept. My frequent appearances were because I was interested in the House and not because I was being a 'policeman'. In reality, they were just trying to see if they could get the new, 'green' House Master to take his foot off the pedal and give them more freedom to do what they wanted.

Almost as important as becoming a House Master was getting onto FIFA. A few years earlier FIFA had announced that the retirement age for international referees would change in January 1992 from fifty to forty-five. This meant that England would lose five of their ten FIFA referees – George Courtney and Keith Hackett (who had been our top referees for almost a decade) along with Allan Gunn, Neil Midgley and Brian Hill. I was desperate to fill one of the places and felt I had a good chance as I was top of the rankings. Among other names being mentioned were Steve Lodge, Gerald Ashby and Mike Reed. I knew that the FA Referees Committee was due to decide in early September.

On the second day of term I returned to Druries from morning lessons and found two messages from Steve Lodge telling me that he had heard from Colin Downey, Secretary to the FA Referees Committee, that he was being nominated for FIFA. I was stunned that I had heard nothing as I really thought I had a strong chance of being nominated. Later, Steve phoned again to say there had been a mess-up at the FA and that I should not worry. I did, of course, until a letter arrived telling me that I was being nominated for the FIFA panel of referees. My pleasure at being nominated was increased when I learned that Gerald Ashby and Martin Bodenham, as well as Steve, were also being nominated. I admired all three and counted them among my closest refereeing friends.

The next few days brought a stream of congratulatory letters from all sorts of people, but my greatest pleasure was the joy my nomination brought to my parents and grandmother. My father was always very proud of my refereeing and I felt I was repaying him and my mother for the sacrifices they made to put me through school and university. I reflected on how much my refereeing meant to me but also what it meant to my parents. My mother loved going shopping and having friends tell her that they had seen me on television, and my father probably bored his friends to death with stories about my matches.

I first had to pass a fitness test and would not get any appointments until 1992 as the FIFA panels run for the calendar year. The reality of the nomination dawned when we met at Crystal Palace athletics stadium. I hated fitness tests and I was more nervous than I had been for a long time but the thought of representing my country overseas carried me through. The tests were conducted by Ken Ridden, Director of Refereeing at the FA and a member of the UEFA Referees Committee, and knowing his standing in the football world, when we passed we knew we were on as no English nomination had ever been rejected. My FIFA badge, a double globe showing all the continents with the word REFEREE above and FIFA 1992 underneath, arrived in mid-December. It had once been the case that you only got a

FIFA badge after refereeing three full internationals so some FIFA referees never wore one. I felt seven feet tall as I strode onto the field the first time I wore it and thereafter it was always a very special moment when I fixed it to my shirt.

Running parallel to this excitement was the growing tension about what would happen to referees with the inception of the FA Premier League. The new league offered the clubs great financial rewards which would increase the pressure on referees whose decisions could, in theory, cost clubs millions of pounds. My records for season 1991/2 vividly demonstrate how the fortunes of individual clubs can change dramatically. I had three consecutive First Division matches involving four teams no longer in the Premier League: QPR v Wimbledon, Luton v Crystal Palace and Notts County v Aston Villa. For clubs like these the desire, indeed urgency, of being part of the lucrative Premier League was great and the end of season relegation battles were all the more fierce, as were the promotion encounters at the top of the Second Division.

I had all this very much in mind when I was appointed to a very tough match on the last day of season 1991/2. It was a Second Division game at Filbert Street between Leicester City and Newcastle United, the latter managed by a beleaguered Kevin Keegan. The different fortunes of both teams hung in the balance. Leicester were assured of a place in the play-offs but if they won and Middlesbrough drew or lost at Wolves, Leicester would be promoted to the Premier League. In contrast, Newcastle had to win to be certain of avoiding relegation to the Third Division. The atmosphere was electric and I have a marvellous photograph of my colleagues and me leading the teams onto the field through a balloon and ticker-tape welcome. The Newcastle fans were squeezed into one corner of the ground and the police were very worried about what would happen if either side lost. There were more than five hundred on duty, many in full riot gear. I loved the atmosphere and relished the challenge of keeping control of events on the field.

The tension caused the players to make many mistakes, creating consternation among the fans, but the errors also produced some very exciting moments. Every attack had one set of spectators in anguish and the others cheering wildly. The first half was deadlocked until, seconds before half-time, Leicester's Steve Thompson underhit a backpass to his goalkeeper. Gavin Peacock, looking yards offside, raced onto the ball and the linesman, unaware that it had been played by a Leicester player, raised his flag. I waved him down and allowed play to proceed. Peacock scored and the goal was greeted by hundreds of Geordie fans invading the pitch in joyful celebration. There was nothing hostile about the invasion, which held up the restart for several minutes, but it was a worrying indication of how difficult it would be for the security people and police to prevent further incursions.

The contest had been very fair, with only one yellow card, and the excitement continued in the second half with the Newcastle fans confidently taunting and abusing the Leicester hordes in the Kop to their left. Seats were being ripped out and as the match moved towards the final stages the exchanges between the fans were turning hostile and ugly. In the eighty-ninth minute the Leicester captain, Steve Walsh, equalised with a simple header and hundreds of home fans invaded the pitch to share his celebrations. The stewards eventually pushed them off the field but were unable to get them into the stands so I allowed play to restart with hundreds standing on the touchlines. Newcastle were now under pressure and I booked Warren Barton for time-wasting. The ninety-minute mark arrived and I had six minutes of additional time on my watch, most of it because of the pitch invasion. The air was shrill with piercing whistles as the Geordies urged me to put an end to their misery and confirm their survival in Division Two.

With ninety seconds to go, Walsh again scored, but this time in his own net and the Newcastle fans went absolutely wild. Hundreds streamed onto the pitch and the players and I ran to the tunnel to avoid being trampled. The pitch was a sea of ecstatic fans in black and white shirts but I had a dilemma as there were still ninety seconds left to play. The riot police formed a thin blue line between the warring fans and skirmishes were breaking out everywhere. The Tannoy announcer was desperate: 'Get off the pitch. If you want us to have to play behind closed doors next season you are going about it the right way. Get off the pitch. That's the green, grassy stuff.' It was frightening stuff and it was later reported that Newcastle's former Leicester striker, David Kelly, had taken refuge among the Newcastle fans until two policemen could escort him to safety. Brian Hamilton, the Leicester manager, and Kevin Keegan were clearly concerned for the safety of their players and met me in the tunnel. They both said, almost in unison, 'That's it, isn't it, David?' 'Yes!' I replied. Kevin, in particular, was delighted and we all sought the refuge and peace of the dressing rooms. On my way up the tunnel the senior police officer said, 'You're not intending to go out again, are you.' It was a statement rather than a question.

I wrestled with my conscience because I had not played the full ninety minutes. No one else knew that I had, in a way, not fulfilled my duties. I thought things through and came to the conclusion that what I had done was morally acceptable. The results from the other crucial matches had come through and no team had suffered as a result of the final ninety seconds not being played; no one had been robbed of an outright place in the Premier League. If I had resumed play there would only have been time for one goal, so even if Leicester had equalised the match would have finished 2-2 and Newcastle would still have survived. More pragmatically, it would have been very difficult to get the field cleared and to do so for what was effectively a pointless period of play could have caused the police and security people huge problems. I felt satisfied with my decision. In the event, Leicester did not win the play-offs but Newcastle had survived and this was the start of an incredible renaissance for them. Meanwhile, I readied myself for the start of the Premier League.

# Chapter Five

# *The Premiership Starts*

'*Elleray insists hard-line discipline is the only answer.*'
TODAY[24]

The introduction of the FA Premier League (known simply as the Premier League or Premiership) and my elevation to FIFA transformed my refereeing career. It was fascinating to be one of the original Premier League referees and be actively involved as it evolved into what is arguably the greatest football league in the world. Certainly, it became the most avidly watched and wherever I went on international duty I regularly came across people with an encyclopaedic knowledge of the Premier League and its clubs.

Before the season started I refereed a pre-season testimonial match between Dover and Crystal Palace. It was an emotional experience officiating on what, when I was a youngster, had been the local hallowed turf of Crabble Football Ground. It brought back memories of walking up the steep slope to the Tannoy playing the *Grandstand* theme tune. Palace won 3-2 and it was a real joy mixing with some of the spectators before and after the game as well as receiving their compliments and good-natured banter during the game. On one occasion, I gave a dubious corner to Palace and one youngster shouted, 'Oi, ref! You won't last long on the Premier League if you give decisions like that!'

The inception of the Premier League brought many changes. A small group of Football League referees were selected for Premier League matches and I was delighted to be one of them. As part of the Premier League marketing we were forced to abandon the traditional smart black and white kit for the controversial 'green shirt'. The new kit design was appalling: the green shirts with thin black stripes resembled pyjamas. Even worse, the shorts were very short and tight which did not flatter some of the more substantially built referees. The green shirts had generated huge controversy at the FA where the traditionalists wanted to keep the black shirt with white collar and cuffs. The problem was that some clubs had diversified their range of kits and had chosen dark blue or black which clashed with the traditional referees' outfits. Commercial interests won the argument but, having refereed in almost every colour possible, I still believe the black shirt with the white colour and cuffs is by far the smartest.

To comply with FIFA statutes which said that the control of referees must be in the hands of the National Association (the FA) and 'independent of clubs and competitions', Ken Ridden was also appointed as FA Premier League Referees Officer. Ridden published the appointments on a monthly basis and it was always a moment of real excitement when the lists arrived. I used to cover the pages with a piece of paper and slowly move it down the pages checking each match carefully to see which game I had. Previously the tension had been about whether I had a First Division match, but now it was the quality of the matches that caused the suspense.

The Premier League referees regularly spent a weekend together to review progress and also discuss any problems which were becoming evident. While refereeing is essentially an individual activity, rather like golf or athletics, we were also part of a 'team' because if someone made a major error it reflected on us all. Ken Ridden took us through videos of incidents from matches, using a balance of good practice and mistakes. He very skilfully created a supportive atmosphere where referees were confident enough to talk about their mistakes without feeling under pressure. The aim was to identify why errors had occurred and establish what action the whole group would take if certain incidents occurred in future games. We looked, for example, at illegal use of the arm and attempted to agree on the distinction between offences which merited only a free kick and those which required sterner action. In general, we agreed that if a player led with his arm or elbow near an opponent's face then it was a yellow card, but where the arm or elbow was used as a weapon the player should be dismissed.

A significant change was that the removal of financial restrictions on travel expenses meant I could now referee anywhere in the country. The distances I travelled increased significantly. For example, I drove to Manchester one New Year's Eve, refereed at Old Trafford the next day, drove home afterwards and returned the following day to referee at Maine Road. It might seem strange driving back and forth but the alternative was to stay in an hotel for three nights. This change meant that I refereed at northern clubs much more often and it was later followed by the relaxation of the practice of the referee being 'geographically neutral'. Previously, I only refereed teams like Arsenal if they were playing another London team but now I could do Liverpool v Arsenal. This meant I was away from Harrow much more so it was therefore something of a relief when, from season 1994/5, Premier League referees no longer officiated in the Football League. I was sad as I had many friends at the Football League clubs but it gave me a few more free weekends when I could be at Harrow.

I also began to see the same teams more often. In the previous six seasons I had refereed Manchester United three times and Liverpool and Leeds one each. In the Premier League's first five seasons I refereed United seventeen times and Leeds and Liverpool sixteen times each. Seeing teams more frequently affected me right from the start as, having refereed Liverpool at Wembley in the Charity Shield, my first Premier League game was at Anfield. I then refereed Aston Villa twice in the space of five weeks. The second time was when Manchester United visited Villa Park when almost 40,000 spectators watched the teams play out a sensationally exciting game with the action ebbing and flowing from end to end. I played huge amounts of advantage and had three yellow cards – Bryan Robson, Paul Ince and Gary Parker – indicating the intensity of the struggle. Ince and Robson were very hard work as they were highly combative in their tackling and in their comments. Ince snarled at you if you penalised him or did not, in his view, protect him while Robson tended to look rather sour and dismissive. In contrast, Gary Parker and most of the Villa players were quite amiable largely because we had established a good rapport in the previous match.

The potential problem of seeing teams regularly became a stark reality after I refereed Newcastle v Everton. I got on the wrong side of Everton and in the space of two minutes in the second half I sent off Earl Barrett and Barry Horne, both for second bookable offences. I also booked John Ebbrell, Neville Southall, David Burrows, Joe Parkinson and David Unsworth, along with Newcastle's Rob Lee, Peter Beardsley and Robbie Elliott. I was due to referee at Goodison Park three weeks later and the invective in the Merseyside newspapers and my post bag promised a hostile reception. Everton demanded that I be taken off the match but the Premier League would not accede if a club publicly called for a change. If clubs made unofficial representations then Ken Ridden might keep a referee and a particular club apart, as I had experienced with Arsenal after the microphone saga. But public protests and requests were a different matter. As ever, Ken found a diplomatic way out by appointing me to referee Scotland v Northern Ireland at Easter Road, Edinburgh, on the day of the Everton game. He had thus publicly rejected Everton's request to have me taken off the game but had then saved me from an ordeal.

I have no doubt that refereeing the same teams regularly helped forge working relationships with many players as they quickly started calling me 'David' rather than 'referee' and I was increasingly treated as an individual rather than just another official.

Television was by now becoming more intrusive and referees found themselves under ever greater scrutiny. In September 1994 I refereed an extremely tough encounter between Leeds and Manchester United at Elland Road. The match was live on Sky TV and it took all my experience and seven bookings, six of them for Leeds, to keep matters under control. Leeds won 2-1, and United scored with a penalty for a foul which TV showed had been committed outside the penalty area. After the match Sky TV asked me to talk about my 'error'. I saw footage of the incident and felt that it might be beneficial to accept responsibility for a mistake so I agreed to be interviewed. I explained how I had made my decision but accepted that I had made an honest error of judgement. The majority of the press praised me for having admitted that I had been wrong but others simply used it as further ammunition for attacking refereeing and called for the use of video technology during matches. Others subscribed to the view that referees should be seen but never heard. I took the view that if we want the thinking, intelligent football watcher to respect referees there is no harm in admitting errors when we are clearly wrong. Of course, it is much easier to admit a mistake when it has not affected the overall result.

The power of television to create controversy grew as more and more television cameras were being used at grounds and an increasing proportion of matches were being shown live or at some length. While it would be wrong to say that they invented controversy, some commentators took pleasure in highlighting mistakes and creating strife where none had previously existed. I experienced this at White Hart Lane in February 1995 when I awarded Southampton a penalty. There was no dispute from the players or the partisan crowd but after the game slow-motion footage showed that the foul was just outside the penalty area. We had all been deceived by the speed of the players' movement. The Spurs managers Gerry Francis admitted that he had been very happy with my refereeing until television told him I had made a mistake. To be fair, the referees and linesmen were not the only ones whose failings were now being picked up by the cameras, but the ability to analyse every incident and every decision meant that errors were more frequently spotted which created an impression that refereeing standards were not as good as they had been. I am sure there were many ex-referees who were delighted that they had avoided such forensic post-match analysis.

Criticism of referees grew but there were times when we did receive recognition. I refereed a Coca-Cola Cup second leg match in 1992 between Millwall and Arsenal in a rerun of my 'microphone' match, having not refereed Arsenal since then amidst rumours that Arsenal had had me 'banned' from their games. There had been problems with coin throwing at Highbury and this time, after only five minutes, Nigel Winterburn was felled by a coin. Afterwards the Millwall chairman Reg Burr banned nine fans from The Den for life, one of whom was later convicted of coin throwing. I was touched when I received the following letter from Chief Superintendent Kenneth Chapman who had been the match commander:

*Dear Mr Elleray,*
*Protocol meant that I could not write to you until after the FA had made a decision on the Millwall v Arsenal match.*
*In days when praise is rare, I wanted to compliment you and your officials on the splendid way you handled the match – you were a credit to your fellow referees and to football.*
*The pre-match discussion with my officers encompassed the most difficult scenario we would have*

*to face – a 1-1 draw after extra-time and that is what*
*happened. However, your positive control which allowed*
*the game to flow ensured that the match, which was a*
*credit to both teams, went off without further problems.*

*My congratulations on the way in which you refereed*
*the match.*

*Sincere regards*
*Kenneth Chapman*

Praise thus sometimes came from unexpected quarters and
this was not the only example. I started season 1993/4 with the
first two Monday night televised matches and for the second,
Aston Villa v Manchester United, the commentators opened
with 'Welcome to Villa Park. It's Monday night so the referee
must be . . . David Elleray.' It was one of the most enjoyable
games I had been involved in. The play flowed from end to end
and a superlative first-half goal from Dalian Atkinson was cancelled out by a brace from Manchester United's Lee Sharpe.
Everyone was in raptures afterwards about the quality of football and I was pleased to have played my part in a match of such
pace, intensity and drama that the excitement reverberated
round the ground for ninety pulsating minutes. The action was
non-stop and the tempo so unrelenting that I had my work cut
out to keep pace with the physical demands. Few stoppages
meant few opportunities to get my breath back and slow my
heart rate down. If I had wanted to show someone why I loved
refereeing I would have brought them to that game and let them
smell and feel the passion and excitement and then ask them to
imagine what it is like being right in the middle of it all.

A few weeks later I won the Carling No. 1 award which went
monthly to 'someone, from a chairman through to a fan, judged
to have made an outstanding contribution to the FA Carling
Premiership'. The panel gave me the August award for my handling of the game, saying, 'It was a text-book performance
which allowed an enthralling spectacle to unfold at breathtaking

speed – for once a referee must take credit.' I was very proud to have won it and felt that it was recognition not only of my performance but also of the contribution that referees up and down the country make to matches and for which they receive very little praise or recognition. Sadly, this was the only time a referee gained such recognition.

The rewards associated with the Premiership were so immense that this led, on occasion, to players literally fighting for success. My first Merseyside derby was at Goodison Park in September 1993. I had heard a great deal about this fixture and the stories of Everton and Liverpool supporters happily coexisting. This was most assuredly one of those games when the nerves do tingle beforehand and I had a very pleasant moment just before kickoff when the two captains, Gary Ablett and Ian Rush, presented me with the Carling award. I then had to make sure I focused on the game ahead and not be complacent because I had won an award. The adage 'You're only as good as your next game' rang in my ears. The match produced a quite extraordinary incident. Midway through the first half Everton scored and the players ran towards the main stand to celebrate. I followed their celebrations and when we kicked off I was slightly concerned by a buzz in the crowd. I thought nothing more of it and concentrated on keeping the challenges within reasonable bounds as the temperature of a game always rises immediately after a goal. At half-time we retired to the dressing room with the home crowd delighted with the score and the quality of the football.

I then noticed one of my assistants, Phil Joslin, looked rather bemused. 'What's wrong?' I asked. 'Well, when Everton scored and the players celebrated there was a fight behind your back,' he replied. 'Why didn't you call me across?' I asked, to which he replied, 'I didn't know what to do because it was two Liverpool players fighting each other!' It transpired that after the goal Bruce Grobbelaar, as was the case with some high-profile keepers, looked for and found a scapegoat. He picked on Steve McManaman who refused to take the blame and the two of them came to blows. Had Phil called me across I would have had to send them both off for violent conduct as players must be disciplined for violence or using foul or abusive language towards a team mate as well as opponents or officials. It was too late to take action but the incident certainly provoked some interesting photos and column inches in the papers.

The Premier League was producing some great matches and when Ossie Ardilles, a proponent of 'the beautiful game', took Spurs to Maine Road in late October 1994 they lived up to their reputation as an attacking side with a weak defence. If football is about scoring goals then Spurs were the team to watch, but their defence did not make it easy viewing for the away fans. The game was one of the most entertaining I ever refereed in the Premier League and was a wonderful feast of football. Spurs played exactly as expected and lost 5-2.

The pressure of the Premier League with all the travelling, media attention and on-field demands was relentless so I enjoyed an occasional break refereeing schools football. One of my highlights was refereeing the first ever Independent Schools Cup Final between Charterhouse and Forest at Fulham's Craven Cottage. The competition had been the brainchild of Mark Dickson who ran football at Shrewsbury School and, as a member of the Independent Schools FA (ISFA) Committee, I had enthusiastically supported his vision of a national competition which would see the traditional northern 'public schools' competing with their southern counterparts in a competition that would evoke the Corinthian spirit and the Old Boys' Arthur Dunn Cup. FIFA officials Martin Bodenham and Rob Harris ran the line and Forest won on penalties after a thrilling 2-2 draw. One of their stars that night was Quinton Fortune, who was to go on to play for Atletico Madrid and Manchester United, and represent South Africa in the finals of two World Cups.

The pressure to play matches was also immense and my reputation as a geographer, or at least a meteorologist, took a bit of a knock at Maine Road when, about ten minutes before the game between City and Ipswich, the heavens opened. I was already changed for the game so went out to inspect a water-logged pitch in my referee's kit with a flat cap and Barbour which produced some good photographs and wry captions in the papers the next day. I decided to play, hoping that the rain would soak into the pitch, but it got worse and worse and I was faced with abandoning the match to protect the players. I had just made up my mind to call a halt when an Ipswich back pass stopped in a puddle and Manchester City scored. With both sides already looking like relegation candidates I dared not risk inciting the crowd by abandoning it just as City had taken the lead. I prayed that no one would get injured as players aquaplaned across the pitch. I fervently hoped that Ipswich would equalise which would make an abandonment easier. However, Manchester City went 2-0 up and then the heavens opened again and the surface became absolutely unplayable. There was a serious risk of injury so, after thirty-seven minutes, I finally abandoned the match. I was confronted by an irate Tony Coton, the City goalkeeper, as we left the field and the crowd went berserk. Fortunately for me, the rain continued and everyone supported my decision. I agreed to give an interview to Jimmy Armfield for Radio 5 Live in which I stressed that my prime responsibility had been the safety of the players. Tony Coton, now much calmer, came to the dressing room to apologise.

Balancing refereeing in the Premier League and abroad with Harrow was becoming very demanding but also very satisfying. On the first Saturday of each School year I entertained the senior boys to a big black-tie dinner. The purpose of the evening was both to bring them together as a year group as they started their final months at Harrow and to give them a taste of a formal occasion. We began with a Latin grace and ended with a glass of port and the loyal toast. These meals were an important part of building relationships with the boys and they often provided a relaxed forum in which I could get my thoughts and philosophies across to the boys and they could tell me what they thought about life and the School. We often had fascinating discussions.

The boys were always keen to know what action I would take in certain circumstances. 'What would you do if you found someone in bed with their girlfriend?' was a regular. My answer was usually that I could not be seen to condone it otherwise there was a danger that the House would be awash with such couplings. If a boy's girlfriend came to visit they should be introduced to me before she entered the House and the two of them should not do anything which would embarrass matron or anyone else should they walk into the room. I would then recount the story of the boy I had had to rusticate after he was found in bed with his girlfriend who regularly climbed into his room at weekends. They are now married with a young family.

In many respects, being a referee helped me in both the House and the form room. The boys saw me as more than just a school-master. By having another life I moved up the scale of 'normality' in their eyes. My Geography pupils used it as a wonderful source of red herrings and regularly tried to deflect me from the intricacies of weather systems onto something far more interesting, such as what I thought about Vinnie Jones or Eric Cantona. They loved the press coverage I attracted, especially the critical articles, and were highly amused when a football magazine conducted a poll to discover the fifty most hated people in football. I was the only referee to feature, coming in at No. 18 between Paul Ince and Gary Lineker. Eric Cantona topped the list followed by Graham Kelly and Alex Ferguson.[25] I was surprised I was not higher as referees, unlike cricket umpires, have never been popular and are widely derided.

The boys in Druries quite liked the kudos of having a 'famous' referee as their House Master. They shared my passion for football and enjoyed my high profile, not least because I let them watch televised matches after prep, especially if I was the referee. They particularly liked it when I had a controversial game or when I was criticised by the commentators. Whenever

I returned from a match they were much more interested in the number of red and yellow cards than goals. They wanted all the gory details and then they would say, 'Sir, the commentators said you missed two blatant handballs because you were not properly up with play. Is that true, sir?'

Most of the boys supported a team and the majority seemed to follow Manchester United who won the first two Premier League titles with some ease, but Jack Walker's Blackburn were challenging them and on the last day of season 1994/5 the Premier League title could have been won by Blackburn Rovers (away to Liverpool) or Manchester United (away to West Ham). For United to be champions they had to win and Blackburn had to lose. There was speculation (but no evidence) that Liverpool might throw the game to stop their hated rivals, United, winning the title and hand it to Kenny Dalglish, the Liverpool legend who managed Blackburn. I was refereeing the Anfield match and the Liverpool manager Roy Evans told me of his concern at these allegations – kidology or not? When the managers brought the team sheets into my dressing room an hour before kickoff you could cut the tension with the proverbial knife.

More than ever, it was crucial that neither I nor my linesmen made any mistakes. My pre-match instructions usually lasted about fifteen minutes. I told my linesmen where I wanted them to stand for corner kicks and penalties. I asked them only to signal for offences that I had not seen (which is why linesmen get so much stick nowadays from the crowd for not flagging for obvious fouls) not for everything they saw. At the end of this particular briefing I said 'I do not want any clever decisions'. This meant I did not want a penalty or red card for something no one else had seen. An official can be on an adrenalin high in big matches and flag without taking a split second to think and play the incident through in his mind. Major errors by linesmen, or referees, often occur because they have been too quick in giving the decision. I wanted that day's decisions to be cast iron certainties as, although a Championship is of course decided over the entire season, the reality was that the Premier League Championship would be decided between 4.00 p.m. and 5.45 p.m. in East London and on Merseyside.

To keep things in perspective I also said, 'Just remember that this is a normal football match. There are twenty-two players; the ball is the same size; the pitch is no different; and the Laws are no different. The only difference is what is going on outside the field so just focus on what happens on the pitch.' With any big event, sporting or otherwise, it is the anticipation and build-up which can cause an almost intolerable level of pressure. This can lead to a performer cracking, so what I was trying to do was remind the linesmen (and myself) that there were no special rules – it was just another match. The consequences of our decisions might be enormous but how and why we made them were no different than if it was a game on Stanley Park or Hackney Marshes.

When we walked down the stairs, passing under the sign reading 'This is Anfield' and then up and into the bright sunlight, I had never felt so much tension among players. It was worse than a Cup Final and, like coiled springs, they just wanted to start the action. Waiting around, doing nothing, was almost unbearable but I could not start early as we had to coordinate with Upton Park so that both matches started at the same time. The Premier League would not countenance one match starting late, thus giving one team the advantage of knowing how the other game was going.

The noise from the fans suggested that they did not quite know what to do. The Kop wanted Liverpool to win but they could not bear the thought of United winning the Championship. The Liverpool players, as usual, were pretty silent while the Blackburn players seemed to have half an ear on their supporters who were relaying events from West Ham. The game was very tense. Then, with the score 1-1 and only seconds to go, Liverpool scored. There was desolation among the Blackburn players as the title seemed lost. The television cameras focused on Dalglish who looked completely downcast and then he suddenly started celebrating as news came through that the United game had finished 0-0. Blackburn were Champions. I have rarely seen such a sudden change in emotions. The Liverpool players started congratulating their opponents and it was almost impossible to get the game restarted. Eventually we kicked off and then I blew for time and let the celebrations get under way. It was a wonderful climax to the season with the title in doubt until the very last minute. The integrity of English football was intact. Blackburn had won the title even though they had lost the match so there could never be any suggestion that Liverpool had thrown the game. Some things never change, however. I had turned down an appeal for a Liverpool penalty and when I came off Ronnie Moran, Liverpool's coach, told me that I would never referee at Anfield again.

As well as officiating in title-deciding matches another major challenge Premier League referees faced was refereeing the top players who attracted so much media attention. The most extreme example was Eric Cantona, as I had discovered when I was appointed to referee Manchester United v Liverpool in October 1995. United were, as usual, dominating the Premiership and Liverpool were desperately trying to recapture the successes that had made them the team of the eighties. This match was extra special as it was Cantona's first following his eight-month suspension for his appalling kung fu kick at a spectator at Selhurst Park back in January. The build-up was more intense than anything I had ever experienced and I too became a focus of attention. The press acknowledged that, as the country's top referee, I was the right person for the game but they also highlighted my previous encounters with United. Somewhat foolishly, I gave a couple of interviews outlining the pressure that I would be under dealing with Cantona. I wanted to get across the difficulty I would face every time Cantona committed a questionable foul. Some would demand he was booked while others would expect me to be understanding. Everything that Cantona did would be analysed to the nth degree and my reactions would be subject to almost similar scrutiny.

One of the interviews, for the *Today* newspaper, was headed 'Ref Elleray in pledge to French star' and, as was increasingly the case, sought to contrast my life at Harrow with my life as a referee. 'The man entrusted with ensuring Eric Cantona neither sins nor is sinned against strode the same street of learning as Churchill, Byron and Nehru. Whether boaterless adolescents or unorthodox Frenchmen, Elleray insists hard-line discipline is the only answer.'[26] I said I would red or yellow card any player who deserved it, regardless of who he was, otherwise my credibility would be lost. I knew Cantona wanted to restore his own credibility in British football but I had mine to think about as well. As a disciplinarian at school and on the field I believed that firmness creates the right environment for positive and creative people to flourish, be they players or schoolboys. Strictness reduces the likelihood of bullying and intimidation in schools and on the football field. I admitted I would be saddened if Cantona quit English football. He was an exceptional talent because of his unpredictability and no one doubted his footballing genius.

The atmosphere at Old Trafford was electric and Cantona received the most amazing reception when, in his imperious manner, he emerged into the sunshine and the spotlight of the world's media. He conducted himself well and the moment most people remember came in the sixtieth minute when he threaded the ball through to Ryan Giggs and, as he drove into the Liverpool penalty area, was pulled back by Jamie Redknapp. Without hesitation I blew and pointed to the spot. There was no doubt who would take the penalty: up strode Cantona and dispatched it with dignity and ferocity. He ran behind the goal and swung on the netting post as the crowd went wild with delight.

The penalty made it 2-2 and with both teams attacking we saw Premier League football at its best. Liverpool were hanging on so desperately that I booked Jason McAteer and Michael Thomas in the last ten minutes for time-wasting. The match ended without anything dramatic from Cantona, that penalty excepted. I drove home absolutely shattered; the pressure had been immense. I reflected on the majestic way Cantona had dealt with the ordeal of returning after committing one of the most shameful acts ever witnessed in English football. It was a great testimony to his professionalism that he had kept himself fit and was able to cope with the intense scrutiny. I, on the other hand, had not done myself any favours by speaking out before the match and my interviews rightly opened me up to criticism. As Roy Evans commented afterwards, 'It's a sorry state of affairs when the referee says he's on equal billing to Eric Cantona as he did in the build-up to this match. Eric came through his test all right but the referee certainly did not. He had only three decisions to make and he got all of them wrong.'[27] Evans felt that I should not have awarded the United penalty and thought I had missed two Liverpool penalties. By speaking before the game I had directed the spotlight onto myself. Worse, I had given the impression that I was as important as the players, something unimaginable. I learned a hard lesson from that and very rarely gave pre-match interviews again.

Stung by losing the title in 1994, Manchester United were determined to regain it and, apart from Liverpool, their toughest matches were away at Blackburn and Newcastle. They were in resurgent mood and eager for revenge when, in late August, they played Blackburn, who had had the temerity to take the title away from them. The battle between the only two clubs to have won the Premiership was live on Sky TV. There was no love lost between the clubs, not least because of a controversial match at Ewood Park the previous season where Henning Berg had contentiously been sent off. This time Rob Hughes of *The Times* described the match as 'Another fractious, contentious, titanic contest [which] disfigured the start to the FA Carling Premiership season. If you prefer the unrefined rush of blood, the near hysterical pace and the clamour of the English game then you may have been satisfied.'[28]

Goals were at a premium in the first half and the players became more combative in their approach. After twenty-nine minutes I produced the yellow card for the first time for Roy Keane's intimidatory tackle. Having sent him off for stamping in the FA Cup semi-final against Crystal Palace four months earlier this did not endear me to the United fans. Neither did it lower the temperature and in the last three minutes of the half I booked Tim Sherwood of Blackburn and the United pair of Nicky Butt and Gary Neville, all for fouls. However, the most significant yellow card was Graeme Le Saux's in the thirty-second minute when he threw himself to the ground in the United area hoping to get a penalty. A growing concern was that the influx of foreign players was bringing with it a culture of 'diving'. Prevalent in the European and South American game, the habit was spreading, as Le Saux's booking emphasised, and I certainly felt that those of us who refereed abroad were more experienced at spotting such offences.

The second half was less combative. Lee Sharpe opened the scoring for United in the forty-seventh minute after Blackburn keeper Tim Flowers had saved attempts from Keane and Beckham as the Rovers penalty area began to resemble a pinball machine. Alan Shearer equalised in the fifty-eighth minute but United scored an exquisite winner nearly ten minutes later when the least experienced player on the field, David Beckham, chipped Flowers meticulously. The dramatic moment came in the seventy-fourth minute. Roy Keane got the ball on the United right and pushed it forward into the Blackburn penalty area. Colin Hendry came across to challenge and, as he did so, Keane began to go to ground. It was a very skilful movement by Keane and his timing was nearly perfect. Had I not been concentrating fully I might easily have awarded a penalty. What convinced me of Keane's intention was that as he fell his arms went out rather like someone diving into a pool. It is this movement which is often the giveaway. If you know you are going to fall over your hands go out to save yourself much more quickly than if you are knocked over unexpectedly.

Before I could deal with Keane, however, Graeme Le Saux

confronted him and was pushed angrily away while Colin Hendry charged at me, gesticulating as if he was a referee showing a card – a reprehensible action. I showed Keane the yellow card followed by the red. The crowd erupted as for the first time in the Premier League a player was dismissed for diving. I had no option as I had booked Le Saux for something very similar and I had to be consistent. Le Saux's booking actually helped because if Keane's action had been the first I had penalised people might have said I had something against him. As I left the ground I was besieged by the press. I said, 'I sent Roy Keane off for diving which he compounded by pushing out at an opponent, Graeme Le Saux. Diving is something we have inherited from the Continent; it is not natural to our game and it is important to stamp it out. The game was played at one hundred miles per hour and I thought it was a great advert for English football.'[29]

The controversy surrounding this decision swirled around for several days but I was pleased when James Lawton of the *Daily Express* wrote, a few days later, 'The best Darjeeling, if not bubbly, should be served to Harrow House Master David Elleray in his study this afternoon. His decision to send off Roy Keane and book Graeme Le Saux was courageous and right.'[30] His sentiments were echoed by Bruce Millington in the *Sporting Life* who wrote, 'David Elleray did superbly to spot both Keane's dive and an earlier one by Graeme Le Saux. Can a referee be player of the year? If so, I nominate Elleray.'[31]

Despite the controversy, it was clear that the millions Manchester United had invested in their youth programme had started to provide a rich harvest; one young talent, in particular, David Beckham, was beginning to score spectacular goals at crucial times in the most hostile of atmospheres.

Blackburn faded in the title race which developed into a battle between Newcastle and Manchester United. Newcastle raced clear but by the end of February they were only four points ahead and the crunch match was on 4 February at St James' Park and I was appointed to the game. The build-up again filled pages and pages of the newspapers and for many it was the season's defining match. Kevin Keegan, the Newcastle manager later famously lost his temper while being interviewed. Eyes blazing, he launched into a tirade about how he would just *love* to beat Manchester United and Alex Ferguson. Clearly Ferguson's renowned mind games had got to him. If Newcastle won they would deal United a great psychological blow and establish a commanding seven-point lead over Ferguson's team. Newcastle's cavalier style of play had won many admirers and the North East was once again vibrant with self-belief. It was a remarkable turnaround from when I had refereed them on the last day of the 1991/2 season against Leicester, when they had been staring relegation to the Third Division in the face.

I don't recall being particularly nervous as I walked onto the field but what did hit me was the noise from the passionate Geordie crowd. It was the loudest I have ever experienced. Indeed, it was so loud that it actually hurt my ears. The match was played at a frightening speed and it was no surprise that mistimed tackles brought bookings for Nicky Butt and Phil Neville in the space of five minutes midway through the first half and for Newcastle's Rob Lee in the thirty-eighth minute. Just before half-time the ball was bobbling around the edge of the Newcastle penalty area and was then hoofed upfield. I started to sprint after it knowing that I would have to get a move on as the pitch sloped down towards the United goal. Whether it was instinct or a change in the crowd noise I do not know, but I glanced back over my shoulder and saw an almighty fracas taking place. I blew the whistle and headed back to the mêlée as quickly as I could. There was a great deal of pushing and shoving and insults flying and I had no idea who had done what to whom. No one was injured but it was unsightly and I needed to get a grip on the unruliness before it spilled over into something much more serious.

I strode purposefully across to the assistant, Ian Blanchard, and said:

'Ian, what's gone on?'

'I don't really know,' he replied.

'Has anyone struck anyone?'

'No, it was just handbag stuff, really.'

'OK, well, who was most involved?'

'I'm not sure.'

Slightly exasperated, I said, 'Look, just name one player from each side who I can go and bollock!'

All the time I had been standing next to Ian so that we could both observe the players in case there was any more trouble while we were talking. I knew that if I did nothing then, in effect, the players had taken control of the game. I needed to re-establish myself as being in charge. I called Butt and Lee across and spoke to them severely, telling them they were very lucky that I was not sending them off. They looked somewhat bemused but said nothing and it did the trick. I had been seen to take action. I believe that after any fracas or mêlée the referee has to be seen to do something to demonstrate that he is in charge and that the game will re-start only when he is ready.

We came off at half-time to almost as much noise as when we had entered forty-five minutes earlier as it had been a wonderful first half. The second continued in much the same vein and the game was sealed with a fine goal from Cantona in the fifty-second minute after Keane and Phil Neville had engineered something special down the left. Cantona had ghosted in at the far post and hit the ball first time past the despairing Srnicek. It was the turning point of the season: Manchester United did not look back after that and won their third title. Newcastle challenged the following year but Blackburn failed to make an impression.

The Premier League had been a great success and I was enjoying my refereeing more than at any stage in my career so far. It was exciting being involved with such great players and the attention and criticism were inspiring and daunting in equal measure. They were also easing the bitter memory of that fateful moment in the Cup Final which was still haunting me.

# Chapter Six

# *The Cup Final*

*'You're a f*****g disgrace, you cheat!'*
CHELSEA FAN

If the 1966 World Cup Final was the catalyst for my love of football, Wembley Stadium was inextricably a part of it. Of all the magical moments of watching football on television the majority were Wembley matches. Like any schoolboy footballer, my greatest desire was to play on the 'hallowed turf'. Looking back, my visits to Wembley were such that when I eventually ref-ereed the Cup Final I was completely at home and comfortable with probably the most historic and awe-inspiring venue in world sport.

My first visit was to watch an England schoolboy interna-tional with my Dover primary school, St Martin's, in 1964. I refused to eat anything and sat on the crowded coach for what seemed like hours. It was as if I was in a dream and was being spirited away to another, magical land. I remember little except that the place was absolutely vast and the noise from thousands of schoolchildren was incessant and deafening. Afterwards, I panicked as I came down the steps to be confronted by a sea of coaches. How would we find our coach and what would happen if I got separated from my friends? The sick feeling of excitement was now replaced by one of irrational fear. Little did I know at that stage that I would return to Wembley many times to watch games and, more importantly, to officiate there fourteen times.

My next visit was a few years later to watch England. My father had somehow managed to get tickets and I had to get permission from the headmaster to miss afternoon lessons. We drove to the Elephant and Castle, parked on a building site and then took the Tube to Wembley. It was probably a really exciting occasion but all I can remember was that I trod in some stinking mud when we parked the car and could not get rid of the smell for the rest of the evening. I can still smell that mud to this day.

I was lucky enough to go to a number of Cup Finals in the mid-1970s, the most dramatic being when Leeds beat Arsenal 1-0 in 1972 in the Centenary Final. The drama was that referee David Smith booked Bob McNab of Arsenal in the first minute – the fastest booking in a Cup Final. He booked four players in what was a tough game and his correct handling of that match made a keen impression on me.

Wembley is only a few miles from Harrow; the twin towers were visible whenever I walked to lessons and it became my sporting Mecca. The stadium is so close that I twice walked home after Cup Finals and the music from Bob Geldof's Live Aid concert drifting through the still summer afternoon in July 1985 could be clearly heard at Harrow. When I went to a Simon and Garfunkel concert I stole a few blades of grass from the pitch which I kept in a small box, like the relics of an ancient saint. I took some Harrovians to the 1978 Oxford v Cambridge Varsity match because my close friend Mel Mrowiec was the Oxford captain; I still delight in telling my goddaughters how their father committed one of the worst tackles I have ever seen at Wembley.

I spent thirty years getting Wembley into my blood and when

I was appointed to officiate there for the first time it was not some distant, unfamiliar stadium but more like a friendly acquaintance. Over the next thirteen years it was to grow into an old and well-loved friend. In September 1984 Reg Paine from the FA rang. 'David, we've appointed you as reserve linesman for England's World Cup match against Finland on 17 October. The match officials are Polish. Please report to White's Hotel at 3.30 p.m. to travel to Wembley with them.' I was taking my first step towards refereeing at the famous stadium. I was meticulous, almost obsessional in my preparation and spent hours polishing my boots. I was the resident House Tutor in Moretons and I asked Anna, the House Master's glamorous Polish wife, to teach me a few Polish words. I enjoyed the surprise on Reg Paine's face when I met Mr Suchanek and his colleagues and greeted them with 'Dowidzenia' – the Polish for 'hello'. I learned enough to ask them if they wanted coffee, tea or water and whether they liked milk and sugar.

The drive to Wembley took me back to that coach journey years earlier and I again felt sick with excitement. We drove up Olympic Way (I prefer to call it Wembley Way), parked at the front of the stadium and walked round to the side entrance at the end of the players' tunnel. Huge wooden doors guarded the tunnel and as we passed through that feeling of entering a magical land returned. Halfway up the tunnel on the right-hand side we went through a door, up two flights of stone stairs to a small landing and there it was, the holy of holies – the referees' room. I was crestfallen. It was a tiny, cramped L-shaped room with dingy decor, dull lights and a small bathroom. I am not sure what I had expected but it was unimpressive. Still, it was Wembley and I was not going to let peeling paint and grubby lino spoil the evening. I did wonder, though, how many other referees, from England and abroad, had had their expectations and excitement dashed by this grotty room. We unpacked our kit and then walked up the tunnel and there I was, about to step on to the Wembley turf. My right foot hesitated for a moment and I felt I was about to walk on holy ground. The turf was lush and springy. If you could not play football on that, there was no hope for you.

The England team that evening was brimming with household names, among them Bryan Robson (captain, Manchester United) Peter Shilton (goalkeeper, Southampton), Ray Wilkins and Mark Hateley (AC Milan), Tony Woodcock (Arsenal) and John Barnes (then at Watford). I was awestruck. I have a photograph of me standing with the Polish officials for the National Anthem and I look as if I am about to face a firing squad. I was simply trying to believe that I was really there. My most memorable moment was holding up Bryan Robson's number and substituting the England captain off. I had great fun the next day telling the boys how I had taken off the England captain because we were winning too easily. England won 5-0 with goals from Hateley (2), Woodcock, Sansom and Robson in front of only 47,234 spectators as England were not playing to a full Wembley. However, I'd have been happy even if the stadium had been empty.

I had to wait two and half years before I returned, this time as linesman for the U15 England v Scotland schoolboy international in May 1987. Fortunately, earlier in the season I lined in front of 95,000 people in Belgrade so officiating with a crowd of over 45,000 did not daunt me. The tension in the dressing room was incredible and I spent much of my time keeping the referee calm. He was concerned because I was senior to him but I made it very clear that I was thrilled to be officiating at Wembley and would give him all the support he needed. England went 1-0 up in the first half but Scotland equalised in the second, much to the disappointment of the English fans whose high-pitched shouts and screams took me back to when I had watched just such a game. I wondered how many youngsters that day were dreaming of playing, or even refereeing, there.

March to June 1991 was really unbelievable as I went to Wembley three times and each match was more important than the previous one. On 9 March, it was again England U15s against Scotland at Wembley, but this time I was the referee. England won 2-0 but I spent most of the game trying to believe that I was actually refereeing at Wembley and desperately praying that nothing controversial would happen. Rather like when I refereed school matches at Harrow, I was tougher on England than Scotland so that I could not be labelled a 'homer'. The dressing rooms were still tatty but that did not matter any more. After the game I just sat in the corner, put my head in my hands and wept. I had actually refereed a game at Wembley and I felt I was the luckiest person alive. Once I had got over the emotion I wondered how many more visits I might have and whether one would one be for the Cup Final itself.

My wait for a return was short-lived: in May I was reserve referee for the Leyland DAF Cup Final, the competition for clubs in the Third and Fourth Divisions. There was a fantastic atmosphere in the stadium with almost 59,000 people treated to a pulsating match as Birmingham, having been 2-0 up at half-time, overcame a resurgent Tranmere to hold on to a 3-2 lead. Throughout, my mind was racing ahead a week as I had also been appointed to referee my first senior Wembley match, the Second Division play-off final between Brighton and Notts County a week later. I used the DAF Final as a dress rehearsal, making sure that I was totally familiar with everything about the ground, the substitutes' benches, the changing rooms and all the protocols. I knew exactly how long it took to walk up the tunnel and how long we could stay in the dressing room to ensure exactly fifteen minutes between the end of the first half and the start of the second.

No one could have organised a better preparation for my first really big game at Wembley. It would be my fifth game there and, more importantly, my third in under three months so I was as familiar with the ground as anyone possibly could be. It was bright and sunny as I led Brighton and Notts County out into the stadium. Most of the players had never played at Wembley before and the ordeal was perhaps greater for them than for me. Steve Lodge, the reserve referee, kept me calm, chattering away in his Yorkshire brogue, and I was fully confident because I had got the game by being top of the merit order.

Most striking that day was the appalling Brighton strip: white shirts and shorts with red blotches. As we chatted in the tunnel I told the Brighton skipper Dean Wilkins that it looked like a reject design from a wallpaper shop. I felt surprisingly relaxed as we strolled up the tunnel towards the great arena. The sudden change from the dull background noise to the wall of sound which assails you as you emerge from the tunnel still took me by surprise. I felt the most incredible tingle go down my spine as my senses were bombarded by noise and colour. I had no trouble keeping my head high as I instinctively looked round and drank in the extraordinary atmosphere. There then came over me a great temptation to start running.

The tension was palpable and the early stages of the game were littered with errors. However, by half-time Notts County were leading 1-0. As I blew the half-time whistle and began to walk towards the tunnel Steve Lodge came running over and shouted, 'If that bloody Neil Warnock doesn't shut up I'm not going to be responsible for my actions. The man's a pillock!' We agreed that if there were any further problems I would come across and deal with them myself. Needless to say, midway through the second half I saw Warnock ranting and raving so I blew my whistle and walked purposefully across to the substitutes' benches which were set back some twenty yards from the touchline. I said to Warnock, 'Sit down.'

'What do you mean?'

'It's quite simple; please sit down.'

Rather stunned, Warnock sat down and to his further surprise I sat down beside him. 'Neil, you've got two choices. You either shut up and stop giving Steve and the rest of us a hard time, or you'll have an extremely long walk into the stands. I don't mind which you choose, it's up to you.' With that I got up and walked back to the field, much to the relief of John Goggins, the Football League Referees Officer, who had looked up from his programme to see twenty-two players but no referee. Afterwards Steve told me, 'That was bloody magic. I've never seen Warnock so gobsmacked. He sat there for a minute with his mouth opening and closing like a bloody goldfish!'

Notts County were too strong for Brighton that day and won 3-0. My heart was in my mouth at one stage when a County forward broke clear, hotly pursued by a Brighton defender who looked as if he was going to foul him. I quickly analysed their positions and decided that if he did he would have to be sent off for denying an opponent an obvious goal-scoring opportunity, the so-called 'professional foul'. One technique I used was that, as soon as a 'professional foul' seemed about to be committed, I would say quietly to myself 'red card, red card'; I kept on repeating it until the situation changed. Thus, if there was a foul I knew exactly what decision to make.

I almost got through the match without any bookings but in the eighty-sixth minute Mike Small committed yet another foul and I booked him. Then, in added time, there was a flare-up when Gary Chivers badly fouled Dean Thomas of Notts County who retaliated. I had three options: send them off, book them or lecture them. The pressure to lecture was quite strong as there were only a few seconds left but I knew I would be failing in my duties if I opted for the easy way out. Sending off would have been harsh so I settled for two bookings. I was mindful not to let my standards fall just because the game had gone well and I certainly did not subscribe to the view that referees should go soft in Wembley matches. I was glad I did book them as afterwards John Goggins said, 'If you had not booked those two idiots at the end I would have kicked your backside as it would have spoilt an excellent performance.'

It had been a wonderful three months: three matches and no controversy. Referees, like players, have some grounds which are lucky, where they enjoy refereeing, and others where they never seem to do well. Fortunately, Wembley had become one of my lucky grounds and I always felt totally comfortable there.

I had a year without going to Wembley and then another season with a hat-trick of visits. Refereeing the FA Charity Shield is the most prestigious appointment after the Cup Final and I was thrilled when I was appointed to the Leeds v Liverpool game on 3 August 1992. The game was more special than usual as it was the final showpiece before the FA Premier League season started. There seemed to be an extra buzz in the air as we stood beneath the twin towers and watched the crowds flood towards the stadium.

It was a thunderously hot day and I sweated so much that at half-time and after the game I could wring my T-shirt out. Pitch-side temperatures exceeded 100 degrees Fahrenheit but the players put on a great spectacle, memorable most for a Leeds hat-trick from Eric Cantona (before he was transferred to Manchester United). Leeds won an enthralling encounter 4-3 and the match was played in a friendly manner, my only yellow card being a rather harsh one for David Batty in the seventy-eighth minute. The game flew by and I remember little of it except that I was delighted at the lack of controversy and pleased that the season had started with a football spectacular. One of the talking points was a new Law which forbade goal-keepers from picking up the ball if it had been deliberately kicked to them by a team mate. The aim was to stop the endless time-wasting which was killing the game where a full back could play the ball to the keeper who could roll it back to him and he could then pass it back again. I was impressed with the impact the change had and felt that it was in part responsible for pro-ducing what was an incredibly exciting seven-goal thriller. It made the game faster but there was less recovery time as the goalkeepers immediately kicked back passes upfield.

Towards the end of that season I refereed Port Vale v Stockport in the Autoglass Cup Final; I had been reserve referee on the final of this competition when it was sponsored by

Leyland DAF. Surprisingly, I also had to referee a Football League play-off semi-final between the teams four days prior to the final. Fortunately, there was no controversy in the game at Port Vale so I went to Wembley knowing the teams well and with no 'afters' to worry about. The kit sponsors provided the officials with yellow and purple shirts for Wembley finals. I chose the yellow but it seemed strange not being in the standard black and white or the Premier League green. However, the shirts made the linesmen much easier to see against the background of the fans. I was well used to the 'Wembley experience' although the most testing moment still remained getting down the stone stairs to the players' tunnel. I always had visions of slipping and being unable to do the game. The match went well and afterwards John Goggins told me that I would be returning to Wembley nine days later, on Bank Holiday Monday, to referee the First Division play-off final between Leicester and Swindon. I was again top of the rankings and I felt as if all my Christmases had come at once as, for the second time in three years, I was going to officiate on that wonderful springy turf for the third time in a season, something few, if any, referees had ever done before.

The build-up was incredible and the game was dubbed the most valuable of the season as the financial rewards for gaining a place in the Premier League were significant. It turned out to be one of a series of remarkable finals. Wembley was almost full to capacity with around 74,000 spectators enjoying a match which ebbed and flowed for 120 minutes. Swindon led 1-0 at half-time and midway through the second half Leicester were 3-0 down and looking dead and buried. They then staged a remarkable comeback and at the end of normal time the score was 3-3 so, on a scorching hot day, we moved into extra time. As the players became increasingly tired they succumbed to cramp and I was desperately hoping that fate would not befall me. Wembley's turf had a bounce in it, rather like a cushioned running track, which played havoc with the calves. As extra time proceeded it was stalemate. Then Swindon had a surging attack and the next moment Steve White was sent clattering to the ground by the Leicester goalkeeper, Kevin Poole. Without thinking I blew the whistle; then, realising that the offence had taken place inside the penalty area, I pointed to the spot. The penalty was duly dispatched and Swindon won and gained promotion. I have many memories of the match, one of the best being Glen Hoddle, the Swindon player-manager, sending a ball floating from one wing almost to the other and it landing perfectly at his team-mate's feet. It was a moment of sublime skill which rightly graced the hallowed turf. It contrasted sharply with the foul which had brought him a yellow card, the 1999th of my career.

Throughout season 1993–4 people kept telling me that I was the clear favourite to referee the Cup Final. I knew my chances had improved because when I refereed Wimbledon v Manchester United in the Fifth Round it suggested that the 'geographically neutral' rule which had ruled me out of contention for the 1993 final had been abandoned by the FA as well as the Premier League. It was tough dealing with that pressure, which grew as the competition progressed, and by the Sixth Round every day that passed without a letter or phone call appointing me to the final was agony. I dreaded opening the paper and reading that someone else had been appointed.

When the call finally came it took me by surprise. On Easter Monday at about 9.15 p.m. the phone rang: it was the FA Referees Secretary, Colin Downey. It was so late that it did not occur to me that he might be ringing about the Cup Final – I suppose I had assumed that such an important call would come during office hours. A dream that I had had for twenty-six years was about to come true but I could scarcely believe it. I remember having to take a deep breath as I was unable to speak. It is impossible to express how you feel when one of your life's ambitions becomes a reality. I was sworn to secrecy until the next morning, but I told my parents and a few friends and, needless to say, I had a sleepless night.

Being appointed to referee the Cup Final set in train an amazing series of events and emotions. Once the news was released the phone rang incessantly. One of the many wonderful things about the appointment was the avalanche of congratulation letters I received. Many were from friends and colleagues or people with whom I had been at school or university, but some of the nicest were from genuine fans I had never met. It was truly touching that so many people took the trouble to write.

There was a hectic round of radio and TV interviews in the days after the appointment and, aware that the media like to have some theme to focus on, I gave them two. One was that I only drank Earl Grey tea and the other that I was House Master of Druries, the House where Charles Alcock, the man who founded the FA Cup, had been a boy from 1855 to 1857. I had a number of photographs taken, one of the silliest of which was for the *Daily Mirror*. I wore my referee's kit with my academic gown and mortarboard, and I was waving a cane!

I was in a something of a daze for much of the time leading up to the match itself. One of my first concerns was who the finalists would be. Manchester United were playing Oldham in one semi-final and Luton and Chelsea were contesting the other. I had a private dread that the final would be Luton v Oldham. It was a selfish thought but the most watched club Cup Final in the world should be between top clubs. Chelsea won easily but Manchester United were rescued by a last-minute equaliser from Mark Hughes in the first game before winning the replay. It was a dream combination of teams as both had a reputation for high quality, attacking play. They were both glamorous clubs and while I had a good rapport with both I got on especially well with Chelsea.

In the days before the final I was anxious to avoid injury. I have a record of every game I have ever officiated in and as the final approached so too did my 2000th match. I was asked to referee Wimbledon v Nigeria on the Monday before the final. I was on 1998 matches and there was a strong desire to do the game so that the final would be the 2000th match of my career. However, the stronger desire to avoid injury prevailed and I declined the game, even though I had never been injured refereeing a game.

The pressure on the Cup Final referee is immense. Whatever else anyone might claim, it is the biggest match of your career and as you only referee the final once you are desperate not to make a mess of it. People are often surprised to learn that you can only do it once but I thoroughly approve of the principle. It is such a special occasion that, like returning to a favourite holiday location or to an old girlfriend, it would never be as good the second time round. I strongly believe that no one should have all the big games and those who have shown themselves capable of refereeing at the highest level should receive the highest accolade of doing the Cup Final.

One of the biggest problems is that the occasion is so enormous that the referee needs considerable big-match experience; almost inevitably that means it has to be a FIFA or ex-FIFA referee as they have been in the middle of major games overseas as well as in England. The Cup Final is so much bigger than any Premier League match that someone who has only refereed in this country cannot be fully prepared for the off-field pressure. In the previous twenty years only three non-FIFA referees had done the Cup Final and on each occasion there was controversy. Peter Willis sent off Kevin Moran of Manchester United in 1985 (the only sending off in a Cup Final), Roger Milford failed to book Paul Gascoigne for a bad tackle in the opening minutes of the 1991 final and this, in part, contributed to Gazza's wild tackle a few minutes later which ruptured his knee ligaments and for which he should have been sent off. Similarly, in 1993 Keren Barratt was criticised for his handling of the Arsenal v Sheffield Wednesday final and, in particular, the rough play he allowed in the replay. Mind you, that is not to say that FIFA referees have a divine right to have a controversy-free match, as I discovered.

One difficult issue I had to face was related to the new kit and boots provided for the Cup Final officials. Unfortunately, by the Wednesday before the game my boots had not arrived. As anyone who buys a new pair of shoes knows, they take time to wear in and become comfortable. For some reason, sports firms and football administrators expect referees to wear brand-new boots for the first time for the final itself and I suspect there are more blisters in FA Cup Finals than in any other round. I decided to wear the boots I had used all season, partly because I was superstitious but mainly because they were comfortable. I did not intend to referee the most important domestic match of my career with my feet in agony!

I had no influence on who the other officials were, but I was delighted with the FA's choice. Gerald Ashby was the reserve referee and a good friend. The two linesmen, Graham Barber and Paul Rejer, had both proved themselves to be excellent officials who knew when to assist and when to stay in the background. Neither had any wish to hog the limelight and could certainly not be described as 'flag happy'. Equally, they would not duck any issues. It was a great team.

The evening before the final followed the time-honoured pattern and we were taken to the Russell Hotel for the 'Eve of the Final' rally. The vast majority of England's referees belong to the Referees' Association, the national organisation for referees of all levels. When you start refereeing you usually join your local RA branch and they help and mentor you through your career. The highlight of their calendar is the rally where several hundred gather to honour the Cup Final officials. We were ushered into a reception room for the VIP guests and a marvellous surprise was that my father was there. Duncan Jackson, who had started me off on this incredible journey, had secretly invited him. It made the evening even more special. I was so busy chatting that I did not notice the room had emptied. Suddenly, there was a fanfare of trumpets and we walked proudly into a packed hall where our colleagues stood and applauded rhythmically as we proceeded to the top table. The RA President Peter Willis paid humorous tribute to the four of us and we were presented with commemorative plaques. I then had to make a speech on behalf of my colleagues. I spoke about those who had started me refereeing and who had supported my career and I touched on Harrow's connection with the FA Cup. Then began an exhausting forty-five minutes as our colleagues queued with the rally programmes and Cup Final programmes for us to sign. It was tiring but very moving as so many of them made complimentary remarks as we signed our names hundreds of times.

We returned to White's Hotel well after 11.00 p.m. and went to bed, agreeing to meet for breakfast at 8.30. As we reached our rooms I took Gerald to one side and said, 'I'm going back to Harrow for the night. I'm telling you just in case there is a fire, but no one else is to know!'

'Your secret's safe with me,' he smiled.

I slipped quietly out of the hotel and drove home in breach of FA protocol. I was probably the first referee for many years to sleep in his own bed the night before the Cup Final. However, I wanted – and got – a good night's sleep in my own bed.

Next morning I took the pre-breakfast call-over and the boys were warm and generous in their good luck wishes. As I left, one said, 'Will you get me Cantona's shirt, sir?' When I started the car the radio came on and I heard an interview I had done a few days earlier. It had been recorded as if it was the morning of the final and it was with great amusement that I drove down the A40 to central London listening to myself describing what I was having for breakfast.

I rejoined my colleagues and no one was any the wiser about my night away. After breakfast we went for a long walk in Hyde Park to calm the nerves. There we bumped into the former England manager Graham Taylor and he generously told us how pleased he was that we were doing the game and how we should do our best to engrave as much of it as possible in our minds as it would go in a flash. 'If you don't make a determined effort, you end up remembering very little of it,' he said. It was excellent advice which I have repeated to many colleagues and friends since.

The sun was shining through a thin cloud layer as we got into magnificent black limousines for the journey. As we got closer to Wembley I found myself focusing more and more on the task ahead. The streets were steadily filling with supporters in their red and blue shirts. I was somewhat surprised at the hostility our car attracted but Colin Downey told us not to take it personally. Some fans resent the swanky VIP cars which they believe carry people who only go to the big matches and are not true supporters. His point was graphically reinforced when we slowed down on Olympic Way and a Chelsea fan pressed his face to the window and shouted, 'I bet this is the only f*****g game you've been to this year, you c***s!' As my grandmother would say, 'Charming!'

The stadium was empty when we got inside. As we walked round the pitch it was silent and ethereal, like being in a vast cathedral. The transformation into a seething mass of colour and noise would be remarkable but there was something graceful and serene about its silent majesty. The dressing room was as cramped as ever but it had a familiar feel and I felt quite at home as we signed boxfuls of programmes. We went to the Banqueting Hall for tea and toast while the dignitaries nearby tucked into their three-course lunch. This was not the right atmosphere in which to prepare for the game so I took my colleagues out onto the balcony and we watched as tidal waves of colourful, noisy fans streamed towards the stadium. I was lost in thought when Graham Kelly tapped me on the shoulder: 'I'm told you prefer Earl Grey so I've brought you these for your half-time cuppa,' he said, thrusting a box of Lipton's finest into my hand. Kelly was a man much pilloried for his lugubrious television interviews and I remember one of the secretaries at School asking me, 'Who is that miserable man who always appears on TV whenever there's a football crisis?' In fact, Kelly is a man of great vision and humour, and the tea bags showed his kindness.

It had been agreed that Sky TV could film part of the pre-match preparations so we went to the dressing room early and did a mock-up of me setting out my kit, instructing my colleagues and then going out of the door. That helped kill the time but the tension was growing and I decided that I needed to touch reality so I walked to the end of the tunnel and stood watching the stadium as it filled up. The noise was building and I realised that the eyes of the football world would be on us all that afternoon. The presence of Manchester United and Chelsea ensured even greater interest than usual and I knew that I was on the threshold of the most important ninety minutes of my life.

The team sheets were submitted, we changed and then it was time to go. I felt incredibly calm as I walked gingerly down those slippery stone steps and then I was in the tunnel, shaking hands with the two captains, Dennis Wise and Steve Bruce. There was an edginess about the players. Some, like Ryan Giggs, kicked balls against the walls; others, like Gavin Peacock, just stood in silent contemplation. We got the signal and then we were off. A deafening roar greeted us and the sound and colour infused my very being with energy and excitement. We lined up, met the dignitaries and then stood proudly and emotionally as the National Anthem was played. The vastness of the stadium meant that the singing was not synchronised; one end finished and started cheering while the other end were singing the last few words.

The teams broke to each end and the four of us had our photographs taken near the touchline before we moved to the centre circle for the toss of the coin. I was remarkably calm and all my nerves had gone. I was composed and ready. I was so focused that I even remembered to tug my left ear lobe just before kick-off as a sign to the boys at Harrow that I was thinking of them. Then I blew the whistle and we were off.

The match started with a crash as after eighty seconds Erland Johnsen clattered into Ryan Giggs with such a fierce tackle that, momentarily, I thought of sending him off. There was no player reaction and I contented myself with the second fastest yellow card in a Cup Final. He was joined by Steve Bruce in the eighteenth minute as Chelsea increasingly dominated the half. In the twenty-fifth minute, while the Manchester United defence was going through a slow and clumsy spell, Gary Pallister cleared the ball straight to Gavin Peacock who, twenty yards out, let the ball drop and fired it against the Manchester United crossbar. A few inches lower and the next hour might have been very different! By half-time it was still goalless but from my point of view the game had gone almost perfectly.

The first fifteen minutes of the second half were also uneventful until Ryan Giggs knocked the ball to Denis Irwin who was spectacularly upended by Eddie Newton. I blew instantly for a penalty and no one said a word. It was as clear a penalty as I had ever given and I had not a moment's doubt. Cantona stepped up and was coolness personified as he slotted the ball home. The mood of the game now changed, as did the weather – the heavens opened and it began raining hard. Five minutes later a long ball was knocked through the Chelsea defence and swooped upon by Andrei Kanchelskis. As he approached the Chelsea penalty area Frank Sinclair challenged him. There was contact but they both kept going and as they entered the area the contact continued and Kanchelskis tumbled to the ground. For the second time in five minutes I blew without thinking.

That was my undoing. I should have given myself time to think but I did not. Perhaps I was carried away by the occasion. As I blew, I knew that was wrong, but what could I do? I could not change my mind so I pointed to the spot and ran towards the goal line to put distance between myself and the inevitable Chelsea protestors. The pouring rain did nothing to dampen the Chelsea ire or that of their captain, Dennis Wise. His protests were such that I reached for my back pocket but, deep down, I knew I had made a major error and refused to compound it by booking him. The furore died down and Cantona again converted the penalty –

the only FA Cup Final in history with two penalties. As I hurried back to the centre circle I wondered whether I should have sent Sinclair off for denying an opponent an obvious goal-scoring opportunity, but that would have taken things too far.

Chelsea and Sinclair's misery continued in the sixty-ninth minute when his slip allowed Mark Hughes to score and in the last minute Paul Ince broke clear and set up an easy tap-in for Brian McClair to make it 4-0, equalling the biggest Cup Final-winning margin ever at Wembley and the largest since Bury beat Derby 6-0 in 1903. Cantona was named man of the match although that honour should have gone to Paul Ince, who had dominated the midfield. It had been a good match. There had only been nineteen fouls (plus the two penalties) but the attacking had been somewhat stifled by the sixteen offsides. There had been eleven corner kicks and Chelsea's Mark Stein had joined Johnsen and Bruce in my list of yellow cards.

I was aware that I might be blamed for Chelsea's defeat but had no idea of the hostility that I would face. As the four officials climbed the steps towards the Royal Box, Chris Saunders, Chairman of the Public Schools FA, thrust his hand out and warmly shook mine. 'Well done, David!' he said. I moved on and from my left a man pushed forward from the VIP area just below the Royal Box. 'You're a f*****g disgrace, you cheat!' he exclaimed and spat in my face. It was a dreadful moment. I just looked at him, took out my handkerchief and wiped my face clean. It was a bitter moment that haunted me for weeks afterwards and I was so stunned that I was unaware of any other reactions or comments.

I received the precious gold medal, not much bigger than a 20p piece, and the four of us quietly walked back to the dressing rooms. I was probably fortunate that the Manchester United fans were at the dressing-room end and I received warm applause from them; this lifted me a little but I was hurting as I had never hurt before. I knew I had made a big mistake which could never be corrected.

I sat in the dressing room feeling as if my world had fallen apart. Of course, everyone was very kind and said that I had had a wonderful match and had been correct with both penalties. I kept up the pretence that I also thought I was right but in my heart of hearts I knew I was wrong. I was asked if I would do an interview for BBC Television and Colin Downey thought it would be a good idea. I asked to see the footage and with that clearly in my mind I spent a long time under the shower working out exactly what I would say. While I was showering Alex Ferguson popped into the dressing room and gave us each a bottle of Manchester United Cup Final champagne. I dressed and readied myself for the interview. I made it clear that I would make a general comment about the quality of the match and was then prepared only to explain both penalties. Using the footage I attempted to show that Sinclair had started to foul Kanchelskis outside the penalty area and had continued his illegal challenge in the penalty area, so I penalised him when Kanchelskis went to ground. It was pretty convincing stuff and I even started to believe that perhaps I had been right after all. Immediately afterwards, there was an interesting debate between Jimmy Hill and Alan Hansen which demonstrated why video evidence is never going to be the solution to such decisions. Jimmy Hill said the footage showed it was clearly a penalty while Hansen said it showed that it was not even a foul, let alone a penalty!

As we left the dressing room and climbed the stairs to go to the Banqueting Hall we bumped into the Chelsea manager, Glen Hoddle. He very generously shook hands and thanked me for the game. We had a cup of tea and met up with our friends and colleagues. I put a brave face on things and tried to dispel my growing depression. The journey to the hotel was quiet as the enormity of the event sunk in, but I could only focus on one thing, 'Why had I blown when Kanchelskis went to ground?' That question haunted me for the rest of the day – the whole Cup Final experience disappeared and only that moment remained.

We were going out for a meal that evening and when I went down to meet everyone else I bumped into Lennart Johannson, the UEFA President. He called me over and his bear-like hand gripped mine as he said, 'Europe needs referees like you. I do not care whether the second penalty was a foul or not. The easy decision would have been to have given nothing but you showed strength and courage. Congratulations!' With that he was gone and my spirits were lifted. The evening took on a more positive tone and the pressure and tension drained away. Later on, as we strolled back to the hotel we met a group of noisy football fans. Dread struck me until I realised that they were Manchester United fans. They recognised me and started chanting my name; and the next thing I knew I was being carried on their shoulders. It was a great moment but I did think how different it would have been if they had been Chelsea supporters.

In the days after the match my disappointment grew. The only comfort I could draw was that it was so tight that whatever decision I made would have been criticised. The Chelsea faithful accused me of handing the double to Manchester United even though they were already 1-0 down, had missed a golden opportunity and were eventually overwhelmed 4-0. Conversely, had I not given it and Chelsea had won, I would have been blamed for costing United the double. Perhaps I would have been the loser either way but, deep down, I knew it was not a penalty and that decision has haunted me ever since. It means that I never look back on my Cup Final with any real satisfaction or pride. Indeed, even now, whenever anyone mentions the game, I always become tense in case they launch into a tirade about that decision. It is incredible how a single blast on my whistle created a black cloud which, even ten years later, has never completely gone away.

# Chapter Seven

# *The European Experience*

*'Only accept gifts if they are small . . . and expensive!'*
UEFA OFFICIAL

With so many senior FIFA referees across Europe having been forced to retire because of the lower age limit, there was a wonderful opportunity for a new generation to make their mark and move rapidly through the rankings. I was determined to try to establish myself as one of the elite group of top referees who controlled the major games. International refereeing was very different from the Premier League so there was much to absorb and adjust to both on and off the field. It was one of the most competitive times of my refereeing career as the new referees would be very quickly judged and it would be difficult to recover from a poor start.

I already had some experience of European football. My first taste had been in 1987 in Belgrade as one of Keith Hackett's linesmen in a European Champions Cup quarter-final between Red Star Belgrade and Real Madrid, two of the best clubs in Europe at the time. As I proudly wore my blazer with its FA three lions badge it took me back to my days as a twelve-year-old when I had coveted that Kent Schools FA badge.

Keith Hackett was a fantastic ambassador and he guided me through the three days with consummate skill. Temperatures were sub-zero but, to my eternal embarrassment, I had not taken an overcoat. The pitch had been covered with plastic sheeting to protect it from the frost and the snow and to my amazement there were about 250 prisoners from a local jail shovelling snow off the pitch under the watchful eye of guards with machine guns. A wonderful game ensued in front of 95,000 people. Red Star were 3-0 up at half-time but Real Madrid fought back magnificently in the second half and the final score was 4-2. Keith had a great game and awarded three penalties, largely as a result of players being unable to keep their feet on the frozen surface. The temperature was –12 degrees and I had never been so cold in my life; but I was exhilarated by the quality of the play and the vast crowd who were singing all the famous English football songs to tunes I could recognise although the words were in Serbo-Croat! It was ironic that my final international appointment would also be played in sub-zero temperatures with Real Madrid again being the away team.

I then lined twice to George Courtney and saw both how top referees are treated in Europe and how some clubs react when things do not go their way. We went to Turin for Juventus v Paris St Germain in November 1989 and when we arrived at the stadium the ball boys carried our bags to the dressing room while George was applauded by the Italian spectators and signed countless autographs. George refereed magnificently and the respect he was afforded exceeded anything I had seen, or certainly experienced, in England. At the end, Michel Platini formerly of Juventus said, 'Courtney, you are the best in Europe!' Almost a year later we were in Greece for Olympiakos v Sampdoria where I saw some of the pressure international referees come under on and off the field. The officials looking after us gave us far too much money when they paid our expenses, but when George questioned this they said they had negotiated a very advantageous exchange rate from the bank. UEFA later decided to recompense match officials directly. At dinner George was invited to bring his family back for a free holiday. 'Why are you offering me this?' George enquired and protestations that they were just being friendly and hospitable drew an icy response from the Spennymoor Head Master.

The match itself was quiet until an Olympiakos forward 'fell' in the Sampdoria penalty area. George could have earned his free holiday but he waved away the appeals. The crowd erupted and Ron Tye, the linesman on the far side, was pelted with objects, one of which gashed his eyebrow. At half-time the Olympiakos players sprinted off the field and as we approached the tunnel with the Sampdoria players there was a hail of bottles, stones, bricks and coins. The police, who had been protecting us with riot shields, suddenly disappeared. An Italian player was hit and fell to the ground and as he lay there a glass bottle full of beer smashed just beside him. It could have killed him. I was unperturbed and did not think that I would be hit, although in the dressing room the shock of what had happened hit home. George was not prepared to restart the match until the crowd was calm and the police reinforced. We took a photograph of Ron Tye's cut eyebrow for evidence – if he had been hit a centimetre lower he might well have lost his eye.

It was the worst crowd trouble I had ever experienced and I certainly needed to breathe deeply and summon all my strength and courage to go out for the second half. Sampdoria won 1-0 and the Greeks were not happy so when we got back to the hotel there was no supper. Next morning, our car to the airport failed to arrive so we took a taxi and then had more trouble as the passport officials made snide comments about 'the English referees' and took ages processing our papers. It had all been an eye-opening experience but when I refereed at Olympiakos some years later they were absolutely charming.

My only European refereeing experience had come in the

summer of 1990 at the Nordic U15 tournament in Finland. I referred the opening game between fierce rivals Denmark and Sweden, and as I stood ramrod straight in the middle of the line of players listening to the national anthems I looked up and saw the flag of St George flying because I was the referee. I got a sense of how medal winners feel when they are on the rostrum and my eyes filled with tears. I felt incredibly proud that I was representing my country abroad and had become an 'international'.

Before I could do my first match as a FIFA referee I had to attend the UEFA course for new international referees in Madrid with Gerald Ashby, Martin Bodenham and Steve Lodge where we were inducted into the on- and off-field requirements and protocol. We ran the fitness test in groups and Steve and I ran together. Towards the end of the twelve-minute run I told Lodgey it would be a national disgrace if we were beaten by the three German referees who were forty yards ahead. We picked up speed and were about twenty yards past them when the whistle to stop running sounded. As we waited to have our distances measured we noticed the Germans getting closer and closer; if the officials had taken any longer the Germans would have been in front of us!

My first refereeing appointment came in early September 1992: an all-German UEFA Cup Winners Cup match between Werder Bremen and Hannover 96. Hannover had won the German Cup and Werder Bremen had won the European Cup Winners' Cup against Monaco a few months earlier. We flew out the day before the game and returned the day after. I took two English linesmen, Kevin Lynch and Roy Pearson, and reserve referee Mike Reed, who were tremendously supportive, although we were rather worried that whenever we went for a walk Kevin somehow managed to get us to stroll past a sex supermarket – they did not have one in Harrogate, he explained, and he was curious to see what they were like!

I resolved to make a strong start to my international career and, when Mike Reed joked that my final mark would be determined by the number of yellow and red cards, I told him I was out to get 10/10. After thirty-three minutes I had given four yellow cards. There had also been three goals and a penalty and as I passed near the halfway touchline Mike shouted, 'Keep going David . . . you're well on your way to your target.' I had been unaware that so much had happened because I was concentrating so hard. I was trying to adjust to the different atmosphere and style of play. In English football in the 1990s everything tended to be blood and thunder and there were rarely truly quiet periods. However, in Bremen there would be long periods when the players played 'keep ball', followed by a sudden, rapier-like attack. This required very careful concentration because just when all seemed quiet I might have to make an instant, big decision. Mike's main job at half-time was to calm me down – I was so hyped up that I could not relax. I just wanted to get back out there but it was essential that I cooled down both mentally and physically, otherwise there would have been a real danger of burning out before the match was over.

As the hour mark approached I had issued six yellow cards. Then, a Hannover player was fouled near the touchline and rolled around in agony. I was sure there was nothing wrong and gestured for him to get up, telling one of his team-mates to take the free kick. He refused and pointed at his injured team-mate. I signalled for the kick to be taken but the player again ignored me. I blew the whistle for the kick to be taken. Again he refused. I blew my whistle again and once more he pointed to the injured player. I reached for my yellow card but as I raised it I realised that I had already booked him so I showed the red card as well and Mr Schönberg went off. Miraculously, the 'injured' player leapt to his feet, fully recovered!

At the end of the game several players came and shook hands. However, I could see Schönberg striding towards us from the players' tunnel. As he towered over me, I braced myself for the inevitable abuse but I had misjudged him; instead, he shook my hand and apologised. As we showered, officials from both clubs came and said, 'Thank you for the game. We are sorry that our players did not realise that when you are the referee they must behave!'

My assessment arrived a week later. European assessments were shorter and less detailed than those of the Premier League. I received a very good mark and the summary read: 'Calm, always in control. He had no trouble because of his strong authority. When players tried to make theatre he acted firmly. My opinion is that the referee's work was of high quality ... and they all did a perfect job.' One of the small pleasures I got from my overseas assessments were the expressions used; the phrase 'making theatre' was a beautiful version of 'play-acting'.

I quickly adjusted to the international routines although the travelling and mental strain, which came from being on show from the moment we met at Heathrow or Gatwick Airport, resplendent in our FA blazers, were very tiring. You could not drop your guard for a moment as you never knew who was watching at you, be it press, officials or fans. One danger area was that travelling Business Class meant alcohol was freely available. Indeed, there were tales of officials overindulging and towards the end of my career some Russians were banned from officiating when they arrived in Israel worse the wear for drink. I always warned my team not to drink too much and I very rarely drank alcohol the day before the match and never at lunch on the day of the game. The importance of conducting ourselves properly was brought home to us when, at the end of one flight, another Business Class passenger came up as we disembarked and introduced himself as the UEFA match delegate. He had been sitting two rows behind us.

We were always met at the airport by a home club official (this later changed to an official from the national FA) who took us to our hotel and looked after us throughout the trip, taking us to meals, usually in very fine restaurants. Often, these officials had only limited English and the strain of making conversation was considerable. Like most officials I had a sleep on the afternoon of the match and once I woke up I focused on the match. I would lie in the bath and reread the instructions in the UEFA referees' booklet and go through the differences between refereeing in England and abroad. I packed my kit and my team would come to my room for tea. Unlike in England, I gave my instructions in the hotel and used a copy of George Courtney's briefing notes. International linesmen were not expected to interfere as much as in the Premier League. They dealt with the ball in and out of play, and offside. They should never set foot on the field and should only flag for fouls if they were blatant. I asked them for subtle indicators – to shake their head if a player went down and they thought it was not a foul, and a shake or nod if there was debate as to whether the offence merited a card.

As well as these off-field differences, the actual refereeing was very different. UEFA and FIFA wanted referees to be intolerant of brutal play. Indeed, I gave many more red and yellow cards abroad than at home. In England the philosophy was that if an offence was midway between a lecture and a yellow card or between a red and a yellow card, the player got the benefit of the doubt. In Europe it was the reverse and if there was any doubt, then for physical offences you gave red rather than yellow.

Routine challenges were sometimes also seen differently. Early in my international career I refereed Borussia Dortmund v Real Zaragoza and learned that referees were sometimes expected to give 'diplomatic' decisions. Play was hectic and swung from end to end and I issued three yellow cards, including one for Gus Poyet of Real Zaragoza (it would not be my last encounter with him), and dismissed his team-mate Solana for two yellow cards. The learning point was a challenge early in the second half when Michael Rummenigge appeared to be brought down close to the away team penalty area and I allowed play to continue. The crowd whistled and howled, and afterwards the assessor told me that I should consider giving 'diplomatic' decisions, that is penalise challenges which in truth are fair but which everyone in the ground deems unfair. This would put me in a dilemma: I invariably see things in black and white and a challenge is either a foul or it is not.

UEFA appointed a neutral referee observer (assessor) and a delegate, responsible for all non-refereeing matters, to each match. My international progress depended on the observers' reports and marks. The key observers were from the UEFA Referees' Committee and I had three committee observers in my first four matches. The most important was when I refereed Italy v France in an U18 match and the observer was Josef Mälke, Chairman of the UEFA Referees' Committee and a member of the FIFA Referees' Committee. He gave me 9/10 and commented, 'Impartial handling with a good eye for advantage. Distinguished teamwork. Altogether an outstanding perform- ance.' Soon after I was rewarded with my first World Cup match.

Before my second UEFA match, CSKA Sofia v FK Austria Memphis in the Champions' Cup, I chatted at lunch with the German observer Hans Ebersberger and asked him, in all inno- cence, what he thought were the major challenges facing referees. He extemporised at length, concentrating on the need for referees to be tough on foul play. Afterwards, Ray Biggar, the reserve referee, commented that I had shrewdly established what the observer's pet interests were and I could referee accordingly. I had not intended this but thereafter I always subtly quizzed my observer to see what he thought referees should focus on.

Most of the observers were ex-FIFA referees and each was dif- ferent. One of the best was Michel Vautrot from France. He was always educative and great fun to be with. After a game in Parma he lay sprawled on the bed rubbing his thumb and fore- finger under his nose in the manner of a chef checking the bouquet of a herb and said, in an Inspector Clouseau-like accent, that it was vital the referee 'smelt' the atmosphere of the game. It was a wonderful way of expressing what in England we call having a 'feel' for the game. It reflected my own belief that the referee is like the conductor of an orchestra. The players are key and the referee merely helps determine the tempo and the flow. Vautrot meant something deeper. The referee needs to sense when to intrude into the game and when to hold back, when to lecture and when to yellow card, when to be pedantic and when to be liberal. It reminded me that the game is always about the players and never about the referee.

It was usual to have a police escort to and from the stadium both for security and to avoid the traffic. One of the most alarming I experienced was in Romania, a three-car police escort with policemen hanging out of the side windows gesturing to the traffic to get out of the way. If cars were slow to pull over they were struck by the police batons. We were travelling at quite a speed when one of the policemen lost his hat and his driver braked so fiercely that we nearly crashed as we skidded to a halt. The most impressive drive was when I refereed a Champions' Cup match, Paris SG v Bayern Munich, at the Parc des Princes. Our journey to the ground took place in the middle of the afternoon rush hour so the police stopped all the traffic as our siren-sounding police escort went up the Champs-Elysées and round l'Arc de Triomphe. People stopped and stared, probably thinking that it was someone important, possibly even President Mitterrand. How disappointed they would have been if they had known who was really in the car.

Europe's FIFA referees are categorised according to ability and in 1993 UEFA introduced courses for the top-ranked referees. I was invited to the 1994 top class referees course in Rome and it was a great opportunity to build friendships with colleagues from other countries. We had lectures and discussion groups to try to reach greater consistency among the referees who would be taking charge of the top matches. Unfortunately, we had to take the fitness test. No one likes these tests so as we passed the Vatican on our way to the Olympic Stadium the Polish referee Ryszard Wojcik said that he would phone his former neighbour, the Pope, to ask for help. As we were getting changed there was a huge thunderstorm, which flooded the track, and UEFA decided it was too dangerous to do the sprints. Everyone applauded Wojcik who just shrugged and, with a smile, said, 'What are friends for?'

As international officials we were treated with enormous respect off the field and sometimes had to cope with extraordinarily lavish hospitality and generous gifts without compromising our independence or losing sight of the match itself. Hospitality abroad contrasted significantly with the Premier League where, before Arsenal v Spurs at Highbury one New Year's Day, we had to get a cup of tea from one of the hot-dog stands . . .

A trip to Romania in 1992 with Joe Worrall for a World Cup match with Czechoslovakia opened my eyes to what I might expect throughout my international career. The country was recovering from the Ceaușescu regime and there was much publicity about the plight of the Romanian orphans. Our hosts took us out of Bucharest for dinner. We drove in convoy for ages and, as we went deeper into the forest, it was like something straight out of a Le Carré novel. I had visions of being shot in a small clearing, leaving Smiley to work out what had happened. Eventually, we arrived at an imposing house where we were greeted by flaming torches and gypsy-like figures playing violins. After champagne and caviar we went inside where, seated on a long, dark-red velvet settee, were twelve women who covered the full range of interests. If you liked busty and blonde, there was one, but if you wanted short, red-haired and petite, she was also there. My eyebrows crawled halfway up my forehead as our host explained, 'These are the singers!' Well, they stayed with us throughout the meal and for the entire evening they never sang a single word!

We were treated to a truly sumptuous feast that evening. More caviar, smoked salmon and then a boar's head appeared on the end of a sword with an apple in its mouth. The wine flowed and after dessert the spirits were brought in. My worst fears were confirmed when 'the gents' upstairs turned out to be a bedroom: the place was clearly a very high-class 'boudoir'. I suggested to Joe that we might make our excuses but our hosts said it was too late and we would have to stay the night. We managed to extricate ourselves by claiming that regulations required us to report in to the FIFA delegate but there was more bad news: one of the linesmen who had overindulged had got rather too friendly with one of the 'singers' and had given her his room number. Back at the hotel, we all sat in his room until she appeared. She was sent on her way very sharply and with that we neutralised a potential 'honeytrap'. Next morning we were taken 'shopping' by our hosts. Most of the shops were empty but we ended up in a state store which glistened like Harrods; here the manager presented us with bags full of crystal animal figures, pottery and glassware.

After the game we were taken to a very impressive Bucharest nightclub which would not have been out of place in London, Paris or New York, where we had more caviar and champagne. At the airport on the way home we met British volunteers who were working in the orphanages and it seemed almost obscene that all the money that had been spent on us could have kept several orphanages operating for months. If you were uncharitable you would say the money was spent to 'soften us up' to lean in favour of the host team; if you were charitable you would say they were merely being hospitable.

To be fair, the hospitality was usually genuine and one of the most enjoyable trips (if not the match itself) was when I refereed Auxerre v Tenerife. It included a fascinating trip to nearby Chablis where we went round a vineyard and after a splendid meal were taken to a private cellar lined with dusty bottles. We had a wine-testing tour of the different Chablis and at the end of a fascinating hour the owner gave me a 1954 bottle of wine and I learned that the gap between the wine and the cork is called 'ghost breath'. Thereafter Chablis was my favourite white wine.

Refereeing in Monte Carlo was the most spectacular experience of all. I went twice, the first time in October 1993 for Monaco v Steaua Bucharest. We flew to Nice and then took a helicopter to the Principality. One of my linesmen, Peter Roberts, had seen nothing like it and was 'dead impressed' with the microwave in his wardrobe – it was actually a safe! The Monaco official looking after us knew everyone and after dinner we had a private tour of the Casino, including the private gambling rooms.

The observer, Marko Ilesic from Slovenia, was worried about the lavish treatment and took us for a walk to tell us not to be influenced by all the helicopters, meals and so on. That I had not been influenced became clear early on when after only 19 minutes I sent off the Monaco captain, Lilian Thuram. Ilesic was delighted with the objective and fair way we handled the match (I also sent off Daniel Prodan of Steaua) and his report said, 'The referee was calm, brave and energetic. Impartial and very intelligent. The referee was the absolute master of a very difficult game. With his correct decisions, intelligence and correct positions and reading of the game, he produced a normal match between two teams who were very nervous.'

Although I stayed in top-class hotels and had wonderful hospitality most of the time, there were exceptions. The food in Bulgaria was so bad that we survived on Mars bars, toast and honey for the entire trip, while in Bucharest we stayed in a very dingy hotel. Everything was orange or brown, even the bath water. There was no plug and trying to bath with the plug hole stuffed with loo paper was not easy. Thereafter I always kept a bath plug in my kitbag.

Dealing with 'gifts' was a difficult problem. Clubs were not supposed to give us anything before the match and only permitted to give club shirts, balls and small mementoes afterwards. The reality was very different and the Southern European clubs were the most generous. Everyone turned a blind eye and while I was sure that no one was influenced by these gifts they could put you in an uncomfortable position. When I refereed Real Madrid we were taken 'shopping' at El Corte Inglés department store where the manager presented us with sherry and salami, after which we visited various departments where we 'bought' things. We were told that we could pay at the end but we all knew the game. The generosity reached farcical proportions when I was told to choose some Lladro. I found a small piece but the club official said, 'No, Mr Elleray. You want to buy something bigger than that.' 'No, I don't.' 'Yes, you do!' In the end I gave in and chose a larger piece, but it all felt rather uncomfortable.

In Parma the four of us arrived to find AC Parma sports bags in our hotel rooms stuffed with Parma ham, Parmesan cheese and wine. On the way to dinner the club representative took us to a menswear shop where they pressed us to accept 'a gift from the shop manager who is a great admirer of English referees'. The scenario developed along predictable lines. He asked us to choose something. I was cautious and chose a tie. 'An excellent choice,' he then said, 'but you need a shirt to go with it.' He produced a selection and all that remained to choose was the colour and designer label. 'You need a jumper also.' I felt very uncomfortable and, despite my best efforts, we each ended up with an Armani shirt, silk tie, and cashmere jumper but I drew the line at trousers and a jacket! They were not finished, however, and the next morning we were taken to a shoe factory where we were presented with a choice of brown or black handmade leather shoes. It brought to mind the answer of the Chairman of the UEFA Referees' Committee when asked about presents: 'Only accept gifts if they are small . . . and expensive!'

By the end of my career I had enough watches to wear a different one every day for a month. We also got large numbers of club pin badges, scarves, pennants, etc, and football shirts or T-shirts for our children; my goddaughters built up quite a collection. All this was in great contrast to England where gifts to FIFA referees were minimal and the usual offer was that the

Aged five with my parents and sister, Karen

Proudly wearing my first 'home-made'
referee's outfit, aged thirteen

By the time I was fourteen I had
the proper kit

In my teaching 'uniform' – suit and academic gown – with four Harrovians in School dress

The Druries team having won the 2000 Cock House Harrow Football final in ideal conditions for the ancient game

Keeping an eye on the subs and the spare Harrow 'footer' ball at the 2003 final

Dicks, Wright, Ruddock suggest I consult the linesman in the 1993 Merseyside derby at Goodison Park

Cantona impassive as I book him at Wimbledon in August 1996 on the afternoon David Beckham scored from his own half

Ian Wright is first in the book in the 2nd minute of the North London derby at White Hart Lane, August 1993

Is there one 'n' or two in Ginola? December 1995

All smiles before the
FA Cup Final in 1994

Andrei Kanchelskis
tumbles under Frank
Sinclair's challenge

For the second time in the
match I award Manchester
United a penalty... but this
time I wish I hadn't

Dennis Wise is none too
pleased with the decision

Greeted by flares when lining to George Courtney for Juventus v Paris SG, 1989

Brazil captain, Dunga, sees red in the Germany v Brazil 'battle' in 1998

International duty took me from the desert heat of Namibia for the COSAFA Cup Final

...to the icy wastes of Kiev where Peter Jones, Dave Babski, Darren Drysdale and I discovered that black tights were 'de rigueur'

Dean Holdsworth (Bolton) and I obviously think the decision was a stinker!

Sent tumbling by Nicky Butt in the Arsenal v Manchester United FA Cup semi-final in 1999

I never was a particularly good linesman, especially when I started waving broken corner flags

In false beard and moustache to avoid the Manchester United fans at Wembley for the 1999 FA Cup Final

"Of course Brooklyn can come
to Harrow, David"

"You're not really going to book me,
are you?"
"Yes, Robbie, I am"

"Yes, Phil, Roy's tackle on Haaland
is worth a red card!"

"Sorry, Wayne, but just because you're 17
it doesn't mean you can't be sent off"

My colleagues Phil Sharp, Dave Babski, Jeff Winter and friends Nick and Doug Keen and Daniel Bennett before my final match – Newcastle v Birmingham, 3rd May 2003

Robbie Savage looks on as I ask Dave Babski's advice in the 41st minute

...the outcome is the final red card of my career for Matthew Upson (for denying Craig Bellamy an obvious goal-scoring opportunity)

The kindness of Sir Bobby Robson and the whole of Newcastle United FC helped make it a wonderful finale

match officials could have staff discount in the club shop if they wanted to buy anything. The mementoes I liked most were those, like engraved salvers or embroidered pennants, which were unique to the particular game.

Looking back at my report forms it is fascinating to see that I refereed many players who would subsequently become Premier League players. In Monaco I yellow carded Jürgen Klinsmann, Youri Djorkaeff and Emmanuel Petit in the space of four minutes but before the second half started Klinsmann apologised for his conduct and that of the rest of the Monaco team. He scored twice in Monaco's 4-1 win and at the end the tall, willowy Monaco coach shook hands and thanked us for the game. That was my first encounter with Arsène Wenger. When I refereed Paris SG their captain was David Ginola and in Parma I got on particularly well with Gianfranco Zola, who scored their opening goal in the twentieth minute. He was prepared to communicate with me throughout the game, as was Dino Baggio, and these matches gave me an early opportunity to earn their respect and helped prepare me for the introduction of foreign styles of play and behaviour to the English game.

International matches meant regular three-day absences from Harrow. Fortunately, the Head Master, Nick Bomford, was happy about me being away provided no one complained, so I worked doubly hard so that no one could criticise my frequent absences. My tutors were fantastic and I also had the support of the boys in Druries who appreciated that I would have to stop refereeing if they misbehaved while I was away. Left unsaid was the suspicion that if the boys forced me to give up refereeing by not behaving their lives would not be worth living! They were excellent and in all my time away there was only one problem. The senior boys saw it as a matter of pride that nothing went wrong when they were 'in charge', which led to the ironic situation that trouble only occurred when I was at Harrow. As I am a hands-on House Master, it was good for them to have the occasional break from me – and it was good for me to have a break from a job which was all the more intense now that I had less time to fit everything in.

Whenever I had been away I had to work hard catching up marking all the geography I had set. Indeed, the boys moaned that they worked harder than when I was there. I also had to get back into the flow of life but I had to be careful. I always felt guilty at being away refereeing but I did not want the boys to feel that a period away led to me imposing a great clampdown as soon as I returned. Although the travelling and pressure were tiring they were also refreshing but I always really looked forward to getting back into the day-to-day life of the School and especially the House. I did my best to keep the length of trips to a minimum. For example, when I refereed Holland v Hungary a few weeks after the Cup Final I caught a late flight from Heathrow the evening before the game and a 7.00 a.m. flight afterwards so that I was back in time to teach at 9.00 a.m., less than twelve hours after the final whistle.

At times Harrow and football clashed and the worst case came when I was selected for the Euro '96 finals. The pre-finals UEFA top referees course coincided with Founder's Day when the inter-House Harrow Football finals are played in the morning and the old boys' matches in the afternoon. It is an occasion a House Master cannot miss. Fortunately, Ken Ridden persuaded UEFA to let me officiate provided I passed the fitness test but when the same clash occurred in later years I missed out on the chance to referee a European final.

One of the joys was refereeing the top teams in some wonderful football matches in Europe's great grounds. I got a very early taste of this in my first season as an international referee, when I refereed a UEFA Cup quarter-final between Real Madrid and Paris St-Germain in the Bernabéu Stadium. It was an almost surreal moment when I first stepped onto the perfectly manicured pitch and looked around and drank in the vastness of one of the world's finest stadiums. The seating was so steeply banked that the whole edifice seemed ready to topple inwards. This was the moment when it hit me that I really was officiating at the highest level of inter-club competition in the world. It was an electrifying and frightening realisation and it took me a few moments to regain my equilibrium. It was like being in a schoolboy dream and then suddenly realising that the dream was in fact reality.

It was Real Madrid's 250th European appearance and I was even more nervous because the UEFA President, Lennart Johannson, the man who was to guide UEFA for more than a decade in a patriarchal but kindly manner, was there to make a presentation. My memories are hazy as it was an almost unbelievable experience. I was stunned by the noise of the 68,000 people, one of the largest crowds I had refereed in front of. The sounds were so different from England, and it was the horns and drums which I noticed most. Full of people, the steep banking of the terraces enclosed me more than in English grounds and the atmosphere was electric.

It was a pulsating game. Real took the lead through Butragueño in the thirty-first minute and the crowd had hardly calmed down when, three minutes later, Zamorano added a second. Paris St-Germain fought back and David Ginola scored only four minutes after the interval. With George Weah looking increasingly dangerous the French looked as if they might get a draw and another away goal to take into the second leg, but with only a few minutes to go Real Madrid were hanging on to their 2-1 lead. Then, a Madrid shot was handled on the line. Fortunately I was ideally positioned and I awarded the penalty and red carded Alain Rioche. Gonzalez dispatched the penalty as the huge crowd roared its approval. It had been a quite incredible match as far I was concerned and had everything that you would expect from two of the great European teams. I walked off feeling immensely proud that I had held my nerve in front of a partisan crowd and with some of Europe's best players. We left laden with gifts, including a silver cigar box with my name inscribed on it; unfortunately it said ALLERAY.

As well as the great matches there were some extremely difficult ones. Auxerre v Tenerife in September 1993 was one of the toughest. The score was 0-0 from the first leg and the exchanges were fast and furious. There was a lot of diving and overreaction and I had to keep a very firm grip on proceedings. Tenerife were especially difficult and by half-time I had issued five yellow cards. Right from the start of the second half the challenges were relentless. In the fifty-sixth minute Julio Llorente of Tenerife chopped an opponent down but when I reached into my back pocket for my yellow card it was empty! I had left it in the dressing room. I called the trainer on and quietly walked backwards towards the halfway line where Paul Durkin had spotted my dilemma. With a magician's sleight of hand he passed me his yellow card and I went back and calmly showed Llorente the card as if nothing had been amiss.

The incident taught me a lesson and, thereafter, I always carried a spare yellow card. I kept one in the back pocket of my shorts and a second with a red card in my shirt pocket. This helped my assistants and the fourth official because they always knew that if I went for my back pocket it was a booking but if I went for my top pocket someone was being sent off for a straight red or a second yellow.

The ferocity of the game increased when Tenerife scored and they then indulged in a series of tactics designed to disrupt the game and waste time; I ended up sending Gomez off for a second booking for kicking the ball away after conceding a free kick. I added on ten minutes for all the time-wasting and 'injuries' and this sent the Tenerife team and officials into a frenzied fury. Auxerre were unable to score and were eliminated from the competition. Tenerife's Argentinian coach Jorge Valdano was later quoted as saying that he thought I was trying to gain revenge for the war over Las Malvinas!

Another 'battle' later that season was the Eintracht Frankfurt v Casino Salzburg UEFA Cup quarter-final caused partly by events in the first leg, the worst being when the Salzburg coach spat at a Frankfurt player. I had Rob Harris and Mark Warren as my linesmen and Peter Jones, who became one of my closest friends, was fourth official. When we inspected the ground in the morning the match officials' flag (which flew alongside the teams' national flags and the UEFA flag) was a Union flag. As a bit of a wind up, I said that unless they found an English flag the match would not take place. When we returned in the evening they presented me with a flag of St George which I draped over my shoulders before they hoisted it onto the flagpole.

The match was a bruising encounter. The score from the first leg was 1-0 to Salzburg. Eintracht scored in the nineteenth minute through Maurizio Gaudino and the game went into extra time and then penalties, which Salzburg won 5-4. Afterwards Peter Jones announced that he was absolutely shattered, having recorded six substitutions, one goal, eight yellow cards and one red. 'I'm glad you didn't come off, because I couldn't have coped,' he said. He confessed that, at one point, he felt as if the whole world was against him. It was wet and windy, and, keen to follow my instructions to the letter, he was forever getting up to keep the benches in order. At one point all his papers blew away and he was scrabbling round, chasing bits of wet paper, while I was battling on the field. I was astonished when the Hungarian observer remarked afterwards that I should have allowed more rough play when UEFA and FIFA directives insisted on skilful players being protected.

Seven months later I had a different problem with Steaua Bucharest in Benfica's Stadium of Light. Perhaps I was becoming complacent or maybe I was shocked that one of the world's most famous grounds had become so dilapidated but I had a bit of a nightmare. It was one of those games where little things went wrong and Steaua steadily lost confidence in me and the match descended into a series of contested decisions. The problem had its genesis when I booked Jose Mozer, the Benfica No. 3, for a bad foul. I mistakenly wrote his number in the Steaua Bucharest column on my card so when the Steaua No. 3 Jonel

Pinu committed a foul and I saw his number already on my yellow card, I sent him off. The Romanians protested so vehemently that I consulted the fourth official and I rescinded the red card. Benfica's Claudio Cannigia then scored and the Romanians were convinced I was biased when I (correctly) sent off Anton Dobos and awarded Benfica a penalty. In England such refereeing would simply be dismissed as poor whereas for the Romanians, whose national league had experienced corrupt officiating, it prompted more sinister thoughts. These may have been partly inspired by our previous encounter when they had lost 4-1 in Monaco and I had sent off Prodan. I was very annoyed with my yellow card mistake and thereafter I was extremely careful when I wrote on the cards and regularly reminded myself which players I had booked. It was the sort of mistake the British press would have crucified me for and one of the good things about refereeing abroad was that you did not see the newspaper reports!

The creation of the Champions League with its huge financial rewards in 1995 significantly increased the pressure on match officials and clubs, as I discovered when I refereed a second-leg qualifying round match between IFK Gothenburg and Legia Warsaw. It was a very tense affair which Gothenburg decided to play in their compact ground, which only held 11,000, rather than the nearby Nya Ullevi Stadium as they wanted as hostile an atmosphere as possible.

Gothenburg took the lead and seemed to have the game wrapped up when one of their forwards scored after the ball had been spilled by the Polish goalkeeper, but Mark Warren belatedly raised his flag for offside. Hoping to encourage more goals, the International Board had earlier declared that as from 1 July a player in an offside position should not be penalised unless he was involved in 'active play', blocked the goalkeeper's view or materially distracted a defender. However, should the ball rebound from the goalkeeper or the goal itself and a player who had been in an offside position become involved in play, the linesman had to flag. This is what had happened and although Mark Warren was perfectly correct it almost caused a riot.

Poor Tony Bates, minding his own business in his first over-seas match on the opposite line, was pelted with coins and the Swedes, having completely lost their heads, then lost the game, conceding two goals, having two players sent off, three others booked and the manager sent to the stands. Afterwards, the police kept us in our dressing room for two hours and we were walked back to our hotel, only five hundred yards away, under police guard. I had armed police posted outside my door and a most uncomfortable time at the airport where even the customs and passport officials treated me as Public Enemy No. 1. However, I learned through my Polish friends in Moretons that I was a hero in Warsaw!

In early 1994 I was selected for the Euro '96 finals and appointed to one of the opening games: Germany v Czech Republic. My close friend Steve Lodge was the fourth official and the linesmen were Pete Walton and Tony Bates, who had been my main European and domestic team. The build-up to Euro '96 was amazing and the whole country seemed to come alive, inspired in part by the theme song 'Three Lions' and its refrain, 'football's coming home'. I had a secret ambition to referee the final but knew that there were several very experienced officials with a better claim. I was thrilled that my match was at Old Trafford, a ground where I always felt comfortable. Security was very tight (rightly so as a bomb exploded close to our hotel several days later) and we got to the ground early enough to have a tour of the facilities and we were each presented with a small Manchester United clock to mark the occasion. We had new dark-blue adidas shirts for the tournament and it was with the greatest pride that we led the teams out onto a perfect, sun-drenched pitch. It was a strange match. The atmosphere was subdued and in the first half the players never really got into top gear. The Germans com-pletely outplayed the Czechs and by half-time they led 2-0, Ziege and Moeller scoring the only goals of the game, and the match seemed over. I had had very little to do but had issued three yellow cards, the third on the stroke of half-time to Pavel Nedved of the Czech Republic.

I am not sure what was said at half-time in the dressing rooms but the players came out in a very aggressive manner. In the space of fifteen minutes I issued another seven yellow cards as I battled to maintain control. I could not put my finger on why a match which had been so placid and straightforward had suddenly become so difficult, but we all felt that we had maintained control and done well. The ten yellow cards established an unwelcome UEFA Finals record. The Belgian UEFA observer, Alex Ponnet, who was known to dislike English referees, was not happy and said I had not been firm enough and that I should have given a red card for a late challenge near Tony Bates. I had been pretty pleased that I had spotted it and in English football I would never have dreamed of issuing a red card but European attitudes were different. Ponnet also had the odd notion that after six or seven yellow cards then you should start issuing red cards for yellow card offences.

In stark contrast the British press lambasted me for being overstrict. I particularly remember Steve Curry of the *Daily Express* laying into me for being unsympathetic and card-happy. I fully understood their point of view; and I was highly frustrated that I had not pleased UEFA because I had not been strict enough and yet the British press said I had been too strict. However, I was not the only strict referee as the other three opening group matches had produced twenty yellow and two red cards. The *Guardian* headline 'Heat on as yellow fever sweeps the tournament' was typical and the German manager Bertie Vogts remarked 'I would have expected an English referee to be more understanding towards the physical side . . . (but) my players have to take some of the blame for getting booked so often.'[32] I felt deeply hurt because I knew that my chances of another game had gone.

It was impossible not to be caught up in the excitement of the tournament and, along with tens of thousands of others I followed England's progress and Gazza's wondergoal excitedly. I was beside myself with anxiety in England's penalty shoot-out with Germany. It was unbelievably thrilling and worrying, and the most awful way to lose. Ironically, England losing meant the final itself was a replay of my match: Germany v Czech Republic. It highlighted the problems of a golden goal (now abandoned by FIFA) because when Germany scored the golden goal in extra time the Italian linesman had his flag up for offside. We will never know whether referee Pairetto would have disallowed the goal had he had the chance but the scale of the German celebrations was such that it was impossible for anyone to do anything but allow them to continue.

Looking back, I had come through a tough international apprenticeship and enjoyed some fantastic matches. The difference between refereeing in England and in Europe occasionally caused problems but I had established myself as a leading European referee and now my focus was on the ultimate goal – the World Cup Final.

# Chapter Eight

# *The World Cup Dream*

*'The inevitable clash had come.'*
DAVID ELLERAY

In 1996, I was ranked in the top ten referees in the world on a football website and prior to Euro '96 I had two major matches outside Europe which broadened my experience, enhanced my reputation and encouraged me to believe that my World Cup dream might become a reality.

In October 1995 I was appointed to referee the World Club Championship (also known as the Inter-Continental or Toyota Cup) in Japan between Ajax of Amsterdam (European Cup winners) and Gremio of Brazil (South American Cup winners) and thus become the only English referee to officiate in the match since it had become a one-off final. I immediately thought of those extraordinary matches in the late 1960s, especially when Nobby Stiles was dismissed in the battle between Manchester United and Estudiantes.

This appointment set in train a series of events which would produce some of the people who are now my closest friends, some wonderful matches and experiences, and rekindled my

Christian faith. The starting point was a moment of serendipity on the afternoon I got the appointment. I went to ask the Head Master for permission to go to Japan and as I crossed the road back to Druries I bumped into a prospective parent, Brian Mahon, who was looking round the School. He introduced himself as the head of the consortium that organised South Africa's friendly matches and invited me to referee South Africa v Brazil in Johannesburg in March. Extraordinarily, within a few hours I had been appointed to referee what was effectively the World Club Cup Final and a match between the newly crowned African champions and the World Cup holders.

I set off for Tokyo on 25 November laden with A level geography essays to correct on the plane. The other officials were a South Korean linesman and Japanese linesman and fourth official. The FIFA pre-match reception brought home to us the enormity of the occasion. We received many presents including three different commemorative watches. I slept well but woke on the morning of the match feeling the eyes of the world on me; as the day passed the pressure grew. On the drive to the stadium I felt completely isolated as my colleagues chattered away in Japanese. I do not think I had ever felt so lonely and isolated before a match and I can still recall the somewhat hollow feeling I had inside. I had not realised how important the inconsequential pre-match banter is in calming nerves and with no one to talk to I felt increasingly tense. My mood did not improve when we arrived at the Olympic Stadium to find that our dressing room had no lavatory facilities and we had to share two urinals and a WC with the entire Brazilian contingent.

The clash of styles and attitudes between the physical north Europeans, managed by Louis Van Gaal, and the volatile and dramatic South Americans, whose coach was Louis Filipe, was potentially explosive. I knew I would have to be on top form to keep control. The pitch was in a very poor state and the ball seemed light. Play swung from end to end and there were a number of chances but no goals. We reached half-time without any serious problems although I had booked two Gremio players. A talking point came in the fifty-sixth minute when Gremio's Catalino Rivarola, who I had booked three minutes earlier, made a wild challenge on Patrick Kluivert but the ball ran to Jan Litmanen who was about to shoot. It is risky playing an advantage for a red card offence but not wanting to deny Ajax the chance to score, I allowed the shot. Litmanen hit it weakly at the goalkeeper and the ball went out of play. I called Rivarola across and showed him the red card and he left the field to minimal protests.

I turned to both assistants and with a clenched fist signalled to them to be on their toes. I did not know how experienced they were and I was particularly worried by the South Korean, on the dugout side, who had only been officiating for five seasons. Three minutes later I penalised Ajax's Marc Overmars near his penalty area. Lots of players crowded round and, behind my back, a Gremio player fell to the ground clutching his face, claiming Overmars had punched him. There was uproar and the South Korean linesman was assailed by the occupants of the Gremio bench. I was surrounded by Gremio players demanding a red card and Ajax players claiming nothing had happened. There was mayhem.

I immediately brought my basic refereeing instincts and techniques into play. I tried to radiate calm and called to mind the famous line about keeping your head, from Rudyard Kipling's poem *If*, as I walked purposefully across to the linesman. I strongly suspected it was play-acting to try to get Overmars sent off to even up the numbers but I was worried that the linesman might have been taken in by the Brazilian reactions. My fears were unjustified and he told me in his broken English that nothing had happened. I returned to the incident and simply blew my whistle and pointed for a Brazilian free kick. The 'injured' player instantly got up and 'disappeared'. When I watched the incident on the video afterwards I saw that my Korean colleague had been absolutely correct. I was delighted when he was selected for the 1998 World Cup finals in France.

The match continued at a hectic pace and Kanu and Litmanen

joined the yellow card list but no one could score. The match went to penalties which Ajax won 4-3. Everyone seemed very happy, even the Gremio players who for some reason called me 'professor' as they shook hands at the end. The sense of isolation returned after the game. I was on an adrenalin high as the match had gone well but I could not share this with my colleagues who were jabbering excitedly in Japanese. The post-match talk about various incidents helps release the tension and I found it highly frustrating that I could not share my happiness and emotions with them. It brought home just how important a release apparently incidental conversations and jokes are in coping with the enormity of officiating at the highest level.

An abiding memory is the extraordinary crowd behaviour. An exciting attack ending in a great shot or save received limited applause or reaction. About ten seconds later, the crowd would suddenly cheer and applaud. It was very perplexing until I realised that they were watching the gigantic screens and applauding the replays!

I was fast asleep at about 3.00 a.m. when room service delivered an urgent fax from Harrow; Druries had convincingly won all elements of the inter-House CCF assault course competition. I was upset I was missing it but delighted with the result until I read that the House Tutor had bought half a dozen bottles of Moët Chandon to celebrate at my expense! I fancied some champagne myself to celebrate successfully coming through my first FIFA match outside Europe.

A few months later I flew south to a country which would soon become very special to me. I arrived at Jo'burg Airport to a carnival atmosphere as the Brazilian team had just arrived and the terminal was alive with dancing and singing children, and a plethora of media representatives. This was clearly a special match for South Africa who were still on a high, having won the African Cup of Nations on home soil, and they were relishing playing the World Cup holders.

I was greeted royally and then whisked off to some TV interviews. My host was Ari Soldatos, a FIFA linesman who later officiated in the 1998 World Cup finals. My assistants were from Angola and Mauritius. The former spoke only Portuguese and the latter spoke English and French so, as in Japan, communication was not easy. The next morning we set off on what I thought would be a sight-seeing tour: it soon became a procession of visits to back-street car dealers as the Mauritian assistant needed some parts for his car back home.

The journey out to the edge of Soweto for the match was a slow one with the highway choked with fans resplendent in the South African colours. We arrived about ninety minutes before kickoff to an almost full FNB Stadium. There was a youth game underway, and as we walked round the pitch to soak up the atmosphere, I bumped into a young linesman called Daniel Bennett. This chance encounter was to have an extraordinary impact on my career and life and made 24 April 1996 a very special day.

The atmosphere was different from anything I had ever experienced – there was so much joy and happiness everywhere. The fans were singing and laughing and there was a cacophony of horns and hooters. The teams were competing for the Nelson Mandela Inauguration Trophy which marked his inauguration as President with an annual match between South Africa, or Bafana Bafana, as they are known locally, and a major (ideally non-African) nation. Proud as I was to be officiating, I was saddened that Mandela would not be present.

We left the dressing rooms ten minutes before kickoff and I was very moved as the South African players held hands and sang a powerful, melodious African song as we walked down the long, narrow tunnel to the pitch. We lined up to meet the chief guest, Thabo Mbeki, South Africa's Vice President. As I looked round the stadium it seemed to be overflowing with people and noise and I was sure the crowd far exceeded the 80,000 capacity. Fifteen minutes passed and there was no sign of Mbeki. With the Brazilians and TV people getting increasingly restless I was faced with a major diplomatic problem. Should I keep everyone waiting in the hope that Mbeki would arrive or should I start the match only for him to appear? I set a deadline and fortunately, with three minutes to go, Mbeki arrived. With the formalities completed we kicked off.

The game began well but South Africa were rather tough and after ten minutes I booked Lucas Radebe, one of their English-based players, for a wild tackle. I was mindful that English referees had been out of favour in Brazil for almost thirty years. As the Brazilians saw it, in the 1966 World Cup Pele had not been protected by English referees. The Brazilians said they would never again let an Englishman referee their national team and, while Joao Havelange was President of FIFA, no one from England refereed them. I was thus the first Englishman to referee the national team for almost thirty years and I was keen to avoid another ban. In the thirty-fourth minute I yellow carded the other English-based player, Phil Masinga. He was on a high having put South Africa in the lead eight minutes earlier with a looping header which beat a somewhat sluggish Dida. The crowd were already wild with delight when, in the forty-third minute, Doctor Khumalo struck a beautiful volley to make it 2-0. There was pandemonium. I have never experienced such a wonderful atmosphere and as we walked off at half-time I saw fans of all races singing and dancing together. It seemed to me that football had transcended all the apartheid divides, demonstrating what a powerful uniting influence sport can be on the lives of individuals and nations.

The fairy tale did not continue in the second half however. Brazil, keen not to lose their unbeaten record against African teams, raised their game. Flavio began the revival with a twenty-yard rocket of a shot in the fifty-sixth minute and ten minutes later Rivaldo rounded two defenders to curl the ball into the net to make it 2-2. A wonderful encounter developed but Brazil were just too classy and, with six minutes left, Bebeto, who had been quite brilliant throughout, volleyed home a Ze Maria cross. It had been a marvellous advertisement for football and I felt as if I had been in a spectacular dream.

Elated, I went upstairs to the post-match reception and met Brian Mahon, and thanked him for giving me the opportunity to be part of such a wonderful match. I also met his stunning wife, Iola, and young son, Michael, who he hoped would eventually come to Druries. Returning to my hotel, I was joined by Daniel Bennett and his parents. He told me I was his role model and that he had been so sure I would be refereeing the game that it was no surprise when I walked out pre-match. The four of us chatted late into the night about refereeing and football and I learned that Daniel had been born in Yorkshire but had come to Jo'burg in 1983 when his father, also a referee, had emigrated. I discovered that South Africans follow English football avidly, not least because they see three or four live Premier League matches every weekend.

The next day I was given a Brazilian and a South African team shirt, both signed by the players, and a case of fine South African wine which began my love affair with the South African vine. I flew home on cloud nine, having refereed one of the most memorable matches of my career. I also took with me indelible memories of happy, singing people and a young referee who would later reinvigorate my career and who would become my number one refereeing pupil.

The success of these matches convinced me that I could referee the 1998 World Cup Final. My first objective was selection for the finals but I had disappointed FIFA by turning down tournaments in Australia and Japan because I could not be absent from Harrow for two to three weeks. I therefore needed to reinforce my standing as one of Europe's top referees by performing extremely well in UEFA club matches and FIFA internationals. Domestic matches would be of limited importance, although as so many Premier League games were broadcast live across the world a poor performance could harm me. Amid all these hopes and ambitions there was the nagging doubt about whether if selected for France I could be away from Harrow, and especially Druries, for six weeks at such a crucial stage in the school year.

My first World Cup match had been Malta v Portugal in Valetta in 1993 and I restarted my campaign in August 1996 in Belgium with a very tense match with Turkey. I was surprised to discover that the FIFA match commissioner was not an ex-referee but the former French coach, Gérard Houllier. Belgium were winning 2-0 at half-time but the police stopped us going out for the second half as there was fighting in the Turkish section of the ground. Apparently, a contingent of Turks from Germany was fighting with other Turks while the bemused Belgian supporters looked on mystified. We eventually restarted and I sent off Yalcin of Turkey for spitting at a Belgian player after he was fouled. Footballers loathe spitting so it was fortunate that I was close to the incident and immediately got the red card out before the Belgian players could react. Houllier had not seen the incident but as we discussed it in the dressing room afterwards it appeared on the TV and he was very complimentary about my spotting the offence and dealing with it promptly and firmly. Little did I realise that he would become a central figure in the Premier League in a few years time.

I then had an important Champions League match in Norway, in Rosenberg, and the whole town was alive with excitement at the visit of the mighty AC Milan. The significance of the match for me was that the observer was Michel Vautrot who was now on the FIFA Referees' Committee. Milan were too strong for the Norwegians and ran out 4-1 winners. I had very little to do but, mindful of UEFA's requirement for referees to be strict, I booked Marcel Desailly for carrying the ball away after conceding a free kick in the thirty-fourth minute and Costacurta for an eighty-fourth-minute foul. Everyone seemed very happy so I was surprised when afterwards Vautrot enquired, 'Why did you yellow card Desailly and Costacurta?' I said I thought they were yellow card offences. 'Of course, they could be but why did YOU use your yellow card?' I was mystified, so he explained. 'When David Elleray walks onto the field everyone knows who he is. They have instant respect for him so he does not need to use the cards.' He believed that I had not needed to book them because the game was totally under control and the offences did not challenge my authority. It sowed a seed in my mind and as my career progressed I increasingly came round to Vautrot's way of refereeing, especially in the Premier League. As we flew home I reflected on all that he had said. While slightly disappointed, I was very pleased that he had been critical in the context of my reputation in Europe. I felt I was moving in the right direction.

Unlike today, there were far fewer European matches to referee and I had to wait over a month for my next trip – Sparta Prague v Fiorentina in the Cup Winners Cup. My two assistants (as linesmen were now called) were Matt Messias, a new FIFA assistant, and Phil Sharp, who would join the FIFA list in January. On the journey to the morning administrative meeting I noticed that Phil had not shaved. I commented on his scruffy appearance and pointed out that, as we were meeting officials of both clubs and UEFA officials, being unshaven hardly created the impression of high-quality, professional referees. Phil was extremely embarrassed. I caught Matt Messias grinning and said, 'And you should know better, Messias!' He had not shaved either, nor, as the senior colleague, had he warned Phil what was expected. It was an incident they never let me forget.

Prague was one of the most stunning cities I had visited and its beauty and tranquillity were in stark contrast to a very competitive and challenging match. By the end I had shown the yellow card nine times and included in the list of culprits were Tomas Repka of Sparta Prague and Gabriel Batistuta and Stefan Schwarz of Fiorentina. I was very touched when, after the match, Schwarz presented me with his shirt to thank me for, in his words, 'being a very fair and honest referee'. This sportsmanship towards referees was a very European feature and when I later refereed another ex-Arsenal player, John Jensen, for Brondby he made a point of shaking my hand as he was substituted off, only minutes after I had booked him.

In early March I refereed Bobby Robson's Barcelona in their European Cup Winners' Cup quarter-final first leg against AIK

Solna of Sweden. It was my first visit to the impressive Nou Camp Stadium. The players' tunnel is divided in two by a fence which prevents the two teams having any contact (friendly or otherwise) when going between the pitch and the dressing room. About a quarter of the way down the tunnel on the home side there is a small chapel containing a statue of the black Madonna. As we lined up for the start several players emerged from the chapel and there was no doubt that it played an important role in their lives and playing careers.

The 65,000 crowd gave the teams an ecstatic welcome and the atmosphere was electric. In the same way that actors rise to the occasion when there is a full house, so players and referees cannot help but be affected by the crowd. When they are noisy and expectant the adrenalin flows that little bit faster. As a referee you have to be careful to control your feelings and emotions, otherwise you have little chance of controlling the players. Solna scored through Pascal Simpson in the second minute and the goal was greeted by thousands of Barca fans waving white handkerchiefs in protest at the sloppy defending. However, Gheorghe Popescu equalised two minutes later. It was 1-1 at half-time and not a card in sight. The players were getting on with the game although Hristo Stoitchkov was constantly complaining but in the second half the tension began to grow as Barca pushed for goals as 1-1, with Solna having that vital away goal, would be a bad result. Barca's frustration was clear and I booked Guardiola on sixty-eight minutes for a late tackle, then Nordin of Solna was yellow carded for blatant time-wasting. Ronaldo scored a quite magnificent headed goal in the fifty-sixth minute but the fans' frustration remained and expressed itself with the players when Barca's Lauren Blanc was guilty of a dreadful tackle and I gave him a straight red card. The crowd went berserk. I was aware of the hooting and hostility but I was not sure whether it was aimed at me, the player or the team. When I yellow carded Barca's De La Peña three minutes later the boos and whistles reached fever pitch. Fortunately for me,

Nordin then steamed into a tackle which was almost worth a red card but I gave him his second yellow followed by the red and the crowd were appeased. Barca seemed to relax: Pizi scored after eighty minutes and they emerged 3-1 winners. It had been a wonderful match and I had enjoyed the theatre of it all. My gestures and signals were becoming increasingly flamboyant with each overseas match, partly because foreign players and officials seemed to like referees who were prepared to be theatrical and to show character.

The wonderful thing about going abroad as an English referee was that I was always treated with the utmost respect. This was partly because I was 'known' as so much English football is watched overseas that Premier League players and referees are almost household names. Moreover, English referees are always regarded as totally fair and honest. If I made a mistake the players seemed more prepared to accept it because they did not believe that as an Englishman I would 'cheat'. Reputations counted for something much more overseas than in England.

The season was going really well and in April I flew with Steve Lodge, Mark Warren and Matt Messias to Tenerife for their UEFA Cup first leg semi-final with Schalke 04 of Germany. My pleasure at the appointment was dampened by the appointment of the Belgian UEFA observer, Alex Ponnet, the man who, I felt, had robbed me of a second match in the Euro '96 finals with his harsh assessment of my performance in the Germany v Czech Republic match.

We arrived at the stadium to find more than 20,000 people already crowded onto the open terraces. Memories of my handling of Auxerre v Tenerife ensured a hostile reaction and when we did our pre-match pitch inspection there were tremendous boos and hoots. On the spur of the moment, I walked to one end of the pitch, stood in front of the goal, raised my hands above my heads and applauded the fans. Miraculously, they applauded back and our inspection became almost like a lap of honour. Unfortunately, by the end of the game I had reignited their hostility!

As expected, the match was very challenging. In the opening stages Schalke were the more difficult team but yellow cards in the eleventh and seventeenth minute quietened them down. The home team warmed to me further when I awarded them a penalty which gave them a half-time lead. The match burst into life after fifty-four minutes when Tenerife's Dorado elbowed an opponent in the face and I sent him off. The crowd went berserk and the atmosphere got to the away team and I quickly booked two of them for rash challenges. Then, in the seventy-third minute, the Tenerife goalkeeper, Ojeda, chopped down an opposing forward and I awarded a penalty and sent him off. The crowd were by now beside themselves and I feared that we might not finish the match. Again, fortune seemed to shine on me and the reserve goalkeeper saved the penalty. I had a couple more yellow cards and when I blew the final whistle I felt physically and emotionally drained. It had been a very demanding match in hot, hostile conditions but Mark Warren told me it was the best he had ever seen me referee abroad and Lodgey thought the same. Unfortunately, Ponnet thought otherwise and again said I had not been strong enough. I thought I had been pretty brave sending off two home players but he obviously did not and his mark robbed me of any chance I might have had of refereeing a European final that year.

My season ended in Budapest with another World Cup match – Hungary v Norway – and I was hugely disappointed that Norway were involved as, to preserve my neutrality, I had to decline an invitation to referee their friendly match with Brazil. There were a number of Premier League players in the Norwegian team, including Egil Ostendstad (who I booked in the closing stages of the game), as well as Oyvind Leonhardsen and Stig Inge Bjornebye. If ever there was a game where one decision gave me almost total control then this was it. In the twelfth minute the Hungarian star striker, Ferenc, went to ground in the Norwegian penalty area. My friend Dermot Gallagher told me later that he was watching the game at home and was amazed when I did not award a penalty but penalised and yellow carded Ferenc. Dermot was convinced I was wrong until he saw the replay which clearly showed the dive. I could not explain exactly why I thought it was a dive but there was just something about the manner in which he fell which did not suggest someone being knocked off his feet. The player did not protest and from then on the Norwegians knew they were going to be treated fairly and the Hungarians realised they did not have a 'homer' in charge. They played out a rather drab 1-1 draw but there had been no controversy.

As I looked back on the season I knew that I had greatly enhanced my chances of being included in the list of World Cup referees which would be announced early in 1998. I now had six months and probably only half a dozen more games to make my case. There was, however, a potential problem as I had started applying for Headmasterships. I made two short lists and in both interviews much of the focus was on whether I would continue refereeing if I was appointed. While I said that I would do whatever the Governors wanted, I think it was clear to them that I hoped to continue refereeing. I withdrew from one post after interview and was beaten by an existing Head for the other one, but continued with my applications.

I only had a short break in the summer; indeed I was in the midst of a spell where, from July 1995 until May 2001, I refereed in every one of the sixty-four months. I did not mind as I was enjoying my refereeing more than ever before. I sensed all was going according to plan when I received another World Cup match. This time it was a relatively low-key appointment – Romania v Iceland – and I was disappointed that I had not been given a more testing match. However, the FIFA match commissioner explained 'FIFA decided that you always have difficult matches so they thought it was time you had a straightforward one!' Romania were much too strong for Iceland and the match turned out to be an historic one as Gheorghe Hagi equalled and then broke the Romanian goal-scoring record. As we approached the closing stages I had only issued one yellow card, to Prodan, but when I awarded Romania a penalty in the eighty-first minute I booked the Icelandic goalkeeper, Gottskalysson, for the crunching tackle and added Siggi Jonsson's name as he protested long and hard. Hagi stepped up and coolly slotted the ball into the back of the net for the record.

A few weeks later I was again off into Europe and this time I was greatly looking forward to my return to Monte Carlo for Monaco's Champions League encounter with Bayer Leverkusen. We experienced some of the most lavish treatment of my international career. We lunched at the Monte Carlo Country Club and stayed at L'Hermitage, where I had one of the great meals of my life in a wonderful private dining room. Beneath an ornately decorated ceiling and in a *fin de siècle* atmosphere we enjoyed lobster salad and coquilles St Jacques, followed by exquisite strawberry, mandarin, vanilla and chocolate soufflés, all washed down with a very fine Corton Champagne 1989.

About an hour before kickoff we were called to the Monaco dressing room and were presented to Prince Albert who is a fervent supporter of the team. I had been told that he had his own football team nicknamed *badajuan* (after a local delicacy) and I discussed their performances with him. All this rather delayed our preparations so when we returned to the dressing room the two assistants immediately went to warm up. Although UEFA expected all match officials to do a warm-up on the pitch before the match I never did. I preferred to rub Deep Heat into my leg muscles to get them warm and to do a series of stretches rather than expose myself to public scrutiny too early. To be truthful, I would have felt extremely self-conscious doing all those stretches and runs. I used to laugh it off by saying that I would get enough abuse during the ninety minutes and I did not need to subject myself to even more before the match started. I was midway through my stretching when Mark Warren returned looking pained and white. He had pulled a muscle doing some warm-up sprints, proof, if I ever needed it, that warming up was a bad idea! He was unable to run the line so reserve referee Graham Barber took the flag; he had lined to me in the Cup Final so I knew he would be fine.

Monaco emerged as 4-0 winners. Although I sent off Kovac of Bayer, it had been another straightforward match and the observer was delighted with our performance.

I was growing confident about my chances of going to France. However, things had taken a significant turn at Harrow where Nick Bomford had announced his intention to retire in July 1999 and the Governors were advertising for his replacement. One or two people suggested that I should apply but as Harrow always appointed an existing Head Master I dismissed the notion. It therefore came as a shock when the Chairman of the Governors said the Governors would like me to apply. He said there was no guarantee that I would be appointed but I would make the final short list at the very least. He outlined the timetable for the appointment and this put me in turmoil as the interviews were scheduled during the World Cup. I spoke to several friends about whether to apply but any hope of being able to make a private decision went as someone leaked the idea and it became common knowledge throughout the School pretty quickly, causing plenty of debate.

I felt under intense scrutiny and was thus delighted to escape at half-term and then, as I was about to go to Prague for Sparta's Champions League game against Galatasaray, I received a phone call from Colin Downey saying I had been appointed to a World Cup match in Riyadh on 6 November. In preparation for the World Cup, FIFA wanted to give referees experience of refereeing outside their own continent and had made a series of 'exchange' appointments. I was to have the honour of being the first European (indeed, the first non-Asian) to referee a World Cup qualification match in Asia. I was thrilled because it showed that I was regarded as one of FIFA's top referees.

Saudi Arabia were playing China, which made the game even more exciting as China were an emerging football nation and this would guarantee, in theory at least, an enormous television audience. I did some research about customs and practices in the Arab world and briefed my colleagues (Steve Lodge, Phil Sharp and Paul Vosper) about various do's and don'ts. I stressed two things in particular: sitting with the soles of your shoes showing is considered very rude, and Muslims do not eat pork. We arrived at lunchtime and after a quick snack we went to the pre-match administrative meeting. The Saudi delegation wore white robes and headdresses and a number of them were members of the royal family. We looked pretty smart in our blazers with the FA badge on the breast pocket but felt rather uncomfortable when the Chinese delegation arrived and we saw that one of them was wearing the same badge. It was Ted Buxton, Terry Venables' right-hand man when he was England manager, who was now working for the Chinese FA as a coaching adviser. He made a beeline for us and chatted away about life in China. After the meeting, the Sri Lankan FIFA match commissioner told me that I should not speak to Buxton as it looked bad since he was wearing the same uniform as us.

The next morning I awoke to find, to my great surprise, that it had been raining heavily – it was strange, but rain often followed me when I had a big match. Steve Lodge was particularly grumpy at breakfast, so much so that we nicknamed him 'Victor' after the moaning Victor Meldrew in the TV series *One Foot in the Grave*. 'I'd just got off to sleep when some bloody idiot outside started screaming,' he complained, unaware that the 'screaming' had been the faithful being called to prayer at the mosque. Steve is a very fussy eater and only likes simple English food and we had great fun teasing him about the sheep's eyeballs and goats' testicles that he would have to eat at the official luncheon. 'I'm not eating any of that bloody muck!' he replied.

A Saudi FIFA referee looked after us and he drove us out to the magnificent King Fahd International Stadium on the outskirts of the city. It was one of the most impressive I had visited. Its roof was constructed like a Bedouin tent and the ground held

70,000, with parking for about 37,000 cars. Everything was immaculate – not a scratch or piece of peeling paint in sight; how different from our own dilapidated Wembley.

The pitch itself was like a luxury carpet and they could raise or lower the water table to ensure perfect playing conditions. Although they said they rarely had any trouble with spectators there was a small police station under the main stand where they dealt harshly with any miscreants. Our host referee recounted a story of one player who argued with a referee and was sent off. When he refused to leave, the police came onto the field, took him to the police station and gave him a 'good beating'. 'He never played football again,' our host added darkly but did not tell us whether he had been banned or had been physically unable to. The players' dressing rooms were immense and each had its own warm-up area which was like a huge gymnasium.

The main stand was on the other side of the field and in the royal box each spectator had his own throne-like seat with a personal television monitor. Everywhere was gold and marble. Downstairs there was a small hospital in case of emergencies and some bedrooms in the unlikely event of people being trapped in the stadium. Once the tour was over we went for a desert drive and, as we passed a huge camel farm, I asked what they kept camels for. Our referee host explained that they were for transport, work and food. I asked what camel meat tasted like and before I knew it Paul Vosper had said, 'I suppose it tastes like pork!' I was horrified but, apart from a slight tightening of his grip on the steering wheel, our host remained impassive.

When we returned to the ground it was already full and the atmosphere was electric. Walking out to the sight of 70,000 Arabs in white robes singing Western football songs and doing a Mexican wave was surreal. The match was played at a furious pace. The Chinese ran around like dervishes and the tackles went flying in. To calm things down I booked two of them midway through the half but the greatest excitement came when I awarded a penalty to China. The stadium went deathly silent but was soon reverberating with cheers as the Saudi keeper saved the kick; at half-time it was 1-1 and I had given four yellow cards. The pattern continued in the second half although no one looked likely to score until China conceded a penalty and I felt able to say that, with one blow of my whistle, I had upset a quarter of the world's population. There was eager anticipation around the ground but it turned to catcalls of derision when the weak penalty was easily saved. There were no more goals and by the end I had experienced one of the most frenetic ninety minutes I could remember. I had booked eight players for fouls, six of them from China. Buxton came in afterwards to thank us and surreptitiously gave us some Chinese football shirts and gifts. We had little time to relax as we had to shower, change, be introduced to the various dignitaries and then leave for the airport for the midnight flight. It all added to a whirlwind experience.

The game in Riyadh had gone well and I felt that I had taken a major step towards France. However, the World Cup and Harrow were on a collision course and I knew which had to take priority. In the second half of the summer term the boys were busy taking their GCSE and A level examinations. They needed a great deal of encouragement and support. Moreover, there were the Common Entrance examinations for prep school boys hoping to join the School that September and then a tea party for all the new boys and their parents. There would also be the Eton v Harrow cricket match at Lord's and the Harrow team included several Drurieans, including the captain, Daniel Hepher. I also knew that I could not be absent on the last night of the term when there was a Leavers' dinner followed by the singing of Harrow Songs in each House, after which I traditionally made a speech bidding farewell to the boys who had been in my care for the last five years. I knew it would be impossible for me not to be at School.

My very strong chance of selection was confirmed when I was appointed to referee the UEFA Super Cup Final between Barcelona and Borussia Dortmund. My assistants were Phil Sharp and Mark Warren, the very best England has ever had as

Mark later lined the 1998 World Cup Final and Phil the 2002 World Cup Final in Japan. Peter Jones, one of my closest and most trusted friends, was the fourth official.

It was exciting to be back at the Nou Camp and the match was very straightforward. I gave only three yellow cards, two after I had played the advantage and then gone back and shown the card. Barcelona had an emphatic 2-0 win and the only talking point was when I let Borussia take a free kick just outside the Barcelona penalty area without blowing the whistle. The Laws only require the referee to signal but on the Continent the teams expect the whistle. Nothing came of the kick but the Barcelona goalkeeper, Ruud Hesp, politely asked me as we came off for half-time to use the whistle in future. There was a nice moment afterwards when Barcelona's Ivan De La Peña came into my dressing room and asked to exchange shirts with me. I said that I was not allowed to do so but he still gave me his shirt. That evening the UEFA observer, Lars Aake Bjorck, who was on the UEFA and FIFA Referees' Committees, said I had a very good chance of going to France but deep down, I knew that I would not be going.

I had several very long discussions with Ken Ridden and explained the problems with the Head Master interview timetable and my commitment to Druries. Ken was very keen that I accept the nomination and then decide what to do. He was concerned that if I did not allow myself to be nominated no other English referee would be selected. Much as I appreciated his confidence it seemed morally wrong to allow myself to be nominated when I knew that I would be unable to accept. I felt it only fair to let someone else have the chance so I sent Ken the following letter:

*Dear Ken*

*Following our meeting last week I have given much thought to the dilemma facing me, and you, about the World Cup Finals in France next June.*

*The present situation is that I have been short-listed for the Head Master's post at Lancing College. I will be*

*interviewed on 12 November and, if successful, will have
a final interview on 24 November with an appointment
being made soon after that. If I am offered and accept the
position there is a possibility that I could resign from
Harrow as from Easter. I would then be free to officiate
in France. However, Lancing College might require me to
be available during June to appoint staff and to receive
briefings before taking over as Head. Additionally, I am
unsure whether Harrow would be happy to release me
during the academic year as this would cause
considerable problems covering my A level and GCSE
teaching as well as the running of the House.*

*If I fail to be appointed to Lancing, or decide not to
accept any offer made, then I am likely to continue with
my application to be Head Master of Harrow. This would
certainly involve at least one round of interviews during
June. Moreover, being away during June would not be to
my advantage as it would be the time when I would be
trying to convince the Governors that I am the man most
suited, and most committed, to taking charge of the
School's future. They might justifiably suggest that
refereeing would seem to be more important to me than
the School.*

*All this means that the chances of my being able to go
to France, even if I was selected, are minimal. You know
that I am concerned that I should not be selfish and
maximise my slight chances and thus deprive the Football
Association of a representative. However, I feel that I
must ultimately leave that aspect of the situation to your
judgement. I am further concerned that being selected,
and then withdrawing, might damage the reputation of
English referees in general and my standing in particular.
Again, you are in a better position to make a judgement
about this than I am.*

*I am most grateful for all your support and advice over*

*this difficult matter. I have been extremely fortunate that*
*the Football Association, through you, and Harrow*
*School, through the Head Master, have enabled me to*
*combine both 'professions' for so long. The inevitable*
*clash has finally come. You know what I feel should*
*happen but I leave it to you as to who you recommend to*
*FIFA. I know that nothing is certain even if you do*
*nominate me.*

> *Yours sincerely,*
> *David*

A few weeks later the referees for France were announced. I was not among them and I felt hollow inside. For thirty years I had believed that I would referee the 1998 World Cup Final. It was not to be and it was very painful indeed. Deep down, I knew I had made the right decision and I have never once regretted it, even though I did not get the Harrow Head Mastership either. The Governors rightly chose Barnaby Lenon, who has done a far better job than I could ever have done but, when it came to it, I knew that Harrow, and especially Druries, came before refereeing. People still ask me if I regret the decision. I do not. Refereeing has been a wonderful part of my life but it has always been second to Harrow and nothing could ever convince me that my priorities were wrong. I had been very fortunate to have got so near to fulfilling my dream. When Mark Warren ran the line in the France v Brazil final it confirmed my long-held belief that, following George Reader in 1950 and Jack Taylor in 1974, an Englishman would do the 1998 final. Mark's appointment gave me great pleasure.

I would love to have been a World Cup referee but that was impossible as I would be too old in 2002. I was left wondering if I would find a new inspiration now that my World Cup dream had ended.

# Chapter Nine

# *Talking Points*

*'Modern-day referees like Elleray require the wisdom of Solomon, the patience of Job, the vision of Superman and the thick skin of Del Boy.'*

DAILY TELEGRAPH[33]

The country was invigorated by the success of the Euro '96 tournament; football had certainly come home. I was really enjoying the Premier League but little did I realise that I was about to enter a period where I would feature in some major controversies as the English game underwent a period of intro-spection and self-examination, with referees often the focus of attention. I was involved in a number of matches which pro-vided major talking points.

I started season 1996/7 with two high profile incidents involv-ing Manchester United. Peter Jones and I officiated at the Umbro pre-season tournament at the City Ground, Nottingham and I refereed the first semi-final between Ajax and Manchester United. During the first half Roy Keane was at his most aggres-sive and difficult. At half-time I had a word with Brian Kidd and said that if he saw me talking sternly to Keane then it was a signal that they should take him off so that I did not have to book him. Sure enough, Keane got involved again and I was delighted when Kidd responded and Keane, to his annoyance, was substituted off in what was described as a 'masterstroke of diplomacy' by one of the newspapers the next day.[34]

A fortnight later, I opened the season proper on a baking hot day in South London when Wimbledon hosted Manchester United. For the most part it was an unremarkable game. I yellow carded Eric Cantona for a foul midway through the second half and as we reached the closing stages Manchester United were in total control at 2-0; we were all going through the motions just waiting for the final whistle and a chance for a cool shower and long, cold drink.

The match had already entered stoppage time when, as I crossed the halfway line, David Beckham looked up from his position on the right flank, just in his own half, and attempted to lob Neil Sullivan, the Wimbledon goalkeeper. For the next few seconds everything seemed to move in slow motion. The ball went extremely high and it was clearly going to beat Sullivan, but where would it land? There was no real expectation in my mind, or, I suspect, any one else's, that Beckham would actually score so we were just watching to see how close he would get. It was rather like a majestic chip shot from Tiger Woods onto the eighteenth green – you do not expect it to drop into the hole but you know it is going to be pretty close. The ball passed behind the goalkeeper's head and out of view and then there was a movement of the net. Had the ball entered the goal or landed on the netting behind? There was a split second of silence – it seemed longer at the time - and then a gasp followed by a roar of approval from all round the ground. Beckham had scored with the most audacious chip. I remember thinking that it was a marvellous piece of skill but, trying not to be swept up in the euphoria, looked across to the assistant to check that it had in fact entered the goal correctly and not through some hole that had mysteriously appeared in the roof of the net. He was running back to the halfway line, the usual signal for a goal, with a surprised look on his face. I looked to my right and there was Beckham with both arms raised and out-stretched, milking the applause. Referees are not supposed to applaud goals but it was difficult not to in this instance. There was genuine applause from all corners of the ground as Beckham was mobbed by his team-mates and several Wimbledon players clapped and I felt minded to do the same. We had about a minute to play and as Beckham passed me I said, 'David – that was sen-sational.' 'Cheers!' he said, looking stunned and delighted in equal measure. The special talent that is David Beckham had arrived in the nation's consciousness and the goal brought comparisons with Pele's similar, but unsuccessful, attempt against Czechoslovakia in the 1970 Mexico World Cup.

When people ask me why I put up with all the abuse and crit-icism I tell them that being on the field when great goals are scored more than makes up for the negative aspects of referee-ing. I have a photograph hanging in my kitchen which shows this goal being scored. Beckham is just in his own half and I am crossing the halfway line. The ball is hanging in the air; there's a look of growing shock on the goalkeeper's face and unalloyed pleasure all around the ground at a moment of such audacious genius from one so young. That goal still brings a glow of pleas-ure whenever I recall it. It was also the only time in my career when I could say that I was not embarrassed at not being up with play, but rather stranded in the centre circle when a goal was scored! Unsurprisingly, it was the goal of the season and was later judged the Premier League goal of the decade.

Sometimes a referee hits a bad patch and that was the case for me with a couple of games. Early that season I first went to the Baseball Ground for Sunderland's visit. This was always a tough ground on which to referee as the partisan Derby crowd was very close to the field and the atmosphere was hostile at the best of times. Sunderland were not on top form that day and neither was I. From the start we did not hit it off and the animosity grew as the game progressed. I squabbled with Niall Quinn and Alex Rae, and after twenty-four minutes I sent off Richard Ord of

Sunderland for an act of angry dissent after he had previously been yellow carded for a foul. This inflamed the Sunderland players, staff and supporters and the rest of the game was very difficult. There are some games, like this one, where you know you are not refereeing well and that you have lost one of the teams. You have to steel yourself to cope with the hassle they are giving you and try to remain calm and confident, even though self-doubt is creeping in. Whenever pundits analyse refereeing decisions they rarely acknowledge that when a referee is having an off day he cannot be substituted, unlike the players. There is no escape and the minutes seem to drag as you become fearful that every time you blow the whistle you will bring more abuse and conflict upon yourself. By the end of a thoroughly unsatisfactory performance I had shown six yellow cards and one red. Few went home commenting favourably about 'Elleray of Harrow' and I deserved their criticism as I had not refereed well. I was particularly cross that I had allowed myself to become irritated by the players and this had disrupted my mental equilibrium. I was snapping at players when I should have been calm and collected. Once you begin to lose control of your emotions when you are refereeing, you make it much more difficult to maintain the dignity and objectivity you need to control the players and their emotions.

The following week I travelled up to Blackburn for their match against Everton knowing I was not Everton's favourite referee following my double dismissal of Barry Horne and Earl Barrett at Newcastle. It was a pulsating game but I had real trouble with Duncan Ferguson, who is a most difficult player to referee. He is ungainly, with flaying arms and legs, and totally unresponsive when you try to talk to him, so you cannot build up any rapport. If you attempt to give him a public rebuke he will ostentatiously ignore you so this management technique could not be used when dealing with him. The game burst into life in the last fifteen minutes. I cautioned Unsworth of Everton and Fenton of Blackburn in quick succession for fouls and then in the eighty-seventh minute Ferguson showed persistent dissent over a straightforward decision and I yellow carded him. This provoked him into an uncontrollable rage and he swore loudly and aggressively at me. Without thinking I said, 'What did you say?' and he repeated exactly the same swear words. I had no alternative but to send him off. Several players looked very surprised at what he said and Craig Short remarked, 'He left you with no option, David.' Joe Royle was incensed and stormed into my dressing room to call me, among other things, a pterodactyl! The Everton fans were so incensed that the police feared for my safety and gave me a police escort to the M6. David Mellor was in full flow on his BBC Radio 5 Live 606 programme and was having a field day taking calls from furious scousers. Referees will tell you that listening to that programme is rather like having a bad tooth – you want to ignore it but, somehow, you can't. I was lambasted in the Sunday and Monday papers and then the abusive letters started arriving from Merseyside. I was pleased I had a midweek match in Europe and could escape.

The season was oscillating between the highly enjoyable and these occasionally unhappy games. Having refereed Liverpool in the 1500th game of my career at Old Trafford, I next went to Anfield for Liverpool v Newcastle. The previous year, Liverpool had emerged 4-3 victors in an amazing game and, while everyone joked that the same would happen again, the odds on a repeat were very long. With the score 3-0 to Liverpool at halftime I remarked to my colleagues that the chances of having another 4-3 thriller were virtually nil. How wrong I was.

Newcastle staged a remarkable comeback and those who remember the game will recall Warren Barton scoring the equaliser and how, in his excitement and pleasure, he kicked the TV sound boom almost into the crowd. It was one of those games which seem to run themselves and all I needed to do was occasionally change the tempo by awarding a free kick. Both sides wanted to attack and no one wanted the game to stop so I could afford to play lots of advantage. There had been a forty-eighth-minute scrap between David Batty and Steve McManaman and I booked them both, but that was the only friction between the players and the only assaults were on the two goals.

We had just moved into stoppage time when Warren Barton asked me how long there was to go. I told him there was just a minute, at which point a Liverpool cross came in from the left and Robbie Fowler scored to make it 4-3. The Kop went wild and once the celebrations had died down we kicked off and I brought a dramatic but hugely enjoyable match to an end. As I relaxed in the large bath in the dressing room I reflected on the part the refereeing team had played in the game. We would get no mention in the press the next day and rightly so, except that we too had played our part in helping to produce a wonderful spectacle. The media are always quick to criticise referees and assistants but when we make a positive contribution we rarely get any credit. Of course the game is about the players but given the criticism we get when we are perceived to have spoilt a game it would be nice if, just occasionally, we got some credit for getting things right. It brought to mind what must be the referee's favourite quote: 'When I'm right no one remembers, when I'm wrong no one forgets!' However, it had been a real privilege to have been part of such a wonderful festival of football and the private contentment of knowing that we had played our part was reward enough.

On 15 February I went to Chesterfield for their Fifth Round FA Cup match against Nottingham Forest. As well as the game being something of a local derby, Chesterfield were beginning to excite the imagination of the public as they, a relatively lowly side, were making excellent progress in the cup. The ground was packed to the gunwales and Chesterfield were very grateful to me as the only goal was a penalty which they scored after Mark Crossley, the Forest goalkeeper, brought down an advancing Chesterfield forward and got himself sent off. Two rounds later Chesterfield and I met up again at Old Trafford for one of the most talked-about FA Cup semi-finals, between Middlesbrough and Chesterfield. It was a fairy-tale match as the small club was only ninety minutes away from Wembley.

It was a sunny Sunday afternoon and the crowd were ecstatic as we emerged to a ticker-tape welcome. Chesterfield, clearly highly motivated by their manager John Duncan, started the better and the game surged from end to end, causing great excitement. Middlesbrough were clearly rattled and Vladimir Kinder committed two late challenges in the space of four minutes and was sent off (thirty-sixth minute) but both teams left the field at half-time to tumultuous applause.

If Chesterfield played well in the first half they played out of their skins in the second; soon they were 2-0 up and looking very secure. Then came the moment that changed my mind about technology in football and which many Chesterfield fans believe robbed them of a place in the Cup Final. Chesterfield were attacking the east end of the ground and a shot from Jon Howard went in which, like that 1966 World Cup Final goal, hit the bar, came down near the line and bounced out. I was positioned on the edge of the penalty area and could not tell if a goal had been scored. Several players turned to claim the goal and I looked across to Alan Sheffield, my assistant, who seemed hesitant. Usually when a goal is scored the assistant moves up the touchline towards the halfway line, keeping his eyes on play. If the ball only just crosses the line he is supposed to stand on the goal line, raise his flag and then point towards the centre. I always encouraged my assistant to hold that signal until I had blown the whistle so that when players and spectators looked at him they could see that he was perfectly positioned on the goal line.

Alan did not flag but shuffled up the line and, as far as I could tell, he was simply getting himself back in line to judge offside. Aware that there was controversy afoot I quickly blew for a foul against a forward and half expected Alan to signal for me to go across to speak him. He did not and I assumed that a goal had not been scored, although he had not given me what you might call a positive negative signal; in other words he had not indicated that a goal had not been scored.

On reflection, I should have gone across and spoken to him as afterwards he said he thought it was a goal. In all honesty, I don't think he knew for sure and, like cricket umpires, we can only give a decision if we are 100 per cent certain. Interestingly, there was little dispute from the players or the spectators at that end of the ground. The pulsating match continued and although I awarded two penalties no one emerged victorious. The match went to extra time and finished 3-3 and everyone had had two hours of wonderful entertainment. I left the field very satisfied with the way the game had gone and everyone seemed happy. There was no abuse as we left the field so it was not until we returned to the dressing room that it became clear that the 'non-goal' had become a major talking point. It was one of those occasions where the media generated discussion and controversy where it did not really exist. That is not to say that they were wrong to do so but the fact was that no one on the field or in the ground really disputed the decision. No one was in a position to say that the ball had crossed the line and in the days before television the incident would scarcely have merited more than a few passing words in the newspapers.

Needless to say, however, Andy Gray on Sky TV was in full flow and, although the TV pictures were not conclusive, they did suggest that a large part of the ball was indeed over the line. But, had the *whole* of the ball crossed the *whole* of the line as required by the Laws of the Game? The ball has to be a long way over the line for it to be 'over' and many of the marginal goal kick, corner and throw in decisions are wrong because the ball has not fully crossed the line. The ball has to go far enough over the line that if the line was extended upwards it would not intersect any of the ball – and that is quite a long way. It was frustrating for everyone that Sky did not have a TV camera exactly on the goal line so the debate raged based on imperfect evidence, the ideal grounds for sustained controversy. To this day I do not know if it was a goal (the same is true of Geoff Hurst's World Cup Final 1966 goal) but for me it was a defining moment as far as technology was concerned.

In general, I believe that football should accept that human error is inevitable. If every decision was referred to a video referee the game would last for hours and there would still be disputes as many decisions come down to a matter of opinion. However, scoring a goal is the fundamental aim of football and deciding whether the ball has crossed the line is a factual rather than a subjective decision. On the rare occasion when the ball hits the crossbar and bounces down and out it has often come from a long-range shot. The referee will not be in a position to judge and the assistant should be in line with the last defender (excluding the goalkeeper) and thus unlikely to be on the goal line. So, through no fault of their own, neither can make an accurate decision. What is needed is something like Cyclops in tennis which will indicate to the referee that the whole of the ball has completely crossed over the line. It seems incredible that in this age of high technology something has not been developed to cope with what seems to be a very simple matter.

The newspapers were full of the controversy and the hate mail began pouring in. What particularly upset me was that Martin Tyler, a commentator I respect greatly, implied that I actively sought controversy, particularly in big games. If he knew the repercussions from controversial decisions he would know that no one would go looking for such trouble. I phoned him to ask what he had meant and, to be fair to him, he apologised and explained that he had meant that controversy seemed to follow me, rather than me seeking it. I could not disagree with that!

Unfortunately, Chesterfield's moment had gone; nine days later at Hillsborough Middlesbrough were too strong for them and, despite a valiant effort, they went down 3-0. The Chesterfield fans have neither forgotten nor forgiven me and whenever I drive north I still avoid Chesterfield.

Midway through the next season I refereed Liverpool v Manchester United at Anfield and United won 2-1 with a convincing display of football crowned by a wonderful free kick goal from Beckham. The pre-match preparations put a lot of demands on me as I had a major function at Harrow on the Friday night; as I was about to set off at 8.00 p.m. I received an urgent phone call from a parent which meant that I had to spend another hour sorting out a problem with one of the boys. The game had a morning kickoff so I travelled halfway there and stayed overnight in Walsall. Early the next morning Mark Warren, England's No. 1 assistant, collected me and we drove to Anfield. We got there so early that we slumped in the dressing room and when Steve Lodge, the fourth official, arrived, he found us fast asleep! That sleepiness did not transmit itself to the players and the crowd and the match had a very fiery start. The tackling was aggressive to say the least and after nine minutes I booked Ronny Johnsen, Nicky Butt and Jamie Carragher for a succession of late, crunching challenges in the space of about ninety seconds. That start certainly ensured I was fully awake.

Amid all the seriousness, however, there are often amusing moments which lighten the atmosphere and relieve the tension. I was at Anfield for a match against Chelsea; as we lined up with the players in the tunnel waiting for the signal from the TV people to go out, cheeky chappie Dennis Wise suddenly grabbed me, said how pleased he was to see me and planted a smacking great kiss on my cheek. This was typical of Dennis – you never knew what was coming next and the best way to deal with him was to talk and talk and talk. I did not referee the game very well and, although there were plenty of goals (Liverpool won 4-2), there were also lots of cards as I struggled to keep the players on my side. I lost the confidence of the Chelsea players and in a stormy four-minute spell midway through the first half I booked Liverpool's Paul Ince for dissent and a few seconds later sent off Chelsea's Lambourde for his second yellow card amid great protests. Chelsea were incensed and dear Dennis steamed into a tackle almost immediately and was also booked. The temperature was then lowered somewhat although Dan Petrescu and Jason McAteer later received yellow cards for fouls.

It had been one of my less impressive performances and I was widely condemned in the papers the next morning. The *Daily Mail*, probably the most widely read paper at Harrow, had the back-page headline 'Elleray, You Blew It!'[35] When I walked into Speech Room at 8.40 a.m. for the Monday morning assembly half the School were holding their papers against their chests with the headline in full view. I got the message!

I was in the news a fortnight later not because I issued seven yellow cards in the Elland Road clash between Leeds and Newcastle but because I refereed most of the first half wearing a blue Leeds United training top. The pyjama-like green and black Premier League referees' kit had been replaced by a choice of one of three shirts: black stripes alternating with either white, red or black. The Premier League told us which shirt to wear for each game. Newcastle's away strip was purple, orange and green and although my shirt looked quite different when we lined up in the tunnel, on the field it looked very similar to the Newcastle kit, especially as they were also wearing dark shorts and socks. While no one actually passed to me, the Newcastle players complained that I was distracting them and when Lucas Radebe mistakenly attempted to mark me at a corner I had to do something about it. I went across to the Leeds United bench and asked if they had any spare shirts and they produced a mid-blue training top. I checked with Kenny Dalglish, the Newcastle manager, who had no complaints, and restarted the game to chants of 'Who's the bastard in the blue?' from sections of the crowd. By sheer coincidence I almost immediately booked Ribeiro of Leeds but I was very conscious of the Leeds crest on the shirt. For about ten minutes I ran round with my left hand covering the badge but then I turned the shirt inside out. Needless to say, the papers criticised me for being unprepared and unprofessional, even though I simply wore what the Premier League had told me to wear.

If that match produced some amusing comments the next game I refereed had a much more sinister undertone. This was the London derby at Upton Park between West Ham and

Crystal Place in November 1997. The visitors dominated the first half and were 2-0 up at half-time. Harry Redknapp must have delivered one of his famous interval talks as West Ham came out with all guns blazing and soon scored. They scored again in the sixty-fifth minute and, as the players celebrated, the floodlights went out. I took the teams off the field and said to one of my assistants, 'Someone must have jumped up and knocked a switch when they scored!' The safety officer came to my dressing room to say they were doing their best to get the lights back on. They managed to get one end working but when they tried the other end all the lights went out again.

A decision had to be taken fairly quickly as the players were getting cold and stiff and the fans were getting restless. I decided to go up to the police control room because evacuating a ground is a major operation and I would not make any decision without the full cooperation of the police. I put a training top on over my kit and walked along the side of the pitch to the control room. Lots of fans wanted to know what was happening and I said I had no news for them. They were pretty patient. When I reached the control room it was clear that the electricians were not going to be able to get the lights back on. The police asked me to delay making an announcement so that they could get extra trains to the local Underground station and more buses into the area. They also wanted to be able to warn all the police and safety stewards, and make sure that the phasing of the traffic lights was changed to allow cars to get away speedily. What I had to do was give the meticulous behind-the-scenes operation time to be brought forward so that the usual final whistle arrangements could swing into action. I went back to the dressing room and told the respective managers and the television people what was happening. I then had a quick shower and agreed to talk to the press.

It took West Ham several days to fix their lights and it later emerged that they had almost certainly been sabotaged. A similar incident occurred at Selhurst Park when Arsenal played Wimbledon and then shortly after someone was arrested trying to interfere with the lights at Charlton. The suspicion was that it was the work of a betting syndicate in the Far East where bets are paid out according to the final score; if the game is abandoned in the second half then for betting purposes the result stands. In both matches the floodlights failed early in the second half when the scores were level. Some months later I was approached by the police to take part in a sting operation. They had intelligence that there would be an attempt to fix the Leicester City v Manchester United match by bribing the referee. The police wanted me to agree to referee the game. They would then leak my name and hope that I would be approached by a betting syndicate. The police planned to wire me up to meet intermediaries so that they could smash the ring. It was all rather frightening and, after consulting the Head Master, I declined as I did not want to be drawn into anything involving gangsters, betting, the triads or whatever. I was quite capable of getting enough abuse and trouble without becoming involved with big-time crime! I also felt that even if it was a legitimate operation I risked being labelled as a referee prepared to take bribes.

West Ham were also involved in a match at White Hart Lane which illustrated, in ninety minutes, both the good and bad aspects of the influx of foreign players into the Premier League. On show were the artistry and magic of David Ginola. His greatness as a player was evident when he created the winning goal for Spurs in the ninth minute. He surged down the left, dropped his shoulder and crossed for Jürgen Klinsmann to take advantage of Rio Ferdinand's slow reaction. His positive and exciting play posed referees some problems as they were linked to a less agreeable side of his game.

Ginola had a reputation for diving and often went to ground too readily for those used to the more rugged style of English football. Certainly, this match reinforced that viewpoint. I needed the courage of my convictions once more and early on I awarded a free kick against Ginola for exaggerating the effects of a challenge. After one spectacular dribble through the defence, Ginola was challenged by David Unsworth, fell, and what started as a stumble became a tumble. I judged it an extreme overreaction to minimal contact and would have booked Ginola except that there had actually been contact, albeit negligible. In contrast, when Spurs' Andy Sinton was clattered by Steve Potts, Sinton quickly jumped up and patted Potts on the back in recognition of a strong, if slightly unfair, challenge.

There may well have been an element of xenophobia in the accusation that diving was a foreign import to the Premiership. But, as my dismissal of Roy Keane at Blackburn in August 1995 had shown, the habit was not confined to the imports and, along with my colleagues, I was determined that diving and overexaggeration should not blight our game. To be fair to Ginola, he was frequently the target for nasty challenges, although he did to some extent invite them. Another 'foreign issue' at this stage was the despicable habit of players indicating to the referee that they wanted a player on the other team to be booked. I felt that both issues needed to be addressed by the PFA and managers as players who overreacted or gesticulated for bookings were effectively attempting to get fellow professionals into trouble.

However, Ginola's antics paled into insignificance just before half-time when, in an off-the-ball incident, Ramón Vega of Spurs pushed Samassi Abou of West Ham who turned round and kicked him. My attention was on the play but Peter Walton, the assistant, spotted what had happened and called me over. I yellow carded Vega and showed Abou the red card but he began protesting and tried to grab my arm and stop me showing the card. He refused to leave the field and started wagging his finger at me. I speak a little French and the gist of what he was saying was that he would not leave. Harry Redknapp, the West Ham manager, came up the touchline to help the situation but his actions were misinterpreted by Colin Calderwood of Spurs and they had an altercation. It was all getting out of hand and I was at a loss at what to do. I wracked my brains for a solution and remembered in the past that referees had called on the police to help but I was reluctant to get them involved. Eventually, common sense prevailed and Redknapp ushered Abou away.

A growing problem for referees at this time was that the exaggerated reaction to fouls often misled their own team-mates into thinking a foul was worse than it actually was. This would then anger the opposition and the scene was set for accusation and counteraccusation and soon there would be confrontation. Harry Redknapp seemed sympathetic to the problem but was upset by Vega's attitude, not least his pulling up of his shorts to show where he had been kicked. 'If it was an English player, he would not have gone down,' Redknapp said. 'Abou deserved to go but I don't think he kicked him hard enough to put him down.' The suggestion from West Ham that Abou's failure to leave the field immediately was because his English was limited cut little ice with me, not least because that is the precise reason why the red and yellow cards were introduced in the first place.

Late summer and autumn 1998 was a very difficult time for me. Although I was greatly enjoying the international matches I had completely lost all other motivation to referee. I knew that I was doing little more than going through the motions in the Premier League. With my dream of refereeing the 1998 World Cup Final now gone, there seemed little else to aim for. My international career would be over in just over a year's time and I had only the Worthington Cup Final left to do. The relentless pressure of juggling Harrow and football was beginning to pall and the abuse and controversy on the field were debilitating. Early retirement became increasingly attractive so I needed new inspirations.

My nadir came on Boxing Day 1998 when, in the final minutes of Southampton v Chelsea, I felt a sharp pain in my calf and I was convinced I had been hit by something thrown from the crowd. We were already several minutes into additional time and, with Chelsea winning 2-0 I blew for time and hobbled off. I went to the Southampton dressing room for treatment and asked them to look at the security cameras to see what had hit me. There was no mark on my calf but when the physio examined me I felt a great stab of pain. I had torn my calf and had not, after all, been hit. I was given ice treatment and some anti-inflammatory tablets and drove home. Being the holidays it was several days before I could get any treatment and I was extremely annoyed that the Premier League had ignored our requests to have physiotherapists available whom we could see as soon as we were injured.

This was the first and only time in my entire career that I sustained an injury during a game. I was very lucky in that respect, especially as I eschewed all the modern theories about warming up beforehand. Rubbing Deep Heat into my muscles and doing a few stretches was good enough for me. I spent a miserable few days and might easily have called it a day there and then had I not received a fax out of the blue from Daniel Bennett, the young referee I had met when I refereed South Africa v Brazil in 1995. We had exchanged the occasional fax since then and, just before Christmas, Daniel faxed me to say that he had just run 2700m in the FIFA twelve-minute test and was really pleased with himself. I faxed back saying that for a twenty-two-year-old it was disappointing and pointed out that I regularly did 2950–3000m and I was more than twice his age. Daniel later told me that my reply really stung him. When he got it he was determined to prove me wrong – so determined, in fact, that he trained hard for a week and then did another run on Christmas afternoon and proudly faxed me to say that he had done 2800m.

Over the next few weeks we made regular contact and he asked if I would help him improve his refereeing. He reminded me that I was his role model and inspiration and he would do anything to achieve half of what I had. He always watched the live matches from England, praying that I would be the referee so that he could study my techniques and man-management. Thus began a regular exchange which not only inspired him but also gave me new motivation and inspiration. I was stunned that someone thousands of miles away was motivated by what I was doing, and it made me determined not to disappoint him or any of the other referees from whom I regularly received letters asking for advice.

I set him a series of fitness targets and started him doing self-assessments so that I could help him improve his on-field performances. The more I got to know him the more he reminded me of the young, enthusiastic referee I was at his age. He had the same hunger for information and ideas, and I felt as if I was reliving my early refereeing days. It made me realise how wonderful youthful enthusiasm is and I found that being his coach reinvigorated me and that my motivation returned. In time I became his mentor and steadily came to treat him like a son.

The time-management conflicts were growing and in mid-February 1999 I found myself triple booked. I should have been at the UEFA Elite referees course as in 1996 but it clashed with Founder's Day at Harrow which is a three-line-whip day for House Masters. If that was not enough, I had also been invited to Johannesburg for Daniel's wedding. Missing that was somewhat compensated for when Daniel asked to come to Harrow for a couple of weeks in March so that I could see him referee. I had not, however, realised when he asked to come that he would be leaving his wife after only three weeks of marriage – dedication indeed.

He arrived at Heathrow at about 11.00 a.m. and within three hours he was running the line for me as I refereed the Harrow 1st XI match against UCS. It was a bitterly cold, grey day and several times I looked across at him as he shivered under several layers, a beanie hat and gloves. By the end of the game he was absolutely frozen although we did manage to get a smile from him when one of the visiting players came up and shook hands with us at the end and said, 'Cheers, ref! That woz just like being on *Match of the Day*!'

For the next few days I put him through a fitness test and then watched him referee the 1st XI. His kit was appalling and the shorts so big that he looked as if he was wearing a skirt. However, within minutes of the start of the game it was clear that he had raw talent. His positioning, signalling and use of the whistle were poor but there was an athleticism about him; there was also an endeavour to work hard and that certain something in the way he spoke to players and his control of the game that told me he had the potential to be a top-quality referee. I could see so much of myself in him and it helped me rediscover all the reasons why I had started refereeing and why, deep down, I found it so fulfilling.

As part of his refereeing education I took him to Newcastle v Manchester United. Having him with me opened my eyes to things that I had come to take for granted. He was fascinated by the number of people who came and chatted during the train journey and he said he was moved by the respect I was shown. Daniel thought his day complete when he met George Courtney (his father's refereeing hero) who was the assessor and managed to get his photo taken with Dwight Yorke. He joined us for the pitch inspection and stayed in the dressing room for the exchange of team sheets and the security briefing. I was really impressed with his unquestionable determination to make it to the top as a referee, but also his humility and ability to conduct himself with quiet dignity when the situation arose, so George and I decided to broaden his experience further. I gave him a tracksuit and asked him if he would like to sit in the technical area with Jeff Winter, the reserve referee. Daniel went as white as a sheet with excitement and shock. He looked after the electronic board for Jeff and spent a most wonderful afternoon sitting only a few yards away from the Manchester United bench.

It was a thrilling match with all the best things about English football, and Manchester United, on display. Solano opened the scoring with a delightful free kick but Manchester United hit back with two goals from Andy Cole in the twenty-fourth and twenty-ninth minutes, both the result of sudden and rapid breaks. The only sour moment was one of sustained dissent from Denis Irwin towards an assistant which resulted in one of only two yellow cards in the game. My day, and I suspect Daniel's, was made complete when afterwards there was a knock on the door and Alex Ferguson came in and shook hands with everyone, Daniel included, and thanked us for the game. 'It's the best I've seen you referee, David!' he said. We were all shocked that he had been to see us and Daniel's estimation of my refereeing rose even higher. The day was rounded off with a highly enjoyable train journey home in the company of Henry Winter, the distinguished *Daily Telegraph* football writer.

Over the next week or so I watched Daniel referee School and House matches. His technical game was dreadful and we had to work very hard on the basics, but he was a quick and determined learner and I was increasingly convinced that he could become a top referee. I drummed into him the importance of positioning, signalling and varying the tone of the whistle, and explained that I wanted all these to become second nature so that he could focus all his efforts on decision-making and man-management. I was tough on him as we had to change a lot quickly, but he responded really well and was as much of a perfectionist as I was. It was exciting stuff and teaching him the basics and answering his myriad of questions helped me re-examine everything I did when I refereed a game. This made me even more focused than before. It also helped me begin to shed the overstrict style I had adopted for much of my career: I felt that I could hardly preach the value of man-management to a young referee if I was not prepared to practise it myself.

It started something of a metamorphosis in my refereeing and as I looked back over these demanding few seasons I thought of the wonderful summing-up of the challenges facing referees from one commentator who said that modern day referees need the 'wisdom of Solomon, the patience of Job, the vision of Superman and the thick skin of Del Boy.'[36]

Fortunately, just as I was about to retire early, disillusioned by the abuse and the constant pressure of two demanding professions, I'd found new motivations and inspirations. I was on fire again.

# Chapter Ten

# *Inspired and Abused*

*'I think the referee must have had some of them magic mushrooms for breakfast.'*

WOLVES PLAYER

I was now back in the groove, my refereeing career revitalised by working with a young enthusiast and, for a short while, I felt that all the controversy and problems were behind me. This feeling was reinforced when I was involved with one of the most exciting matches in FA Cup history – the Manchester United v Arsenal semi-final at Villa Park in April 1999.

In the weeks leading up to the game the media helped build the atmosphere to fever pitch. I was excited at the prospect of doing the game but I was also mindful of all the controversy that had dogged me after my last semi-final appearance. Semi-finals are, I firmly believe, always the most challenging matches of any cup competition. A place in the final is only ninety minutes away and yet losing is ignominious; as they say, no one remembers the losing semi-finalists. For reasons of security and crowd safety the match was scheduled for a Sunday afternoon with a lunch-time kickoff. Arriving at Villa Park early in the morning,

I had a strong sense of *déjà vu*. My mind went back four years to when I refereed the Manchester United v Crystal Palace semi-final at the same venue; that game and the replay were memorable for a number of reasons. The kick off was delayed because of the time it took to clear the pitch of all the balloons the FA had issued to the fans and I was blamed afterwards for kicking off late! The replay was boycotted by many of the Palace fans because one of their number had been killed before the first game but the most memorable incident came in the fifty-second minute of the replay when a huge brawl culminated in me sending off Roy Keane for stamping and Darren Patterson of Palace for reacting violently to Keane's stamp. Before I sent them off I checked with Dave Horlick, the linesman closest to the fighting, to see if I had missed anything but he was so hyped up that he gabbled so fast in his Scouse accent that I could not understand a word he said, even though he repeated himself several times.

The match kicked off in blazing sunshine and after about two minutes Gary Neville committed a blatant foul but I wanted to keep my powder dry so I called him across and spoke to him reasonably sternly. In big matches I felt a responsibility to reduce rather than increase the tension so I was anxious not to produce the yellow card too early if I could avoid it. Unlike his brother, Phil, Gary is not the most receptive or docile of players so the words were less relevant than the action of being seen to be warning him. Almost immediately he brought down Marc Overmars and I reached for the yellow card. On the Sky TV commentary Andy Gray remarked that I had given the player a chance which he had ignored and therefore the card was fully justified. In other words, the action I had taken was 'acceptable' to the vast majority of those watching, even the Manchester United fans. Of course, some said that had I booked him for the first foul he would not have committed the second, while others argued that I should have booked Neville for the first foul and sent him off for the second. I did what I judged best for the game and for my control.

Like many semi-finals, it was rather dull for the first half hour or so. The players were tense and afraid to make mistakes and the crowd seemed hesitant and anxious until the match burst into life in the thirty-eighth minute. Giggs attacked down the left wing, pretended to cross to Dwight Yorke and used this dummy to ghost past Parlour and pull the ball back from near the goal line. Yorke knocked the ball to Keane who finished emphatically to give Manchester United a 1-0 lead. I never whistle for goals but instead look at the assistant before moving upfield and I was surprised to see Graeme Atkins' flag aloft. I moved quickly across to him followed by a posse of Manchester United players. Graeme told me that he had flagged for Dwight Yorke being offside but had dropped the flag and then raised it again when the goal was scored. I was confused and felt uncomfortable with what he was saying but he insisted that Yorke had gained an advantage and been interfering with play (either is essential for a player to be penalised for offside) and he thought the goal should be disallowed.

Unlike the press, TV commentators and, later on, the managers and fans, I did not have the luxury of a TV replay. I was in a dilemma. I could accept the assistant's decision as he was in the correct position and I had no factual knowledge on which to overrule him. Conversely, I could trust my instincts and allow the goal but, if I was proved wrong, on what basis could I justify my decision? How could I persuade anyone that I was right to allow the goal 'on instinct' when there is nothing in the Laws of the Game about instinct? Although deep down I was not happy I disallowed the goal because on the evidence I had before me at the time that was the only logical decision I could take. Manchester United were unhappy and the players became very fractious for the next ten minutes or so.

Chances were rare in the second half and all the way through extra time. The heat seemed to drain the players of their stamina and stoked their tempers and during extra time I had to dismiss Vivas of Arsenal for elbowing Nicky Butt. The match ended 0-0 and we were faced with a replay. This was historic – it would be the last ever in an FA Cup semi-final as the FA had announced earlier in the season that to reduce fixture congestion there would in future be no replays in FA Cup semi-finals.

The debate over the disallowed goal raged for days. Ferguson called the decision 'Quite amazing. Ridiculous', while Wenger retorted, 'I don't know what you can complain about. It was offside indicated by the linesman but the referee didn't see the flag.' In those days the same four officials usually controlled the replay but there was much discussion as to whether Graeme Atkins should remain on the match. Beyond that, the main question was, why had I not overruled him? The decision marked the start of a period when Manchester United players and fans decided that I had something against them. This was to be an ironic sea change of opinion since most non-Manchester United fans had always believed that I favoured Manchester United.

I arrived very early for the replay at Villa Park the following Wednesday and told Mike North and Alan Wilkie (the other assistant and fourth official) to wait in the dressing room while I walked round the pitch with Graeme. This was a vital conversation as he was still suffering from the aftermath of his decision. I said, 'Look, Graeme, you know you got it wrong on Sunday but we cannot change that decision. What you mustn't do is let it influence you so that you make more mistakes tonight. I could have had you taken off this match but I have total confidence in you and I know you will perform magnificently. You will show everyone why you were appointed to this semi-final in the first place. I am going to keep you running the same side of the field as Sunday and you will be excellent.'

Some may have thought it wrong that I did not smooth over the decision. However, both Graeme and I knew that he had got it wrong in the first game and it would have been the worst thing possible for me to ignore his error. I had to be honest and say that he was wrong and then build him up so that he performed on the night. I exaggerated the option to have him removed (although I suspect that, if I had insisted, he would have been taken off the match) as I wanted to show him that I had total confidence in him.

As we walked onto the field we were probably more tense than the players. The first twenty minutes were very challenging and I continued to referee according to the principles I had adopted in the first match. If I had refereed by the book I would have had at least seven yellow cards in that opening spell but I worked really hard to try to take the heat out of the situation. Some players you can talk to while others, like Teddy Sheringham and Dennis Bergkamp, would not listen and just answered back if I tried to reason with them. Manchester United opened the scoring after seventeen minutes when David Beckham latched on to a Sheringham pass and from twenty-five yards out curled the ball past a despairing Seaman. It was the first goal Arsenal had conceded in 660 minutes. The second half was just as exciting and Solskjaer and Blomqvist should have put the result beyond doubt in the opening stages. Arsenal fought back and after sixty-eight minutes equalised when a low shot from Bergkamp deflected off Jaap Stam's thigh past Schmeichel.

I began to sense that I was in the middle of a classic encounter but I did not realise that in the next fifty minutes it would develop into one of the greatest FA Cup semi-finals of all time. Ahead of me lay four major talking points. The first came a minute after Arsenal's equaliser. A stinging shot from Bergkamp was parried by Schmeichel only for Anelka to net the rebound. As Arsenal celebrated I looked across and the assistant was flagging. This time it was Mike North's flag and it was the Arsenal posse that pursued me. Mike explained that when the initial shot was struck Anelka was offside. Had the ball gone straight into the net the goal would have been allowed but as he had scored from the rebound the goal had to be disallowed. I had no hesitation in supporting Mike and the TV replays showed him to have been absolutely correct. What was disappointing, but not surprising, was that the press hardly made mention of Mike's excellent decision. What a contrast to the reaction to Graeme's decision in the first match. It is sad that when officials get it right they receive little praise.

Shortly after this, Roy Keane slid in late and recklessly on

Overmars near the Manchester United penalty area, and, as I had already booked him for a foul on Bergkamp, it meant a dismissal. Before I could get the yellow and red cards out, Keane was walking to the tunnel. It was the third time I had sent Keane off but certainly the least controversial and even Alex Ferguson agreed with it after the match. It was the second time I had sent Keane off in an FA Cup semi-final replay at Villa Park.

We moved into additional time with the score still 1-1 and extra time looking certain. Then Ray Parlour dribbled into the Manchester United penalty area and fell to the ground under a challenge from Phil Neville. I was in a good but not ideal position but my instincts told me that it was a penalty so I blew and pointed to the penalty spot. I moved quickly towards the goal line to put as much distance as possible between me and the Manchester United players. Those who have watched me referee say that whenever I have given a big decision I gently nod my head several times in a subconscious action which indicates that I agree with what I have done! I was aware that I had almost certainly handed a place in the FA Cup Final to Arsenal and I waited and mentally braced myself for the inevitable pack of dissenters. To my surprise there was no argument at all. In fact, when I later saw the incident on TV, it was a blatant penalty, a much clearer and more simple decision than had been the case from my position infield of the incident. Dennis Bergkamp stepped up to put Arsenal through to Wembley only to be denied by a spectacular save from Schmeichel. Moments later I blew for the end of normal time.

I was having increasing difficulty moving as I had been in pain since the first match when I was accidentally knocked over by Nicky Butt and jarred my back. There was nothing for it but to keep moving to prevent it stiffening up. We kicked off to an amazing crescendo of noise from the fans. The match remained delicately poised until Giggs intercepted a pass from Vieira midway in the Manchester United half. He dribbled upfield, passing Vieira, Dixon (twice), Keown and Adams, defeating them as much with the movement of his hips and shoulders as anything else. He reached the penalty area through a combination of pace, dummies and feints and as Seaman set himself for a low shot Giggs' left foot hit the ball with incredible ferocity into the roof of the net. It was one of the most spectacular goals ever seen in an FA Cup match. 'Truly awesome,' I thought at the time. Giggs took his shirt off and twirled it round his head as he ran in celebration down the touchline. The reaction from the crowd was unforgettable and after that Arsenal were completely demoralised and no further goals were scored.

Giggs' wonder goal was interesting from a number of refereeing viewpoints. FIFA have introduced, withdrawn and reintroduced the yellow card for a player removing his shirt when he celebrates. Showing a yellow card for celebrating a goal in a manner which does not offend is very difficult to justify. Ryan Giggs had scored a sensational goal at the end of a wonderful FA Cup semi-final. How would I and refereeing in general have looked if I had booked him for celebrating? What would have been worse was that, if he had been yellow carded earlier in the game, it would have meant that I would have had to send him off. I would have done myself and refereeing a huge disservice if I had applied the letter of the Law.

More significantly for me, Giggs' goal helps explain why we referee. I am often asked why I subjected myself to so much abuse and criticism. Of course, we referee for many reasons and the desire to be actively involved in the game is the strongest of them. However, I also believe that we get something very special from actually being there when the great moments happen. When asked why I put up with all the negativity I sometimes ask people if they remember Giggs' goal. Most football fans do and some tell me how fabulous it actually was to have been at Villa Park that night. I then ask them to imagine what it was like to have been about ten yards from Giggs when he started his run; to have been ten yards from him when he scored; and to have been in the centre of the cacophony of noise that heralded the celebrations. Having been on the pitch when Giggs scored that goal and when Beckham scored his from the halfway line against Wimbledon were two sublime footballing moments that I was privileged to have experienced, not vicariously from the stand or in front of the TV but from almost touching distance. How can you better that apart from actually playing?

After the match my more immediate concern was my back. I was in great discomfort and needed treatment from the Aston Villa physiotherapist just so that I could get showered and drive home. Those late-night journeys down the motorway were always a time for reflection and this time I knew that I had been involved in an amazing match. As usual, I played the game through in my mind searching for the mistakes I had made and trying to work out whether I could have avoided them and how I could have refereed better. I have always been highly self-critical and have never been fully satisfied with any of my performances. There are always mistakes but the best referees make their mistakes on the small decisions and get the big ones right. That is why the Italian referee Pierluigi Collina is regarded as the best in the world. Whenever I made an error I tried to analyse it to see whether it could have been avoided. Sometimes, it is simply a misjudgement based on a split-second view; at other times it is because I was at the wrong angle or did not have a clear enough view of the incident. However, the most frequent cause of error is loss of concentration, especially when a game is going well.

When I gave the last-minute penalty for Ray Parlour I based my decision on what my brain was telling me about the speed and relative movement of the two players, the movement of the ball before and after the challenge. If the ball continues in the same direction then the player making the challenge almost certainly missed the ball so the likelihood of it being a foul is very high. But sometimes the offended player is guilty of 'diving' or 'simulation'. The mind analyses these components in much the same way as it analyses speed and movement when a driver decides whether or not to overtake when traffic is coming in the opposite direction. You are not always aware of the mind's analysis and, sometimes, as with the penalties in the FA Cup Final, you find you have blown before you are aware that you have thought at all. Often, on big decisions, there seems to be a slight pause before the referee blows the whistle. This can lead to accusations that referees are influenced by the crowd but the referee is probably rapidly replaying the incident in his mind before deciding. Commentators sometimes say 'he seemed to think about that one' and they are correct.

Looking back, this was one of the most satisfying matches of my career. I had been under considerable pressure because of the events in the first game. I had then been faced with several major decisions and the opening twenty minutes had presented me with considerable challenges. In the end, I got the major decisions right and had contributed to what would go down in FA Cup history as one of the greatest matches ever. Few people remember that I refereed the game and that adds to my pride as I still believe in the old adage that the best referees are the ones that you do not notice. There is nothing more satisfying for a referee than to have been part of a wonderful match. The last ever FA Cup semi-final replay will live long in the memories of those who watched it live on the day, not only in Villa Park but on television sets throughout the world. It also helped keep alive my new-found commitment to refereeing.

For days after the match I was swept along by the warm glow of having been involved in such a match. It was somehow fitting that the FA Cup, with its wonderful history and magic, had produced such a footballing feast for the last semi-final replay. I was touched that so many people were complimentary about my handling of the game and there was a feeling of immense satisfaction that I had contributed to making the match so enjoyable for so many. It was one of those occasions when I had e-mails and phone calls from referees, friends and Old Harrovians from all over the world wanting to know what it felt like to be involved in such a match. Most special was an e-mail of praise from Daniel. I wonder if he realised how much my performance was due to the inspiration and renewed motivation he had given me.

I was content that I had produced possibly my finest refereeing performance in one of English football's greatest matches. What I was unaware of, however, was that the disallowed goal in the first match had started to turn the tide of opinion against me among the Old Trafford players, management and fans. A few weeks later that tide was to become a flood of condemnation and the most frightening abuse I ever experienced.

Fans screaming at the referee or his assistants are part of the game. Indeed, I was not beyond making the odd comment myself when I coached the Harrow 1st XI. As I moved through the ranks I coped with the abuse as best I could. During a big game it is relatively easy to block out most of the crowd noise as it is just a wall of sound although if the whole stadium erupts it is impossible not to be keenly aware of the upset caused. Walking off and being verbally abused was always unpleasant but I accepted it as part of the job. I could even accept the comments from spectators as I made my way to my car afterwards.

Worst, and entirely unacceptable, were the letters and phone calls after controversial matches. I found it disturbing that people could cold-bloodedly take their time before communicating their rage by telephone or letter. Some letters were cogent and I would often answer them. Others were so crude that they were almost funny, but some were so downright offensive that I destroyed them immediately. The usual theme was that I was not so much incompetent as biased and that hurt.

The Cup Final also produced some amusing letters, the best of which purported to come from a vicar who ran a scout group in Chelsea who proudly told me that the guy being burned on Bonfire Night would have my photograph for a face! I assumed this was a joke but was never really sure. Often the comments were so amusing they could not be taken seriously. After one of my matches a Wolves supporter was reported to have said, 'We were crap, they were crap and the referee was even crapper', while a Wolves player allegedly said, 'I think the referee must have had some of them magic mushrooms for breakfast.'[37] One of the most amusing comments was when I arrived at Stamford Bridge and one fan said loudly to another, 'Look who's reffing today. It's Satan!'

I experienced plenty of trouble after the Cup Final when a group of Chelsea fans came up to Harrow to try to find me. The boys in Druries were very clever and sent them on a wild-goose chase to another part of the School. However, a more disturbing campaign of abuse soon followed, the most sinister aspect being the phone calls. Someone, or a group of people, started phoning me each night, every hour, on the hour, until I slept with the bedroom phone switched off and the answerphone/fax in my study switched on. So disturbing were these calls that even today I still switch off my bedroom phone at night. I did not referee Chelsea for almost a year after that, and then it was a midweek match at Maine Road. My first visit to Stamford Bridge came almost two and a half years after the final. When I walked onto the pitch the PA announcer said, 'Please give a warm welcome to our old friend, David Elleray.'

Having thus endured more than my fair share of abuse I thought I could cope with almost anything but nothing prepared me for the venom and hatred which exploded after a match at Anfield. Before that, however, I was reserve referee in an extraordinary match between West Ham and Leeds United where there was mayhem on and off the field, culminating in the referee, Rob Harris, being attacked as he drove away from Upton Park.

The match came to a head in the sixteenth minute when Rob sent off Ian Wright, who had recently joined West Ham from Arsenal. Having been shown the red card, Wright looked as if he might attack Rob. He was dragged away and led to the tunnel. Anticipating a volley of abuse I stood to one side and let him pass. A few seconds later I heard an almighty commotion and turned to see Wright being led away from the referees' changing room. I went to see what had happened and found the door wide open. Inside the television had been knocked onto the floor, and most of our clothes had been thrown after it or into the shower area. 'Who allowed him to get in here?' I asked one of the stewards as I knew the room was always locked as soon as we left it. 'No one!' he replied, pointing to the damaged door frame. He then explained that Wright had kicked the door open, smashing the Yale lock.

It was carnage. Meanwhile, Rob was getting considerable abuse from the fans for sending Wright off and as I did not want his confidence undermined by what had been done to the room I asked the steward to help me tidy it up. Rob did not notice that I had been away, such was the intensity of what he was having to deal with on the field. I resolved that no useful purpose would be served by telling him what Wright had done until after the match.

Rob left the field at half-time to a torrent of abuse and I had a cup of tea ready for him in the dressing room. He looked shell-shocked. We talked about the Wright sending-off and I mentioned that there had been a bit of a scuffle in the tunnel but that I had a record of everything and would give him the details afterwards. Matters got worse in the second half. First Shaka Hislop, the West Ham goalkeeper, came out of his area and brought down Jimmy Floyd Hasselbaink with a late tackle and was rightly sent off. Then Steve Lomas lost his head and committed a dreadful tackle and became the third West Ham red card. In addition, Rob showed eight yellow cards, so you can imagine the reception he received at the end of the game as the West Ham players trudged off having lost 5-1.

In the relative calm of the dressing room I outlined the Wright incident. We left the dressing rooms very late, hoping the crowds would have dispersed. When I got to my car I followed my usual routine and removed my tie and blazer. I then put on an old jumper and a pair of sunglasses to reduce the chances of being recognised. Another precaution I always took was to fill up with petrol at a garage near the ground before the game to avoid any post-match forecourt encounters with disgruntled supporters. (The potential problems of such encounters had been brought home to me at about two o'clock one morning when, driving home from a game in Manchester, I bumped into some fans at a service station in the Midlands. Fortunately, they were from the winning team and started cheering me but it might have been rather different if they had lost controversially!)

After the West Ham match, I turned left out of the ground, drove about five hundred yards down to the traffic lights and then turned right onto the A124 towards central London. Waiting at the traffic lights can be a little hairy as the Boleyn pub is on the corner and is always full of West Ham fans drowning their sorrows or celebrating, depending on the result. The atmosphere this time seemed quite ugly so I was grateful for my disguise and I was pleased that the police had told Rob to turn right when he left the ground. However, as I neared home word came through that his car had been attacked as he left the ground. Later that evening I rang Rob and he explained that, thinking there would be no trouble, he had turned left out of the ground and got stuck at the traffic lights. Rob had been recognised and a number of fans had attacked and kicked the car. Fortunately, the lights changed just in time and he managed to roar away but it had been a lucky escape.

The long-term repercussions of that game were that from the start of the following season the Premier League decided that match officials would not drive to the ground, but would instead meet at a designated hotel and then be transported in a people carrier. Ironically, my first taste of this new system would be on the opening day of the new season – at West Ham!

Before that, however, I would have to endure by far the worst abuse of my career after Liverpool played Manchester United at Anfield on 5 May. It was a crucial game which would have a major influence on the outcome of the Championship. Despite the recent troubles in the FA Cup semi-final, I was looking forward to another thrilling encounter. It was an evening match and the atmosphere was intense as we took to the field. I sensed no great hostility from United and the Liverpool players were, as usual, rather distant and diffident.

The match was played at pulsating pace and the temperature rose after Manchester United took the lead in the twenty-second minute when a delightful cross from Beckham was headed in by Dwight Yorke. United looked in total control when, on fifty minutes, I awarded them a penalty after Blomqvist was brought down by a high boot from Carragher. Players from both sides squared up to each other and, as usual, Schmeichel was not slow to get involved, running seventy-five yards to make his point. Denis Irwin kept his cool and scored from the spot. Tempers began to flare and Liverpool's Paul Ince, once of Manchester United, had to change his ripped shirt, but I felt in control and was enjoying the atmosphere.

My problems began in the seventieth minute when I awarded Liverpool a penalty after Jesper Blomqvist brought down Oyvind Leonhardsen. It was another of those very tight decisions which could have gone either way, and whichever decision I gave would have been criticised heavily. Redknapp scored. The tempo and passions went up a gear. United were under pressure, and I was feeling it as well. I always try to remain calm and collected as passions rise but this game was becoming a real challenge. Then came the incident which was to turn Manchester United against me and generate debate and controversy for weeks. With twelve minutes to go Irwin was dribbling the ball near the touchline well within his half, trying to relieve the almost incessant pressure on the Manchester United goal. He strayed too close to the touchline and the assistant flagged that the ball had gone out for a throw-in. I blew the whistle, Irwin hesitated for a second and then kicked the ball a long way upfield. I had to decide whether he had heard the whistle and deliberately kicked the ball away to waste time or had kicked it as the whistle was blown and was thus innocent of any offence.

Given his proximity to the assistant, the length of my whistle blast and the obvious desire to relieve the pressure on his defence, I was certain that Irwin was guilty. I blew my whistle again and moved towards him. I must have lost my concentration as I went to my back pocket to get out the yellow card. Nothing wrong in that you would think, except that Irwin had already been booked and I should have been going to my top pocket where I keep a yellow and a red card for dismissals. I had forgotten that I had already booked him and it was only when I raised the yellow card that it clicked. I have often reflected on what I would have done had I remembered that I had already booked him. I am still not sure. Deep down, I believe I would have made the same decision because I was convinced that he had deliberately kicked the ball away. However, sending a player off is a major decision and to do so for something technical can be harsh.

Irwin's dismissal galvanised the Liverpool players and fans, and the atmosphere reached almost fever pitch when, two minutes from time, Riedle turned Stam and laid the ball to Ince who placed the ball past Schmeichel. The draw left Manchester United three points and one goal behind Arsenal in the title race. At the end Alex Ferguson was angrier than I had ever seen him. He was screaming at me and had to be physically dragged away up the very narrow tunnel and stairs that lead from the field to the changing rooms. I had cast myself into the eye of the storm. To compound matters, Irwin was now banned from the Cup Final.

The next few days were tough. Ferguson sounded off in the press, declaring, 'We'd have won but for the referee, but we are not going to let him deny us winning the League.'[38] It was getting very personal and his remarks inflamed the Manchester United fans. Incited by Ferguson's outburst, I was inundated with hate mail and I had a series of threatening phone calls. The most worrying incidents came at Harrow where I would be walking to teach a lesson and a car would stop and someone would fire a volley of abuse at me before driving off. For the first time in my life I was genuinely frightened. I realised that being at Harrow School made me very visible. I walked along the main street between my House and form room many times a day so I was constantly exposed to the public, some of whom were enraged by my refereeing. Things slowly calmed down until the weekend when, in an interview with the *Mail on Sunday*, Martin Edwards, Chief Executive of Manchester United, stated that if Arsenal won the Championship they should give me one of their medals.[39] It provoked a flood of condemnation which did nothing to ease my mind or reduce my post bag.

I became particularly concerned by some very threatening letters (which included several death threats) and I handed them over to the Harrow School security department which had started screening my mail for me. The local police were alerted and having spoken to them for less than ten minutes I suddenly found myself being interviewed by several rather senior police officers; within three hours Home Office alarms had been installed in my private quarters. I had not been overly concerned until the police started taking the letters seriously.

While all this was going on, there was also a debate raging about Irwin's dismissal and the resulting suspension which included the FA Cup Final. There was intense pressure on me to reconsider my decision and revoke the dismissal so that he could play. I was on the horns of a dilemma. I had the greatest sympathy for Irwin and genuinely felt that it was not right that an offence in a League match should result in a player missing the Cup Final. It seems unfair and it surprised me that nothing was subsequently done about it then or in 2003 when Sol Campbell also missed the Cup Final, ironically after being sent off in a League match against Manchester United. However, referees do not make the rules and I was convinced that my decision to dismiss Irwin was correct so I stuck with it. My refusal to change my mind did not help my standing with the Old Trafford faithful and I was condemned in many quarters; I did, however, gain a degree of support from those who felt that the big clubs always got their own way and I was given credit for not bowing to the immense pressure I was under.

As the end of the season approached I was still badly shaken by the abuse and death threats. Ten days after the Anfield dramas I refereed a televised London derby between Spurs and Chelsea at White Hart Lane. In the tunnel beforehand Dennis

Wise asked if I was all right given the battering I had taken. It was a tough and rather irritable match and I was not on top form. Although I had thought I could blank out everything that was happening I was feeling mentally tired and beleaguered by all the abuse and pressure. My morale was low and I was feeling extremely negative about refereeing and football in general, despite the strong support of many colleagues and friends.

Preying on my mind was the fact that I was due to referee Arsenal v Aston Villa on the last day of the season. The problem was that the Premier League title would be decided that day and would depend on the outcome of the Arsenal and Manchester United matches. I kept envisaging a scenario where Manchester United drew or lost and Arsenal won because of a controversial decision (a penalty, perhaps) that I had given them. That would then have fanned the anti-Manchester United conspiracy theories; my position would have become untenable and my sense of being under verbal and physical siege would have become unbearable.

The appointments had been published and the press were already speculating about whether my own should stand. I received several letters warning me not to referee the game at Highbury unless I wanted to suffer 'severe physical harm'. The police were concerned for my safety and the Premier League had to decide whether to take me off the game for my own protection (and the integrity of the competition) or leave me on the game to show that neither they nor I would be intimidated by threats from the public and pressure from the clubs. I thought it was up to Philip Don, the man in charge of Premier League referees, to either change my appointment or tell me to do the game but he would not commit himself.

Ultimately, I decided not to do the game. Was I frightened off? I suppose I was. The threats and abuse had worn down my resolve to a level lower than I had ever before experienced and I was genuinely concerned about what might happen if it all went wrong. I felt that it was wrong to expose myself and those around me, including the boys in Druries, to the potential dangers which the police and Home Office had perceived as credible. Could I forgive myself if some lunatic set fire to the House and boys were injured, or worse? In the end my first loyalty had to be to the School. More than that, I was in no mental state to referee the game.

On the last Sunday of the season I was in turmoil as I knew that if Arsenal won the title I would still be blamed. I started listening to the match commentaries but the pressure was so immense that I went for a long walk round the School cricket fields. I am often asked which team I support. I have never supported a team, apart from England, but I have to confess that that afternoon I wanted Manchester United to win. It is the only time in my life that I have 'supported' a club and in this instance it was purely for self-preservation. Events unfolded in my favour and, with United winning the title, the pressure began to ease but it did not disappear. Daniel was flying in from South Africa to watch his first FA Cup Final and with Peter Jones, one of my closest friends, refereeing the match, I had to be there. But would I be able to watch the game without being subjected to constant abuse, or worse, from the United fans?

As the final approached, I became more and more concerned for my safety both at Harrow and at the match itself. Harrow-on-the Hill tube station is only three stops from Wembley Park on the Metropolitan Line and, until it closed, the King's Head Hotel, near the middle of the School, was a major rendezvous for fans. There had been some wonderful scenes in the past when the School and the football fans met. I particularly remember one bright Saturday afternoon when England were playing Scotland and the match coincided with Harrow Speech Day. At exactly the same moment, all the Harrow parents, in their Speech Day finery, emerged from the Speech Room as about fifty Scottish fans in their kilts and painted faces were making their way from the pub to the tube station. The fans were chanting their songs and, for a split second, both groups stopped and examined each other as if they were from different planets. I am not sure which group thought the other the stranger but within seconds the fans continued their merry singing and the parents their chatting. It was a marvellous moment as kilt and war paint met chiffon and Revlon.

This use of Harrow as a meeting place concerned me as it was common knowledge that I taught at Harrow School. I was worried that I would bump into Manchester United fans or that some might come looking for me if they lost the final. I warned the School's security department and told the boys not to get involved with anything; if there was any trouble they should call security and the police. I was distressed at the potential danger to which I felt I was subjecting the boys.

No matter how frightened I felt I was absolutely determined to go to the match. I decided, however, that I needed a disguise. The drama department gave me a false beard and moustache and some glue. At lunch-time I put them on, donned wraparound sunglasses and a baseball cap, and felt sure that no one would recognise me. My major concern was that the glue would not hold so, instead of the usual packet of Polos in my pocket, I had a tube of make-up glue! Daniel and I reached the stadium without mishap, only to discover that our tickets were in the United section. I queued among the United fans and I was more frightened then than I have ever been in my life. I have too fertile an imagination for that sort of thing and I just stood there with my head bowed, praying that the beard and moustache would hold. I had awful visions of what would happen if my identity became known. If I could have escaped then I think I might well have done so.

We survived the queues without incident and found that our seats were in a relatively neutral area. A few rows away I noticed a couple of refereeing colleagues and I went up to them and said hello. Apart from a polite response I got no flicker of recognition and felt confident that the disguise was working. The match was not a particularly good one. Newcastle did not seem to compete but I was delighted for Peter Jones that it passed without controversy. When the final whistle went we left quickly knowing that most of the United fans would stay for the lap of honour. With Manchester United winning the double, which later became the treble, I began to relax. I felt that the worst of it was over although there was still the question of Martin Edwards' outburst which the press seemed to be clamouring for the FA to deal with.

I subsequently discovered that Edwards was shocked when he heard what I had been through and that he had, as I expressed it, 'unleashed the dogs of hell' on me. The FA were keen to resolve matters and during the summer holidays asked if I would be prepared to speak to Martin Edwards. I happily agreed and a few hours later Martin telephoned me and we had a conversation which I promised would always remain private. All I can say is that he came across as a truly genuine man and by the time we had finished speaking the matter was closed as far as I was concerned.

So ended the most turbulent few weeks of my career. It left me scared and permanently scarred. I had genuinely feared for my safety and the whole affair brought home to me how some fans will do almost anything if they feel a slight or an injustice. While I have always been prepared to take abuse during matches I found the systematic nature of some of the abuse and threats both sinister and unsettling. I became wary of groups of fans or admitting to strangers that I was David Elleray. The experience left me cautious about opening letters with a postmark from an area whose team I had recently refereed and thereafter whenever I refereed Manchester United, I always hoped that I would not have to make a decision which would again unleash such hatred. Although I did not want to be kept away from Manchester United I only ever refereed them at Old Trafford once more during the remainder of my career.

The whole experience took the gloss off the final stages of my career, leaving me with a dread of controversy and a feeling of great vulnerability. Thereafter, it was a relief when there was no trouble in a match.

# Chapter Eleven

# *Refereeing Around the World*

'*These are your bodyguards ... to protect you from the players.*'

BRAZILIAN OFFICIAL

My 1998 World Cup disappointment brought unexpected advantages and by the time the finals started I had refereed four international matches, experiencing Brazilian football three more times. In early March the FA asked if I was available to go to Germany for a friendly match in Stuttgart later that month. 'Of course, who are they playing?' I replied. 'Brazil,' came the answer. I was stunned and delighted. Having refereed the World Champions against the Champions of Africa, now they were playing the European champions in a match that had taken three years to arrange because of disputes between the two kit sponsors, Nike for Brazil and adidas for Germany.

I expected an exhibition match between two of the best teams in the world but had I been able to read the German newspapers I would have discovered that the German coach, Bertie Vogts, wanted a psychological victory over the Brazilians. The World Cup draw meant that they would avoid each other until the final. Unfortunately, what could have been a wonderful encounter, full of exciting, attacking football between the proponents of the beautiful game and the efficient German machine, turned out to be very different in reality.

The tension was palpable as we lined up for the national anthems. I looked down the German line and recognised Ziege, Helmer, Bierhoff, Hamann, Klinsmann and Babbel while in the Brazilian team I picked out Taffarel, Roberto Carlos, Rivaldo, Ronaldo, Júnior Baiano, Denílson, Romario, Aldair and Cafu: a wonderful display of talent. What also caught my eye were the advertising hoardings. One half was adidas and the other Nike. The manufacturers' dispute was settled by having two sets of cameras on opposite sides of the field. One side was for Brazilian television and all the advertising hoardings facing those cameras were Nike while the reverse was true for European television and the adidas advertisements.

The match started with an explosion of attacking moves and crunching tackles. I was immediately struggling to control tempers and stop personal feuds breaking out. Every challenge was greeted by complaints and I was not helped by the players' willingness to roll round in agony whenever they were fouled. The game was spiralling out of control and, much as I did not want to, I had to get the yellow card out early on. Christian Ziege was the first, for a bad foul in the fifth minute, and less than sixty seconds later Dietmar Hamann committed a rash challenge and I flashed yellow again. The Brazilians were very angry at what they saw as intimidatory German tactics and demanded that I book every foul. Brazil were no innocents and in the ninth minute I booked their captain, Dunga, for a nasty challenge. This calmed things down somewhat but there remained an undercurrent of hostility.

Both sides had chances but Brazil looked stronger and took the lead in the twenty-seventh minute when an unmarked César Sampaio crashed a Cafu corner into the German net from about ten yards. The temperature rose and the challenges became fierce but remained largely fair. However, out of nowhere Jürgen Kohler went right over the top of the ball and caught Cafu above the knee with a quite dreadful foul. I immediately sent him off. As he passed the German bench no one looked at him but to his credit he apologised to the Brazilian coach, Mario Zagallo, on his way to the tunnel. It was one of the nastiest fouls I had seen in my international career but fortunately Cafu was not seriously injured.

I expected another burst of confrontations but the players remained controlled and we reached half-time with only one more yellow card – Denílson for a foul. We were all rather shell-shocked as we sat in the dressing room at half-time. The ferocity of the exchanges had taken me by surprise and I admitted to my colleagues that I was not enjoying the match at all. My biggest fear was that we were only one bad tackle away from a brawl and I knew I had to keep a very close grip on proceedings, even if that meant a hatful of cards. How different it was to the festival atmosphere when Brazil had played South Africa.

The second half began quietly but flared up fifteen minutes into the half and I had no option but to book Júnior Baiano and Sampaio for fouls in the space of ninety seconds. Then Dunga chopped down Kirsten and, without a moment's hesitation, I showed him the yellow card followed by the red. I had done it now. I had sent off Brazil's captain and another thirty years in the Brazilian wilderness looked on the cards. My mind went back to the time I met Havelange, the FIFA President, at White Hart Lane before a moving minute's silence for Bobby Moore. He had a look that seemed to go right through you and although he was stepping down as FIFA President he wielded great influence and I was sure that, just as had happened following the 1966 World Cup, English referees would not referee the Brazilian national team for a long time.

I did not have time to dwell on that because the match was now in full flow. Within nine minutes Kirsten, apparently unaffected by Dunga's challenge, took advantage of indecision between Aldair and Taffarel and slid the ball under the Brazilian goalkeeper. Game on, as they say! I was really worried that there would be another red card. I was hating the game and just wished that the minutes would pass as quickly as possible and without controversy. I could scarcely remember enjoying a match less and my mind was in turmoil as each challenge came in. I yellow carded Helmer in the seventy-fifth minute and then, just as the game seemed to be petering out into a draw, there was a moment of sublime pace and skill. With two minutes left, Ronaldo, who had hardly featured in the match because he had been so successfully stifled by Worns, raced on to a perfect through ball – but was he offside? I looked across to Peter Walton who kept his flag down as Ronaldo surged towards goal. He slotted the ball home with precision. I glanced at my watch and there were ninety seconds left. I played a couple of minutes of stoppage time and then blew the final whistle to end a match that had started out as a dream appointment and had become a living nightmare.

The dressing room was again subdued although our mood was lifted when television replays showed that Ronaldo had been onside. It was a small crumb of comfort but although everyone was complimentary about the way the game had been handled I felt physically sick that what should have been one of the highlights of my refereeing career had been so lacking in enjoyment. Salt was rubbed into the wound when, on the flight home, I picked up a tabloid which was scathing about my excessive use of the red and yellow cards!

In the days that followed I reflected on what had happened and believed that even if I had been aware of the pre-match build-up I could not have refereed those opening minutes any differently. After all, how many friendly internationals have had three yellow cards in the first nine minutes? I was especially concerned that sending off the captain of Brazil would leave an indelible black mark on my record, so when the phone rang some time later and a voice at the other end said, 'This is Raoul from FIFA', my blood ran cold. However, my dread turned to delight when he continued 'We are sending you to Brazil to referee a Cup Final on 3 May. Further details will follow soon.'

A few weeks later I flew down to São Paulo for the first leg of the Paulista Cup Final between local rivals Corinthians and São Paulo. I was met at the airport by a senior Brazilian FA official who asked, 'Do you know why you were appointed?' 'I have no idea.' 'Top club matches in Brazil are fraught with difficulties and to prevent referees being bribed or physically threatened we use referees from other South American countries for the semi-finals and a referee from another continent for the final. We knew this year's final was going to be very difficult and as you were strong enough to send off the captain of Brazil we asked FIFA to appoint you!'

I woke up on the morning of the final to find my name and photograph plastered all over the newspapers as the two coaches were worried that I would be too strict because I had shown so many cards in Stuttgart. I had three Brazilian colleagues and we all had to wear blue shirts, shorts and socks, with the sponsor's name, Penalty, on them! As my Portuguese is non-existent and my colleagues' English was limited, I gave my instructions using a mixture of drawings and demonstrations. There was no doubt they were excited at the prospect of working with someone from England, 'the home of football!' as one of them kept saying.

We left for the stadium about three hours before kickoff; the traffic was so chaotic that our driver simply drove down the middle of the road with his lights full on and the horn blaring. I arrived feeling rather sick – was it the driving or nerves? Everywhere was a riot of noise and colour. We were greeted by armed policemen and taken to our dressing room. In England and most of Europe the two teams and the match officials use the same tunnel to get to and from the pitch. Things were very different in the Murumbi Stadium: our dressing room had its own tunnel to the pitch and the two teams each had separate tunnels as well.

About an hour before kickoff an official handed me an envelope bulging with Brazilian banknotes. I politely gave it back to him and reminded him that FIFA had instructed that my expenses were to be paid in US dollars. He shrugged and said something about it being a problem and disappeared. The dressing room was like Piccadilly Circus with all sorts of people coming in to wish me luck, ask for press interviews and speak to my Brazilian colleagues. About twenty minutes later the paymaster returned and said it was impossible to pay me in dollars. I had been told not to accept local currency so I said firmly, 'No dollars, no referee!', and started to take off my referee's shirt. He shrugged again and disappeared but, a few minutes later, reappeared; this time the envelope contained dollars.

As in Tokyo, I was feeling very isolated as all the Portuguese chatter and noise gave me a sense of remoteness. My mind was assailed by images of South American matches where the referee had been assaulted, or worse, and I knew the fans tended to riot if things did not go their way. With these thoughts to the fore the door was opened and in came four huge policemen in full riot gear – shields, helmets, batons, the lot. 'These are your bodyguards,' I was told. It was very comforting. They explained that if I thought I was going to be attacked I was to use a special sign which for all the world looked like pulling a lavatory chain! 'I don't understand why I need protection as there is a huge fence and deep moat keeping the fans at bay.' 'These men are to protect you from the players, particularly the losing team who often attack the referee at the end of the game,' came the reply.

The next thing I knew I was being hugged by my Brazilian colleagues and we were off into the cauldron. It was raining but that did nothing to dampen the excitement of the 100,000 spectators. The match started off at a furious pace. The tackles were flying in and players rolling over and over. I decided that I needed to cast off my reserved British manner so I became increasingly flamboyant and demonstrative with my signals. The first yellow card appeared in the eleventh minute for Valencia of Corinthians and by half-time both teams had scored but I had issued only three cards. The players were responding and I was stimulated by the noise, the smoke from the flares and the tenacity of both teams. Players fell to the ground much more easily than in the Premier League but everyone was happy if I gave the free-kick. The second half continued in the same vein but the mood changed when Corinthians took a 2-1 lead. I cautioned their captain, Surcin, for time-wasting at the first opportunity for I knew all the tricks they would use as they tried to hold on to their slender lead.

The match sprang to life in the final stages and I had to work very hard as one or two players seemed to be losing what little self-control they had. I felt my own control was at best precarious and the atmosphere became increasingly volatile when, ten minutes from time, Das Chagas of Corinthians launched himself into a tackle and I sent him off. He was not keen to leave the field but was ushered off quickly. The frenetic battle continued and I booked Dos Santos, the São Paulo captain, in the eighty-sixth minute as his team desperately fought for an equaliser. Corinthians were doing all they could to use up time and I booked Pavon and Santos in the closing minutes for acts of gross time-wasting. With a great sense of relief and a warm glow of pleasure inside I blew the final whistle. True to their word, the riot police rushed towards me. A Corinthians player came over and I am sure all he wanted to do was shake hands but before he could do so he was smacked over the head with a truncheon.

The atmosphere in the dressing room was happy and emotional. One of the assistants, a huge man, came up and bust into tears as he embraced me in a bear hug which almost squeezed the breath out of me. Through his sobs he said how proud he was to have refereed with 'the famous Engleesh referee'. Many people came to thank us for the way the game had been controlled and one of the reporters said that for the first time ever the press were going to give a referee 10/10. The biggest compliment was when one of the Brazilian FA officials asked if there was any possibility that I could return the following week and do the second leg.

I was on cloud nine and when we went out for dinner we were applauded and spent half the meal signing autographs. As part of the security measures I was booked on a flight home that same night. The check-in girl at the BA Business Class desk recognised me and as her team had won she upgraded me to First Class. I had a wonderful flight home but decided that as everything had gone so well I should not tempt fate and return for the second leg. However, given the problems I had the following Sunday at Blackburn, I might have been better going back to São Paulo.

My Brazilian encounters were not over and three weeks later I refereed Atletico Bilbao's centenary match with Brazil primarily because the club had been founded in 1898 by Englishmen, most of them Sunderland supporters, hence their red and white striped shirts. It was another festive occasion. This was one of Brazil's last matches before the World Cup began and Mario Zagallo fielded a very strong team which included Cafu, Júnior Baiano, Rivaldo, Roberto Carlos, Ronaldo and Bebeto. Aldair was now the captain and there was no sign of Dunga! Forty thousand people packed the stadium and by half-time they were in raptures as their team were winning 1-0. But as in Jo'burg, the Brazilians upped a gear in the second half and Rivaldo scored in the forty-ninth minute. The match ended in an honourable draw.

Exciting appointments continued to come my way and I was thrilled when FIFA appointed me to referee between a FIFA All Stars XI and a Bosnia-Montenegro XI in Sarajevo to celebrate the end of the conflict in Bosnia. Sadly, the match was cancelled because of the deteriorating political situation in the Balkans which meant that the symbolic purpose of the match would be lost.

I was now approaching the end of my international career and got a measure of the respect afforded to English referees when, at the administrative meeting for a Champions League match – Porto v Olympiakos – Paolo Casarin, the Italian UEFA observer, said, 'Gentlemen, please respect the referee today. He is Mr

David Elleray and he is one of the best in Europe. What your players must remember is that they, like me, are from the Mediterranean. We are hot-blooded, emotional people who do not always behave well. Mr Elleray is from England and he is calm, controlled and precise. He will enforce strict English discipline so please tell your players to behave.' Needless to say, I had very few problems that evening.

My last few matches were marked by great climatic contrasts as I went from desert heat to Arctic cold. They began on Saturday 2 October 1999 with the COSAFA Cup Final between Namibia and Angola in Windhoek. My colleagues, fourth official Absalom Goseb (Namibia) and assistants Khayelihle Lukhele and David Nsibandze (Swaziland), and I stayed in a good hotel but had to buy our supper at the local supermarket with the meagre daily expense allowance. This was a far cry from my UEFA experiences where I had wined and dined in some of Europe's finest restaurants. However, it was what my colleagues were used to and it reminded me that not all football is awash with money and unlimited expense accounts.

The Friday evening pre-match administrative meeting was marked by considerable tension between the Secretary of the Namibian FA and the Match Commissioner, Leo Mugabe, nephew of the Zimbabwe President. The Namibian Secretary had recently been a Match Commissioner in Harare and had upset Mr Mugabe with his constant fault-finding so it was revenge time and there were heated arguments over petty matters. I also sensed that Mr Mugabe did not approve of a white non-African refereeing the final.

The pre-match routine was totally different from that in Europe and I went with Mr Mugabe to each dressing room where the team sheet was read out and every player presented himself so that I could check his name and appearance with his passport photo. By the time we took to the pitch at 2.45 p.m. it was searingly hot with not a hint of a cloud in the azure blue desert sky. The match was exciting with a skill level akin to that of the Nationwide Third division. The players were energetic and, at times, overenthusiastic and I had to issue nine yellow cards, seven for the home team. The pitch was hard and bumpy and the heat unbearable. Fortunately, it was a dry heat but I felt as if I was roasting and took every opportunity I could to take on water, ignoring my usual refusal to drink anything from a tap. As luck would have it the game went into extra time before Angola emerged as the victors.

My most difficult decision came during the post-match presentations which, like the match itself, were televised live throughout Africa. As I was about to step up to the podium to receive my medal someone draped an Angolan flag round my shoulders. What should I do? If I took it off I risked offending the Angolans; if I left it on I could upset the Namibians. I was saved when a Namibian put a large velvet-like top hat in Namibian colours on my head. Resplendent in floppy top hat and flag, I received my medal to cheers from both sets of players and supporters. I tried to carry it off with aplomb but felt a complete idiot!

The showers in the dressing room were cold so we returned hot and smelly to the hotel. It was still sunny so I went to relax by the pool, whereupon it started to rain. Having refereed the Brazilian Cup Final in a monsoon, and having brought rain to Saudi Arabia, I suppose it was no surprise that I should experience rain in the Namib desert! That evening I dined with friends and my journey home was precarious to say the least as my driver was drunk. He was careering all over the road and during what can only be described as a white-knuckle ride he lurched along the dark, potholed, unlit roads narrowly missing cyclists and pedestrians. The next morning a replacement driver appeared and I was shocked to learn that my driver was in prison after having knocked over and killed someone.

I arrived back at Harrow on Tuesday morning for two days' teaching before setting off for Moscow for a vital Euro 2000 match between Russia and the Ukraine. It was the last round of qualification matches and as France looked certain to win the group it would decide who qualified for the play-offs. The game had the added spice of being a 'local derby' between 'Mother Russia' and the now independent Ukraine, and as our BA flight approached Moscow I thought of all the spy books I had enjoyed and wondered how much of that side of Russian life I would see. Would we be spied upon at every turn? Would they attempt to compromise us so we would be pressured into refereeing in their favour? Or did I just have an overfertile imagination?

Dave Babski, Dave Bryan, Mike Riley and I were met by a former international referee, Alexei Spirin, who hosted us on behalf of the Russian Football Federation. We were whisked off into a VIP reception lounge where we were offered champagne, smoked salmon and chocolates while our bags cleared customs. Our transport was a cross between a stretch limo and a minibus with curtains to protect us from prying eyes but we had to run a gauntlet of photographers and autograph hunters as we walked to it from the terminal. This gave us an idea of the interest in the game.

From our hotel in central Moscow we could see Moscow's White House, the scene of the shift in the balance of power in modern Russia when Boris Yeltsin had earlier toppled Gorbachev. We had dinner in the hotel. The meal was good and the entertainment afterwards hilarious as the Russian folk group wanted us to join in the dancing. I delegated Mike Riley to oblige on our behalf and the photos of him in traditional folk dress dancing on the restaurant tables continue to bring back happy memories for us, if not for him!

Next morning, Alexei's phone rang and he went rather pale and whispered, 'You've been called to the Kremlin.' Outside the Kremlin walls we decamped from our bus into two large black Zil limousines. I went with Alexei and his pallor increased when we drove through a gate which he informed me was reserved for Heads of State. I suspected he was exaggerating but he seemed to become even paler when we were met by a huge man called

Pavel Borodin who, he explained, was Yeltsin's right-hand man (the equivalent of Alastair Campbell to Tony Blair).

For the next hour Borodin gave us a personal tour of the wonderfully restored Kremlin palace with its stunning polished wood floors and intricately painted ceilings and murals. He explained that all records of the palace had been destroyed during the Revolution and they had been able to restore it to its original glory only because Queen Elizabeth had a set of plans which had been given to Queen Victoria by the Tsar. Such was the magnificence of the restoration that Borodin told us that at a recent G7 summit in the Kremlin to discuss financial assistance for Russian reconstruction Bill Clinton was heard to remark to Helmut Kohl, as they moved from one stunning hall to another 'And they want money from *us*!'

Throughout the tour Borodin's phone would ring and, according to Alexei, he would say that he was with the 'English referee' and could not be disturbed. We saw Yeltsin's cabinet room and his private office where, I convinced myself, I could have picked up the handset of the red telephone and spoken to Bill Clinton. At the end of the tour I said, 'Mr Borodin, thank you so much for a wonderful tour.' He replied in his thick accent and without a trace of irony, 'Thanks are not necessary. The only important thing is the result tonight!'

When we arrived at the magnificent Luzhniki Stadium we were immediately surrounded by security guards armed with machine guns. They accompanied me everywhere I went. We inspected the pitch as best we could with this phalanx of guards and the only time I shook them off was in the dressing room.

Lining up in the tunnel I exchanged greetings with Smertin and Karpin of Russia and Luzhny and Rebrov of the Ukraine. When we led the teams onto the pitch the stadium, full to its 85,000 capacity, rose as one and the atmosphere fizzed. I had expected an England v Scotland-type battle but the players were very disciplined and the atmosphere by half-time was ecstatic as news came through that France were losing to Iceland. The match continued in a good spirit in the second half, possibly helped by the only yellow card of the game for Dmitry Khlestov of Russia. With fifteen minutes remaining Russia's Valery Karpin scored to send the crowd wild with excitement. The stadium was still buzzing when, three minutes from full time, Andrey Shevchenko floated the ball into the penalty area where, inexplicably, the Russian goalkeeper Alexander Filimonov tried to catch it above his head but only succeeded in allowing it through his hands into the net. Eighty-four thousand five hundred Russians went completely silent while five hundred Ukrainian supporters were jubilant.

There were no more goals and as we left the field, still surrounded by guards, it was announced that France had won: Ukraine were in the play-offs and Russia were eliminated. We sat in the dressing room not sure how the Russians would react but knowing deep down that the blame could not be laid at our door. Or could it? After what seemed an age Alexey arrived and said that President Yeltsin did not blame us for the defeat and the President of the Ukraine sent us his congratulations on a well-controlled match. That evening during dinner in a restaurant close to Red Square we had, however, a timely reminder of how precarious our position might have been had we got it wrong. A large gentleman came across with a glass of vodka and raised 'a toast to the English referee'. We exchanged greetings and toasts, and when he left I asked Alexey who he was. 'Officially, he is the head of the Russian Basketball Federation but, in reality, he is number two in the KGB!'

The next morning we visited Red Square and Lenin's tomb and were routinely approached by Russians wanting their photo taken with the 'English referee'. At the airport I felt relaxed as I stood in line at passport control. When it was my turn the passport officer took my passport, looked hard at me and then left her booth. She was gone for what felt like an hour and then returned with a superior officer who looked at me and my passport several times. I was beginning to lose my studied, phlegmatic poise when, to my huge relief, she returned my passport with a curt nod. I often wonder how that encounter would have ended if Russia had been eliminated because of a dubious penalty. We celebrated on the flight home for a match well done but also at having 'escaped'! It had been a wonderful experience and its importance had been summed up by one of the Russian officials who had said beforehand, 'There will be 38 TV and radio commentators; 564 accredited journalists; 124 photographers.' 'So many?' I remarked. 'Of course, this is the "match of the millennium" for us,' came the reply.

Later that week I was appointed to one of the play-off matches: Israel v Denmark. I was thrilled that I was returning to Israel for my final full international and I asked for Peter Jones to be my reserve referee; like me, he was also retiring from FIFA at the end of the year.

I had happy memories of my previous visit to Israel just over a year earlier when they had played Spain in a Euro 2000 group qualification match in Tel Aviv. I had always wanted to go to Israel and my renewed Christian faith made my desire to visit the holy places even stronger. I had therefore booked an overnight flight to arrive in the early hours of Friday morning to allow us a full day sightseeing and still plenty of rest before the match.

Peter Jones had been the reserve referee on that occasion as well and, along with Phil Sharp and Mark Warren, we had arrived at Ben Gurion Airport at about 4.00 a.m. and, having cleared immigration and customs, emerged bleary-eyed looking for the referee liaison officer. He was nowhere to be seen. We waited for half an hour and matters became worse when a siren sounded a bomb alert and everyone evacuated the terminal. We managed to get a taxi to our hotel and I suggested a short sleep before a 9.30 a.m. breakfast. I had just fallen asleep when the phone rang.

'Mr. David?'

'Yes.'

'I am Ari, your liaison officer. What are you doing here?'

'What do you mean, what am I doing here? Why weren't you at the airport to meet us?'

'I was not there because I was told your flight arrived at four this afternoon! Anyway, I am free now so I will see you when you are ready.'

I agreed to meet him at 10.00 a.m. and went back to sleep. When Ari arrived he apologised and said he had been out late at a party but he was ready to take us wherever we wanted. He was very worried that I would report him to the Israeli FA and UEFA and when he went off to arrange some things Peter observed, 'If he thought we were arriving at 4.00 p.m. why did he phone you at 8.00 a.m.?' We concluded that he had partied too well and had overslept and we decided to make him pay for the trouble he had caused us!

For the rest the day we had him running round all over the place. He repeatedly asked if I was going to report him and all I would say was 'I haven't decided yet.' The result was one of the most fantastic and spiritually uplifting days of my life. We visited the old part of Jerusalem, had a private tour of the Knesset and then it was off to float in the salty waters of the Dead Sea. I had always strongly believed in God but had never been a particularly public worshipper. On one of my trips to South Africa I had gone to a couple of charismatic churches and I had, in a sense, been spiritually 'born again'. Certainly my faith had been strengthened and I read the Bible last thing every night without fail. Unsurprisingly, therefore, visiting the site of Our Lord's crucifixion was incredibly moving.

The atmosphere in the Ramat Gan National Stadium the next night was unbelievable. Forty-four thousand people packed the stands – the largest crowd to have watched the national side for decades – drawn by the prospect of seeing a formidable Spanish team containing the likes of Hierro, Canizares, Raul and Luis Enrique. There had been a tangible air of anticipation as Israel had not lost at home for five years and both sides had their sights on a place in the Euro 2000 finals. During the national anthems I had a physical attack of nerves brought on by the powerfully emotional singing of the Israeli national anthem. My left leg started to twitch and I could do nothing to stop it. I looked across at Peter Jones and there was a sense of emotion and wonder on his face as well.

The opening stages saw both teams warily trying to get the measure of each other, rather like boxers in the opening round of a championship bout. After four minutes Engonga of Spain brought Nimni crashing to the ground and I showed him the yellow card. Six minutes later a brilliant pass from Eyal Berkovic to Revivo set up a promising attack which was only thwarted by an illegal shirt tug from Hierro, whom I booked. Play was tentative but both sides had their chances. The home fans were on the edge of their seats (or, more likely, jumping up and down on them) in the twenty-sixth minute when Revivo glanced a Nimni cross past Canizares but Hierro cleared off the line. Minutes before half-time it seemed as if Kiko's header had crossed the line before being reclaimed by keeper Cohen but Phil Sharp indicated no goal.

Spain came out for the second half really fired up and Raul should have done better from deep inside the Israeli box. Israel were rattled and Hazan became the fourth yellow card for a foul. Then, in the sixty-fifth minute, Berkovic surged up the left wing and slipped the ball inside to Revivo who sent a brilliant cross to the other side of the field where Hazan was unmarked. He knocked the ball forward, strode into the penalty area and hit a powerful, precise right-foot shot past Canizares. The crowd erupted and Hazan took his shirt off and leapt over the advertising hoardings in a Giggs-like goal celebration. The ecstasy was palpable but removing a shirt and leaving the field was punishable with a yellow card. As I had already booked him that would mean sending him off. Could I send off the man who had just become a national hero? There are times when referees have to think about the game in a wider context. You may think that I was cowardly but to have sent Hazan off on a technicality would have been unthinking and, dare I say it, irresponsible, so I let it pass.

As often happens when a team scores, Israel then lost their concentration and within seconds Luis Enrique was brought down just outside the Israel penalty area and Hierro, with immaculate precision, caught the goalkeeper unprepared with a shot to the top right-hand corner. Joy turned to lamentation and the Israel fans were further disheartened when in the seventy-eighth minute substitute Joseba Etxeberria met an arching cross from Luis Enrique and beat the desperate Israeli keeper with a relatively weak header. All seemed lost but the fans had a moment of hope when Mizrahi fell spectacularly in the penalty area but I waved away the appeals. Spain were clinging on with some desperation and Kiko took so long going off the field when he was substituted that I booked him for time-wasting. At last the match was over and the roller-coaster ride of excitement and emotion left us all drained.

That match, then, had been a wonderful experience and Peter and I were greatly looking forward to going back for the Denmark match. On the way we joked about how, a month earlier, I had been in Moscow refereeing the group decider in front of 85,000 while he had been doing the wooden spoon match in the same group between Andorra and Armenia in front of 250 people. Our trip to Israel followed a similar pattern to the previous one almost a year earlier except that we were met at the airport and there was no bomb alert. However, the sightseeing highlight this time was going to Bethlehem and visiting Christ's birthplace.

The Ramat Gan National Stadium was once again packed but Israel did not show the spirit or fire that we had witnessed when they played Spain. In fact, they were very poor. Denmark scored after two minutes through Jon Dahl Tomasson. He added a second in the thirty-fifth minute and, despite it being a two-legged tie, Israel's hopes of qualification were long gone by the time Nielsen scored Denmark's fifth with twelve minutes to go.

Symbolic of the reverse of fortunes, Haim Revivo, who had been such a star against Spain, let himself and his team down very badly when he chopped down Jes Høgh in the fifty-ninth minute and I gave him a straight red card. During the second half Eyal Berkovic said to me, 'We are terrible. I am so embarrassed.' Afterwards there were dark allegations that the Israeli team had been partying the night before the match, ironically in the hotel next to ours. When we left the stadium there were hundreds of youngsters clamouring for autographs and Peter Jones still talks of how I spent fifteen minute signing scarves, books and shirts and he marvelled at the respect we were shown by the fans.

I still have very clear memories of the trip. We visited the site of Yitzhak Rabin's assassination and then drove to the old part of Jerusalem, spending a long time walking along La Via Dolorosa. We stopped in Mohammed Ali's shop where, over several cups of mint tea, I bought a huge number of souvenir T-shirts for my goddaughters and friends. We had parked in the square by the Wailing Wall and when we got back to our people carrier it was dark. As we got in we suddenly found ourselves surrounded by armed police. We did not look like terrorists so I could not understand the problem until our driver explained that, because the Sabbath had started, we were not allowed to start the engine so close to a holy place. It looked as if we might have to abandon the vehicle but once the police learned who we were they became less hostile and ended up helping us push the people carrier silently out of the square.

The funniest moment occurred on the journey home. As we made our way through the airport terminal Phil Joslin dropped his bag and we heard a bottle smash. Sherry started leaking everywhere and then he put his hand into the bag and cut his finger. So there he was trailing a bag reeking of sherry with his hand covered in blood and alcohol. He could not take the bag on the plane and all the check-in people could offer him was a couple of transparent dustbin bags. He stuffed all his possessions in the bags and, I think partly because they felt so sorry for him, we were upgraded to First Class. Phil was then stopped at the security check probably because they could not believe that someone stinking of sherry and carrying their clothes in a dustbin bag could possibly be a First Class passenger. I had to persuade them to let him through as by this time Peter Jones was almost beside himself with laughter. When we got on the plane I asked the stewardess to serve a large sherry to the gentleman in seat 4B. 'Very funny, Elleray,' came Joslin's voice when the drink arrived and Peter Jones again had a fit of the giggles.

Returning home I discovered that my final international game was a Champions League fixture between Dynamo Kiev v Real Madrid. It brought my international career almost full circle because, like my first match, it was to be in a bitterly cold Eastern European country and the mighty Spanish team were the visitors. I asked for Peter Jones, Dave Babski and Phil Sharp to make up my team but unfortunately Phil was unavailable; I was delighted to take Darren Drysdale instead. We were stunned by our reception at Kiev. My appointment had made front-page news and we were mobbed by youngsters demanding autographs and football pin badges. Having been the referee when Ukraine had knocked Russia out of Euro 2000 had been enough, it seemed, to make me a temporary national hero and everywhere we went we were treated lavishly.

It was again bitterly cold with plenty of snow on the ground and in the air. Memories of how cold I had been in Belgrade came flooding back with such intensity that we had to go to an adidas shop to buy hats and gloves for the match. Our liaison man also suggested that we should wear tights but I was having none of that. I always wore short-sleeved shirts and I was too macho to wear long sleeves, let alone tights – how ridiculous!

There was concern as to whether the match would go ahead as the undersoil heating was having minimal effect. In reality, we had to play as there would be no chance of rearranging the match before the next phase of the Champions League started in

March. Matters were made worse by UEFA's insistence that all group matches are played at the same time, so our kickoff was at 9.45 p.m. When we inspected the pitch the electronic scoreboard showed the temperature to be −10 but in the icy wind it felt more like −20.

The UEFA observer insisted that we wear tights and plenty of T-shirts and the lengths we went to to keep out the cold were best exemplified by Dave Babski's 'wardrobe'. First, he put on a pair of thick tennis socks and then put his feet in carrier bags over which he put another pair of tennis socks and then his refereeing socks. Next it was a cotton T-shirt followed by a black dustbin liner with holes cut for his head and arms. Then two more T-shirts, black knitted tights and then his green referee's shirt and black shorts. He covered as much of his face and hands as he dared with Vaseline and finally donned black gloves and a black woolly hat. We all looked like Michelin men by the time we emerged into the windswept tunnel.

As we marched towards the snow-covered pitch about 20,000 hardy souls cheered a welcome and the scoreboard registered −11. Dynamo were in white and Real Madrid in black and we used an orange ball which stood out against the snow. Both teams started gingerly on the rock-hard pitch. A good run by Raul was halted by an offside flag while at the other end a twenty-five-yard screamer from Rebrov hit a defender who must have felt the sting for a long while afterwards. My UEFA fair play and FIFA referee badges started to come off my shirt as it was too cold for the double-sided Sellotape. I ran round trying unsuccessfully to hold them on but when the ball went out for a throw-in near the halfway line I went across to Peter and gave them to him. He offered me his badge but when I tried to stick it to my shirt it also fell off.

The pitch was like concrete and whenever a player fell to the ground I feared he might break a limb. I decided to reduce the physicality of the game and in the tenth minute yellow carded Julio Cesar for a routine foul on Rebrov. A minute later I did the same to Yashkin for a rough tackle on Salgado and in the fourteenth minute rather harshly booked Khatskevich for tripping Guti near the Real penalty area. The players got the message and the rest of the match was like a pre-season friendly, with minimal physical contact.

The match came to life in the eighteenth minute when Roberto Carlos intercepted goalkeeper Shovkovsky's long clearance, made a good solo run and crossed from the left for Morientes to score from eight yards. Kiev responded immediately and Rebrov 'scored', only to be denied by an offside flag. Both teams continued to launch penetrating attacks but by half-time there had been no further goals.

My main concern at half-time was Peter Jones. He was absolutely frozen and looked ill. The little hut they had given him to sit in was so small that he could hardly move and it was difficult to keep the blood circulating. However, if he left the hut the icy wind cut through him like a knife. Still, there were only forty-five minutes to go and it would make his final international appointment one he would never forget – if he survived!

Real attacked from the first whistle and three minutes into the second half Savio crossed to Raul who saw Shovkovsky off his line and chipped the ball over his head into the top left corner for an exquisite goal. The game ebbed and flowed. Real looked superior but Kiev steadily came back into the game. The pitch became increasingly dangerous and the air so cold that whenever I breathed in it felt as if thousands of little pins were pricking my lungs. As the match entered the last ten minutes Kiev were easily the stronger team and when Rebrov broke through in the eighty-fourth minute it took a desperate and illegal tackle from Ivan Campo to stop him. Yellow card number four. The free kick was easily cleared but Kiev continued to press and when Rebrov crossed to Shatskikh he headed the ball to Dmytrulin who was comprehensively flattened. I had enough unfrozen air in my lungs to blow for the penalty and although Bizzarri went the right way Rebrov's penalty was too powerful.

Real counterattacked and a wonderful free kick from Roberto

Carlos was spectacularly saved by Shovkovsky. In the dying minutes it was all Kiev. Khatskevich shot over the bar when it was easier to score and a powerful shot from Rebrov was deflected wide. Suddenly it was all over. I blew the whistle and my international career had ended.

It took us an hour to warm up afterwards, although it did not stop us enjoying the caviar and champagne that we were offered. Peter eventually thawed out and to mark the end we had our photographs taken with the electronic subs board showing forty-five twice. My abiding memory is of the cold and of looking up at the scoreboard just before the end to see it showing the score as 1-2, the time 11.30 p.m. and the temperature −11.

My international adventures had started and finished in sub-zero temperatures and in between I had travelled from Brazil to Japan and from South Africa to Norway. I had not made the World Cup but I had done better than I really could have hoped; I was thrilled years later when I chanced upon a website which ranked the world's referees to discover that I had entered the top ten in 1995 and in my final year was ranked fourth in the world.

It is impossible to express how much pleasure I got from my international career and how grateful I was to Harrow for letting me go away so often. I had refereed the world's great players in some of football's best stadiums. I had the possibly unique honour of refereeing a Cup Final in each of the world's major footballing continents. There had been disappointments, of course, but these were more than outweighed by the people I met and the friends I made, some of whom became among the most important people in my life. How proud I had felt every time I put on that simple white FIFA badge and represented England. I had been extremely lucky and privileged, but now my refereeing was restricted to England and I only had just over three years left.

# Chapter Twelve

# *In the Spotlight*

'You've not sent him off for that, have you, David?'
STEVE HOWEY (MANCHESTER CITY)

Just before the start of season 1999/2000 I spoke at the launch of the *Rothmans Football Yearbook* as I had written the foreword. It gave me an opportunity to open up the debate about refereeing and to deal with issues which are still being discussed today.

Having been actively involved for thirty years, it has become increasingly clear to me that the fundamental problem football has to address is how important perfect decision-making by referees is to the game and the price football is prepared to pay to achieve it. Football is played, managed and refereed by human beings who make mistakes. Players like Alan Shearer and David Beckham are not expected to score every time they shoot even though they are consummate professionals who are paid huge salaries. If their salaries were doubled they would still not win *every* tackle, pass perfectly *every* time and score with *every* free kick or penalty. Yet, unrealistically and unfairly, referees are expected to get *every* free kick, throw-in, penalty and red- or yellow-card decision right *every* time. All possible improvements to the game need to be seen in this context.

I am frequently asked if I think certain decisions should be referred to a video referee. For decisions of fact, such as whether the ball crossed the line or whether an offence occurred inside or outside the penalty area, a correct decision could be achieved this way. But at what cost? How long would each review take and how many might there be during the game? Cricket, rugby and American football use video replays for decisions but have natural breaks so stopping to look at replays does not affect the game. In contrast, football is almost non-stop action, more so in recent years, with players no longer being treated on the field and goalkeepers being limited to holding the ball for only six seconds. One of the fundamental attractions of football, almost constant action, would be undermined by lengthy stoppages. More problematic are those decisions which are not questions of fact but of interpretation. Deciding whether a player in an off-side position is interfering with play or an opponent or whether a foul is worth a red or yellow card are subjective judgements, often based on things not evident on a television screen. With fouls the video does not show the verbal exchange between the two players just before the foul, or the look in the player's eye as he goes into the challenge. I would only support the use of technology when the decision is whether the whole of the ball crossed the line for a goal because that is a key factual decision. Beyond that we must accept human fallibility otherwise the game will become a sterile, stop-start affair lasting several hours. That is not to say that improvements cannot be made, and football can learn from other sports, especially rugby.

Rugby is held up as a game where referees are afforded much respect by the players and I agree with many people that advancing a free kick ten yards if a player shows dissent, stops the kick being taken or deliberately kicks the ball away would eradicate a blight on football at all levels which does more to harm the game's image than almost any other on-field behaviour. If the advanced free kick becomes a penalty so much the better. The current experiment is not as effective as it should be as the free kick is only advanced if the dissent or time-wasting is serious enough for the player to be booked. I would advance for every offence and then yellow card if the player's conduct is persistent or serious.

The most significant change with which I would love to see senior football experiment is to replace the yellow card with the sin bin so that justice is done *during* a game not afterwards. Surely if a player commits offences when playing against, say, Arsenal, any suspension should be during that game so that Arsenal, who probably suffered as a result of the player's misconduct, benefit and not another team, possibly a major rival, later in the season. It is illogical and unfair that the team which benefits from a player being suspended is not the one disadvantaged by the offence(s) in the first place. The use of sin bins would also reduce ill discipline because if a side has a player in the sin bin they would be less likely to commit further misconduct for fear of being reduced to nine men; that would act as a deterrent and measures that prevent rather than merely punish have to be good for the game.

Having expounded these views, it was, therefore, somewhat ironic that the first controversy I had centred on one of the very measures introduced to speed up the game. Six minutes into the second half at Highbury, David James, the Villa goalkeeper, collected the ball but a knee injury prevented him from kicking it. He had plenty of opportunity to throw it to a team-mate but he just held onto it. I started counting the seconds and when I passed six I became concerned. No defender made himself available and although James was probably not deliberately time-wasting, when I reached twelve I had to penalise him. I awarded the indirect free kick which Bergkamp knocked to the Croatian international Davor Suker who lifted the ball over the

Villa defenders massed on the line to make it 2-1 to Arsenal. I was roundly criticised afterwards but how long was I supposed to wait?

Around this time, Barnaby Lenon started his Headmastership of Harrow and asked me to consider retiring early from Druries to become Second Master, i.e. Deputy Head. I did not want to do that and our discussions led to me being appointed Director of Boarding, with responsibility for the pastoral and boarding life of the School, and an extension to my tenure of Druries. I was delighted and pledged that I would stop applying for Headships and would remain at Harrow for the foreseeable future. Harrow had changed so much in the previous twenty years and the demands of parents and inspectors for the highest levels of pastoral care were increasing. For Harrow to maintain its position as one of the best boarding schools in the country it was vital that we swept away the remaining vestiges of 'Tom Brown' to create a school which was modern in outlook and teaching, and provided a supportive environment for the boys, one in which tradition and old-fashioned values were still respected and valued.

In late September I was asked by the FA to be one of several referees who might be filmed as part of a Channel 4 documentary on refereeing. I met the producer, Ross Wilson, and I was impressed with his plans, although the Millwall microphone experience still lurked in the back of my mind. I suggested that he come to watch one of my games, the north London derby at White Hart Lane, to observe what went on behind the scenes. I thought it would be a great match for him to see. Little did he know what he was about to witness.

Spurs v Arsenal matches are always tough on and off the field. This encounter started extremely quietly which worried me because I had no opportunity to impose myself on the game or on the consciousness of the players. Iversen gave Spurs the lead after six minutes and Sherwood added a second in the nineteenth from a free kick for a foul by Petit, whom I booked. A few moments later, Petit committed another foul and threw the ball down in disgust at himself. It looked like dissent but I could tell that it was genuine frustration and took no action. Seven minutes before half-time Vieira pulled one back when he headed a Petit free kick past Walker. The temperature steadily rose on and off the field, especially after the half-time pep talks from the manager.

The fireworks went off in the fifty-second minute when Justin Edinburgh's foul on Ljungberg caused a mass confrontation during which Ljungberg punched Armstrong and Ginola was cut on the forehead by a coin. I sent Ljungberg off and was so worried that the game was exploding into uncontrollable violence that I summoned the two captain, Campbell and Adams, and told them in no uncertain terms that they needed to get a grip on their players and help me otherwise the match would spiral into chaos. I could feel myself almost shaking with concern as I sensed that some of the players were spoiling for a fight.

For the next ten minutes I penalised every foul, no matter how trivial, hoping to quieten things down. That and bookings for Keown, Vieira, Clemence and Carr briefly restored some sanity but my control still felt superficial and, worryingly, the Arsenal players no longer appeared to regard a yellow card as any sort of deterrent as whenever Spurs attacked Arsenal scythed into the tackles. I had to keep in check my growing sense of panic as nothing I tried seemed to be working. My authority seemed to be becoming impotent. It was no surprise that there was another sending off: this time it was Keown for a wild foul on Dominguez. The appalling spite and confrontation were reflected in Adams and Suker trying to stop the Spurs physio getting onto the field to treat Dominguez. Meanwhile (I discovered afterwards) behind my back, Sherwood elbowed Petit in the head.

Afterwards Arsenal wrongly claimed I had sent Ljungberg off for headbutting Ginola and the media rounded on the Swede for his V sign to the crowd, while TV footage showed him kicking the dressing-room door. The match fuelled the debate about

Arsenal's disciplinary record as exemplified by Patrick Vieira, who was one of ten players to receive the yellow card that afternoon and was about to start a six-match ban after a spitting offence at West Ham.

The game and my response to it were admirably described by David Miller in the *Daily Telegraph* the next day. Commenting on my refereeing he wrote that early on I 'exercised admirable restraint' and had used 'avuncular benevolence to quell emotions'. He observed that my restraint and attempts at quiet influence had little impact and the second half quickly blew up into a vicious match full of persistent fouling. 'Arsenal unquestionably set the tone, with relentless, cynical challenges . . . David Elleray faced an unenviable dilemma: if he blew for every offence there would be no play at all.'[40]

Of course, I was not blameless and I had made mistakes. It had been a frightening experience as never before had I felt, as I did in those last twenty minutes, that the players were beyond my control. Nothing I tried seemed to have any effect. Being understanding and sensible had had some success in the first half but there had still been four yellow cards. In the second I tried everything: being tough, pleading with the players, summoning the captains to help, but they all failed. Football had appeared only intermittently and I felt a great sense of sadness and frustration.

Ross Wilson loved it and decided that the programme would focus on me alone as he felt there was enough material from my refereeing and Harrow to make an interesting programme. Unfortunately, for some reason, Philip Don would not allow him to film at Premier League matches so Wilson had to confine himself to FA Cup and also Football League matches, which I had started refereeing again. He selected a range of matches to film and was cross that he did not come to the Abbey Stadium in Cambridge on Saturday 28 December 1999. The afternoon witnessed a poignant moment as I put the FIFA badge on my shirt for the last time.

Although it was not my intention, that badge saw a lot of action as in its final appearance I sent off three Cardiff City players. The events of the afternoon were amusingly described by a Cardiff fan on a radio phone-in programme which I listened to as I drove home. The conversation went something along these lines:

'I'm phoning about David Elleray who was dreadful today. He sent three of our players off.'

'Oh, what happened?' asked the presenter.

'Well, first Russell Perrett chopped someone down and was booked and then just before half-time he was sent off.'

'Did you see what he did?'

'No, I was getting a cup of tea and a pie but one of my mates said he deserved to go.'

'So, what's wrong with that?'

'Well, nothing. But then Elleray booked Craig Middleton for a foul and when he then tripped someone he sent him off as well.'

'Was that deserved?'

'Yes. I suppose it was but then he sent another one off.'

'What happened this time?'

'Well, Cambridge had a shot which was goalbound and our centre back, Lee Phillips, dived across the goal and pulled off a brilliant save with his hands.'

'So. He had to be sent off.'

'Yes, I suppose he did, especially as the penalty was saved and the match ended 0-0.'

'So, you've agreed with all the ref's decisions. So why are you complaining?'

'Well, because it's wrong. He shouldn't have sent three players off from one team!'

This match apart, I was doing my best to avoid controversy and keep out of the headlines as the scars from the Liverpool v Manchester United furore were still pretty raw. I had a real dread every game that something would happen to force me back into the headlines. My mental resolve was tested to the full when, in late February, I was appointed to referee Manchester United at Wimbledon. I felt under huge psychological pressure as I was terribly afraid of upsetting the United fans and being subjected to another barrage of abuse and threats. However, I knew I had to do the game. If I pulled out I would be finished and I tried to find the mental strength which had served me so well on that torrid afternoon at Spurs almost ten years before. I was really stressed in the days before the game and experienced huge emotional turmoil as I prepared myself. Somehow, the boys in Druries sensed my apprehension and did their best not to annoy or frustrate me. I was pleased, though, to discover that, probably to the relief of both of us, Roy Keane was suspended! To my amazement the Manchester United players and David Beckham in particular were superb. Beckham came up before the kickoff, shook my hand and said, 'No hard feelings, David.' I had been anticipating reactions ranging from aloof coldness to outright hostility but the players were immaculate, although the Manchester United fans, who filled most of the ground, were far less forgiving and howled with rage whenever I gave even an obviously correct decision against them.

It was a pulsating match and with Wimbledon leading 2-1 it looked as if an upset was on the cards. Then Ryan Giggs got the ball in his own half and went on one of his surging runs down the left wing. Reminiscent of his famous semi-final goal, several players tried to take him out but he kept going and I was able to play the advantage. He continued his run and crossed to Andy Cole who scored his 100th goal for Manchester United. It was another magical footballing moment and its importance was put in perspective when I heard one of the Wimbledon staff berating his players afterwards for not dealing with Giggs properly. 'I f*****g told you at half-time that if Giggs or any other f****r went on a run you were to stop him, even if it meant chopping him down and getting sent off!'

Referees were very much in the firing line at this time and TV cameras claimed to have caught Mike Reed celebrating a

Liverpool goal at Anfield. As Liverpool attacked the Leeds defence Vladimir Smicer was fouled. Mike played the advantage and the ball went to Patrick Berger who fired home. Mike clenched his fist in delight at his decision which was misinterpreted as him celebrating the goal. The newspapers loved it. The *Daily Mirror* produced some very amusing spoof photos of referees celebrating goals. One had the classic Beckham celebration except that they superimposed a ref's kit and Paul Alcock's head and in the background Sol Campbell had become Uriah Rennie. I was shown with my shirt off in celebration with the caption 'Pecs Appeal: David Elleray's a double for Paolo Di Canio'. When Alex Ferguson claimed that referees were more interested in showboating than controlling the game efficiently, and former World Cup referee Clive Thomas said, 'You have to be egotistical to want to be a ref', the *Daily Mail* produced the top ten Premier League showboaters. I was in second place with 'Known as "Lord Elleray" to his colleagues he swans around the pitch as if it is his private lawn. He's a housemaster at Harrow and treats the players as if they are his pupils.'[41] It was all amusing stuff.

The media attention was a minor distraction as I was more concerned with the Channel 4 documentary and the move towards professional referees. The initial attempts to persuade the Premier League clubs of the merits of a system whereby referees could train and focus on refereeing free from the distractions and pressures of their jobs failed but, pressured by some senior referees, Philip Don tried again and during season 2000/2001 the introduction of 'professional' referees became inevitable. I could not countenance leaving Harrow School to become a full-time referee, especially as I only had two years left before I reached the retirement age of forty-eight. The only way I could secure my future would be to demonstrate that I was still one of the best referees in the country in the hope that the Premier League would be forced to retain me.

By mid-season I was the top-ranked referee on assessors'

marks and club marks and I felt reasonably confident of negotiating a place in the new structure. I had come through some tough games pretty well, notably a ferocious encounter at Elland Road between Leeds and Liverpool and an equally combative match between Derby and Manchester United. I was really comfortable with my more relaxed style of refereeing and it was eliciting a favourable response from most players. Arsenal v Chelsea was another good example and although I had five yellow cards they were for isolated incidents and I worked really hard talking to players like Dennis Wise and Patrick Vieira. Communication was integral to my strategy and I chatted to players a great deal as play developed and particularly during stoppages. I worked hard to shed my image as a remote, authoritarian figure and it seemed to be successful. After the Highbury game Barry Knight, my fourth official, remarked, 'I don't know how you get away with it. You float round the pitch as if you are at a drinks party and the players seemed to accept everything you do. It's remarkable!'

I felt my new approach fully justified when I was appointed to referee the Worthington Cup Final. I was delighted at the appointment because it meant that I had achieved the 'big three' – FA Charity Shield, FA Cup Final and Worthington Cup Final. It would be a historic match being the first English Cup Final to be played in another country as the Millennium Stadium in Cardiff had become the new venue now that demolition work had started at Wembley.

My 'love affair' with Wembley had continued until almost the very end. I refereed the last FA Cup semi-final there, when Aston Villa played Bolton. In the dying moments of extra time Bolton's Dean Holdsworth missed a sitter after the Villa defence had been sliced open, partly because they were down to ten men as Mark Delaney had been sent off. Holdsworth blasted the ball high and wide after which the game went to penalties and Villa won. There was much sympathy for Holdsworth but if I had made an error of that magnitude which affected the result it would have been a very different story! My final Wembley visit had been to referee a business charity competition but by then they were playing half a dozen matches a day on the pitch and it resembled a ploughed field. I collected a few blades of grass and some mud and put them with those I had collected at the Simon and Garfunkel concert. It had been sad to see the stadium in the final throes of her life. Refereeing the first final in Wembley's temporary replacement was, however, very special.

I took Philip Sharp and Kevin Pike, the two assistants, and Paul Danson, the reserve referee, to the Millennium Stadium the day before the final to inspect the facilities and to begin to adjust to the atmosphere. It is so important to have a picture in your mind of the pitch and the surroundings so that you have some sense of the security which comes from being familiar with the setting. It is rather like an actor seeing the theatre before performing. Our supper that evening was punctuated by requests from Liverpool and Birmingham fans to sign menus and autograph books, although any illusions of being a celebrity were quickly dispelled when a fan approached me and said, 'Would you be kind enough to autograph my napkin, please, Mr Durkin'!

I woke next morning to find Cardiff covered in a light dusting of snow. The pitch was fine and a decision about whether to close the roof or not would be taken about two hours before kickoff. Once taken, there could be no change as the roof takes so long to close that it cannot be moved during the match. In the end, it remained 90 per cent open because the mechanism jammed. By kickoff it was bright and sunny and there was a tremendous atmosphere in the ground. Unlike Wembley, where the track separated the crowd from the pitch, in the Millennium Stadium the crowd is very close to it and the steep banking of the seats creates a much better atmosphere. It reminded me somewhat of the Bernabéu Stadium in Madrid.

Some expected Liverpool to swamp First Division Birmingham but this was not the case and the opening exchanges were pretty even. After about fifteen minutes came the first crucial moment when Steven Gerrard ran on to a long ball and, as he broke clear, he was brought down by Martin O'Connor – a clear red card. As I blew I felt the buzzer on my left arm vibrating (assistant referees had electronic flags and if they wanted to get the referee's attention they pressed a button on the flag handle which activated a vibrating buzzer which the referee felt). I looked across to see Kevin Pike flagging. Gerrard had been offside before the foul occurred so play was restarted with an indirect free kick to Birmingham and no red card for O'Connor.

After thirty minutes Robbie Fowler scored with a spectacular twenty-five-yard shot and half-time arrived with little controversy. I was busy talking to the players and was keen to avoid any unnecessary yellow cards. Referees often officiate rather more diplomatically in finals and are very keen not to send anyone off if at all possible, so I had been highly relieved when the offside flag had saved O'Connor.

The second half ebbed and flowed and as we reached the ninetieth minute Liverpool were withstanding the pressure well and seemed destined to lift the cup. I had a sense of relief that the match had passed without controversy and I was feeling fit but, understandably, a touch weary. Suddenly, with Paul Danson having already indicated that there would be three minutes additional time, there was a collision in the Liverpool penalty area and Birmingham appealed for a penalty. Before I could decide what to give, Henchoz brought down O'Connor with a dreadful tackle and I awarded the penalty without thinking twice. I probably should have booked him for the foul but all my attention was on O'Connor who was quite badly injured. He eventually left the field and the penalty was scored. Within ninety seconds I had blown for time and we were into extra time.

I was happy with the way the ninety minutes had gone but knew that the next thirty would mentally and physically test everyone. You train and prepare for an hour and a half's play so in extra time you have to draw deeply on physical and mental reserves. When you are physically tired your mental processes also slow down and you are prone to error, so I was determined to keep Kevin, Phil and myself fully focused. Players get tired as well and are more likely to make mistakes and get frustrated, so the pressure really is on the referee.

The ebb and flow of the match continued with neither side really looking like scoring. The third and final crucial moment centred on another penalty area challenge. Johnson rounded Henchoz who put in a desperate lunging tackle. Johnson went down and the ball spun away for a corner kick. I did not have the best view to make what was a critical decision. In an instant I had to decide whether Henchoz had played the ball or the man first. Phil Sharp's body language suggested no foul. As the ball had slightly changed course after the challenge I decided he had played the ball, just, and I awarded a corner kick, to the delight (relief?) of the Liverpool fans massed at that end. Like a cricket umpire who must give the benefit of the doubt to the batsman, referees should only penalise a tackle if they are certain it was a foul. TV replays proved inconclusive – one angle suggested I was right, another that I was wrong; yet another example of how referring such incidents to a video referee would not help. There were few protests from Birmingham although I was subsequently excoriated by a section of the Midlands!

No more goals were scored and we went to penalties. Players from both sides and both managers shook my hand and were complimentary and Trevor Francis, the Birmingham manager, did not question the non-penalty. There was upset among the Birmingham fans when the goal at the north end, where the Liverpool fans were massed, was used for the penalties. They claimed this was because Liverpool were the Premier League club and were being favoured, but the police had decided before the match that they wanted that end for security reasons. I had told both managers about this when they presented the team sheets an hour before kick off.

The shootout was dramatic and it took twelve penalties

before Liverpool won 5-4. The real disappointment was that we then had to hang around on the pitch for ages while the presentation podium was erected. Jim Ashworth brought us our cream sweatshirts as it was cold and we were pretty tired after a demanding two hours. I received my memento from Sven-Göran Eriksson and we returned to the warmth and comfort of the dressing room, happy that we had acquitted ourselves well. I knew I had refereed my last major Cup Final and I was delighted that Phil, Kevin and Paul had performed with the professionalism and dignity I had always expected of them. Yet again, though, I had had a difficult 'penalty' decision to make and, like the FA Cup Final, it was one of those decisions where whatever I gave would be wrong in some people's eyes and right in others. One of the great attractions of football is that there are decisions which are not clear-cut and which provoke debate for years after the rest of the match has been forgotten.

My more benevolent style of refereeing continued to please players, managers and assessors alike and I was refereeing well enough and had been sufficiently rehabilitated with Manchester United that in April I was appointed to referee the Manchester derby. It would be my first visit to Old Trafford for almost four years. It was a key match for both clubs as United were on their way to the title and City were desperately trying to avoid relegation.

Several weeks beforehand I had refereed Manchester City at Everton in a difficult match which saw Paul Dickov (Manchester City) and Alessandro Pistone (Everton) sent off in the dying moments after Dickov charged into a tackle and Pistone retaliated by kicking him. Joe Royle, with whom I had had many spats earlier in my career, asked me to look at the video of the incident. When I did there was sufficient doubt about the seriousness of the tackle for me to ask the FA to downgrade Dickov's red card to yellow. Joe Royle telephoned to say how much he appreciated me having the courage to change my decision as it released Dickov from a three-match suspension at a key time. It marked a turning point in our relationship, reminding me that communication is the best way to stop trouble and antagonism. The game needs more dialogue between referees and players and managers.

The Old Trafford ground and pitch looked immaculate as we prepared for a crucial derby which was being televised round the world. I had a long pre-match chat with Martin Tyler of Sky who made much of the fact that I had sent Roy Keane off three times. He was also interested in an article in that morning's *Daily Mail* in which Joe Royle heaped lavish praise on me as a referee and also said that he thought it was scandalous that I was being forced to retire. I am not sure how well that went down in certain circles but it certainly seemed to help me during the game as the Manchester City players treated me with great respect.

I was pleased the referee assessor was Mick McGuire of the PFA as he does not like lots of cards for technical offences and appreciates that big matches need diplomatic handling. If you referee exactly by the book then you can make matters worse and you need to keep the major disciplinary sanctions for physical offences and other 'hostilities'. McGuire is an astute judge of referees and it was always fascinating to hear his post-match analysis as it gave an intriguing insight from the playing perspective. Given the pressure I felt about refereeing at Old Trafford it was comforting to have an assessor who would judge my overall performance and not be fussy about trivialities.

In the tunnel before the match I had two interesting exchanges. I bumped into Paul Dickov who thanked me warmly for rescinding the red card at Everton. 'I'm not as bad as you thought, then, Paul!' I joked. 'No, David, you're okay. I owe you one,' he replied. 'You can repay me by not causing me any trouble today,' I said. 'You're on,' he replied and he was true to his word. As the players lined up I also spoke briefly to Roy Keane who was captaining Manchester United. 'I suppose you've already got my name in your book,' he said. 'I've not booked you in our last five matches and I hope today will make it six.' He just shrugged.

The match had a lively start and I was soon busy talking to the players, trying to take the heat out of the exchanges while focusing on appearing totally calm and collected. City's Paulo Wanchope looked dangerous and was thwarted by Jaap Stam after eight minutes and might have had a penalty ten minutes later. Roy Keane had several run-ins with City players and I spoke to him quite sternly to the fury of the Old Trafford faithful, but by half-time I had issued no yellow cards, although I probably should have booked David Beckham in the forty-first minute for clipping Dickov's heels. I contented myself with a few stern words as the atmosphere on the field was good, but was I subconsciously avoiding the fans' opprobrium?

The second half developed into a free-flowing match and Manchester United seemed too strong for City. Just before the hour Beckham put Wes Brown through and he was pushed to the ground by Dickov. I had no hesitation in awarding the penalty which Dickov and City accepted without complaint. Scholes hit it wide of the post. The sting went out of the game and both sides concentrated on playing good, attacking football. United took the lead on seventy minutes when Dunne clipped Solskjaer's heels and I awarded a second uncontested penalty. This time Sheringham made no mistake in front of the Stretford End. Then, in the eighty-fourth minute, City equalised when Steve Howey scored from close range. There was still no perceptible rise in temperature and I still had not issued a single yellow card. There were no feuds, no animosity between the players (or hostility to me) and the match had lost its bite and was drifting to a peaceful conclusion. Or so I thought.

It is always fatal to think a match is going well and to keep my concentration I have always refereed as if trouble is about to flare up and I do all I can to prevent it happening. What I did not realise was that I was about to endure the most pressured fifteen seconds of my life and be faced with making a decision which, if I got it wrong, could not only destroy my reputation and my career, but would risk provoking hate mail and death threats to rival those I had endured in 1999. What surprises so many people is that one of the easiest decisions of the season was so difficult to make because of the potential repercussions if I got it wrong.

We were five minutes from the end of a great derby match in which I'd not booked anyone and there was no apparent animosity between any of the players. All was quiet. Roy Keane got the ball on the United right flank, pushed it infield towards the City penalty area and suddenly there was a collision between him and Alfie Haaland. My initial reaction was that it was a dreadful tackle but almost simultaneously a number of questions flooded into my head. Where did that tackle come from? Had I seen the incident correctly? Had I imagined it? Was it a red card?

If it had been a bruising, spiteful, physical battle with half a dozen yellow cards, such a tackle would not have been out of context, but this had been a remarkably sporting match. The realisation that it was Roy Keane hit home hard. I was confronted with the prospect of sending off the Manchester United captain and hero, at the Stretford End and in a Manchester derby. More significantly, I would be showing him the red card for the fourth time. None of this would matter if the red card was the correct decision. But had I misinterpreted the tackle in the split second in which it occurred? If I wrongly sent Roy Keane off the rumours that he was a marked man would gain credence. Conversely, if it was a dreadful tackle and I failed to send him off I would be accused of cowardice for not having the courage to send him off for a fourth time. All these thoughts swirled round my head in seconds and I felt pressure the like of which I have not experienced before or since. It was a seminal moment in my refereeing career. If I got it wrong my reputation would be irreparably damaged. I could not call for a video replay – I had to make an instant judgement and it had to be right. I felt as if everyone could read my mind and see the turmoil I was experiencing. Everything seemed to be happening in slow motion. I cleared my mind of all those thoughts and replayed the incident in my mind's eye. My instincts were that, inexplicable as the tackle was, it was a red card.

I followed my usual procedure and moved towards the players and then through the throng so that I was standing with my back to the touchline. I always do this when I am going to take disciplinary action so that I have, as far as possible, all the players in view. This instinctive positioning proved to be crucial, as I was to discover a few seconds later. As I turned David Beckham and Gary Neville both arrived screaming at me, 'It's only yellow, it's only yellow.' Given that players rarely suggest that a team mate should receive a card of any colour, their comments helped confirm that it was a red card. I called Keane over and reached into the top pocket of my green shirt where I kept my red card. As I did so Jim Devine, the assistant, sidled up to me and simply whispered, 'Straight red.' That was the confirmation I needed.

I raised the card high in the air and braced myself for the torrent of abuse from the fans and protestations from Keane and his team-mates, particularly Phil Neville who was nearby. None came. Keane turned and walked across to the prostrate Haaland and, in what became one of the most talked-about moments of the season, bent down and said something to him. I had no idea what he said. In his autobiography, Keane confuses the sequence of events but reveals what he did say: 'I fucking hit him hard. He went down. Don't you ever stand over me sneering about fake injuries. And tell your pal Wetherall he can fuck off too. I didn't wait for Mr Elleray to show the card. I turned and walked to the dressing room.'[42] The stadium did not erupt and Keane left the field to rather muted applause. I was convinced I was right but my confidence was shaken when the City captain Steve Howey came up and said, 'You've not sent him off for that, have you, David?' 'Of course I have,' I replied.

Haaland received treatment but returned to the field and the rest of the match passed without incident. At the end of the game many players from both teams shook my hand and as I walked towards the tunnel at the south west corner of the field at the Stretford End I again braced myself for a storm of abuse from the United fans. Following my father's advice early in my career, I walked with my head up but there was scarcely a comment as I left the field. As soon as we got back to the dressing room we switched on the television and watched the replays of the incident. It really was an horrendous tackle and each time I saw it it got worse and worse. I was so thankful that I had made the correct decision. If I had lost my courage and ignored my instincts I do not think I could have lived with myself or the justified criticism that would have followed. I also reflected on the exceptional assistance from Jim Devine who, instinctively, had given me that extra confirmation that it was a red card. His split-second thinking and advice were invaluable and, for me, marked him out as an assistant of the highest calibre.

Mick McGuire arrived, having been in the City dressing room, and said that Joe Royle and his team thought I had had an excellent game. Mick was very forceful in his condemnation of the Keane tackle, saying it had no place in the game. He then enlightened us on the probable reason why Keane had committed what almost amounted to an assault on a fellow professional. Several years earlier, Leeds had played Manchester United at Elland Road and Keane had brought Haaland down with a bad challenge which had earned him a yellow card from my great friend Martin Bodenham. Keane injured himself badly making that challenge and Haaland allegedly made some comment to Keane while he was lying injured. Keane had apparently waited several years to exact his revenge. Cynics have also suggested that it was at a stage in the season when the title was almost Manchester United's and that Keane would not be missed for the final few matches. The press made a lot of the tackle but fortunately very little of the fact that I had dismissed Keane for the fourth time. It was the last time I refereed Manchester United at Old Trafford.

People often ask me about the tackle. 'Is it the worst you've ever seen?' is the usual enquiry. It is among the worst three or four certainly, but more crucially for me it was a moment where I was tested to the full. I experienced unbelievable pressure and felt that I had my career precariously balanced in the palm of my hand. People think that it was the easiest decision of my career but for those few seconds it was the most difficult. It is strange that, looking back, I can remember everything vividly and, like a car accident, those few seconds seem to take for ever.

Around this time the Premier League finally confirmed they were introducing professional referees for the coming season. I was invited to apply but Philip Don, the Premier League Referees Officer, made it very clear that if I did not give up my position at Harrow I could not continue as a Premier League referee. The crunch had come. I asked if I could continue as I had done for the previous fifteen seasons but I was told that it would create a dangerous precedent and would not be acceptable to the Premier League or to my colleagues. I knew the latter to be largely untrue but did not know the position of the League. I was given a fortnight to make a decision but there was none to make. I had shown where my loyalties lay with the World Cup in 1998 and I could not conceive giving up the job I loved for two seasons as a professional referee. When I was young I had dreamed of spending all my life refereeing but as the years passed I had developed grave doubts about the wisdom of full-time officiating.

I was left in a state of limbo for several weeks and became increasingly concerned until a chance encounter with Richard Scudamore, Chief Executive of the Premier League, at the Royal Television Society annual awards. The Channel 4 documentary *Football Stories: Man in Black* had been short-listed in the 'Best Sports Documentary' category, competing with a programme about Sir Steven Redgrave's fifth gold medal attempt and one about black athletes. I sat with Ross Wilson and his production team watching clips of the programme before that moment of suspense when the envelope is opened and the winner announced. Ross had previously won several awards with pro-grammes on Gordon Brown and Lockerbie and was quietly confident. In the event his confidence was justified: *Man in Black* was the unanimous winner.

Scudamore offered his congratulations on an outstanding pro-gramme but was somewhat surprised that I had not been filmed at any Premier League match until I explained that Philip Don had refused permission. Scudamore said I was refereeing excep-tionally well so I expressed my concern that it appeared I had no place in the new system as I could not commit to the fortnightly training meetings or unlimited availability. I will always remem-ber his words: 'We will accommodate you in whatever way you want. You will be one of our referees for the next two seasons.' He proved to be a man of his word and within days I was offered a contract. Don was very upset at being told to include me. His subsequent treatment of me and what I heard from other referees and assessors cast an ever-darkening cloud over my final two seasons.

However, my refereeing future seemed secure, which was the most important thing. After watching Steve Lodge referee his final game at Portman Road before he retired, I finished with a very difficult game at Elland Road where Leicester City were the visi-tors. I issued seven yellow cards and came close to sending off a couple of players. Almost the last thing I did was lecture Robbie Savage and Alan Smith, who had been having a running battle all afternoon. I ended my lecture with 'Do you realise that if I send you both off I'll be very popular as you are the most disliked players in the Premier League!' They looked shocked but it was true: at that time they both had dreadful reputations.

English refereeing was changing and the clamour for profes-sional referees had been answered. In many respects I would truly be 'the last amateur'.

## Chapter Thirteen

# *Players and Managers*

'All right, Dave?' – 'Fine, thank you, Vincent ...'
DAVID ELLERAY AND VINNIE JONES

One of the fascinating aspects of refereeing in the Premier League and overseas was that I gained an insight into the characters of so many players. It is perhaps oversimplistic to put them into categories but there were the class acts and the nightmares; the hard men and the gentlemen; the moaners and the silent types; some I dreaded refereeing and others I looked forward to seeing.

In my early years football seemed to be dominated by the mercurial geniuses and the hard men. Eric Cantona and Vinnie Jones epitomised the two breeds so when in February 1994 Wimbledon drew Manchester United in the Fifth Round of the FA Cup the press was full of 'Eric v Vinnie'. I had my work cut out early on with a really forceful foul from Jones on Cantona. One of the difficulties with Vinnie Jones was that he tackled with his whole body and not just his feet. Deciding whether or not it was a foul was not easy as he would play the ball cleanly but the inevitable follow-through seemed deliberately intimidatory.

I had experienced Vinnie's aggressive intentions some years earlier when he played for Sheffield United at Maine Road. Pre-match the press reported that Peter Reid (the Manchester City player-manager) was carrying a knee injury and when the ball was knocked back to Reid from the kickoff Jones immediately fouled him. The game had been going only five seconds and I yellow carded Vinnie – one of the fastest on record. I later sent him off but Vinnie had achieved his aim as Reid limped off shortly after that first foul. Unbeknown to me at the time I had guaranteed myself a place in Vinnie's controversial video – *Soccer's Hard Men* – in which he glorified some of the dirtiest footballers in history.

Jones' foul on Cantona was like the one on Reid: it was calculated intimidation but it was so skilfully done that it was what I sometimes call an 'orange' – halfway between a red card and a yellow card. Cantona's reaction was measured and with United quickly proving themselves too good for Wimbledon Jones' tactic did not have the desired effect. Humour was never far away with Vinnie. I was amused when I refereed him just after he captained Wales for the first time. As he came for the toss-up I greeted him in Welsh with '*Iechyd da*'. 'You wot?' he replied. The boys at Harrow always wanted to know how well Vinnie and I got on and I conned them into believing that our usual pre-match greeting was 'All right, Dave?' from Vinnie to which I responded in my poshest voice, 'Fine, thank you, Vincent, and how are you?'

A highly publicised hard man v gentleman clash had been when a John Fashanu challenge badly injured Gary Mabbutt at White Hart Lane in 1993. I was not the referee that day but the incident summed up one of the problems referees faced as they tried to protect the skilful players against those players and managers who felt the only way to neutralise skill and creativity was with aggression. It was this clash of styles and attitudes which ultimately led to FIFA cracking down on the illegal tackle from behind and other crude challenges, sparking a period in the mid-1990s which saw a deluge of red and yellow cards as referees followed their mandate to clean up the game.

Fashanu was the perfect gentleman off the field and he brought his studied manners and what came across as affected courtesy onto it. He would greet you like a long-lost friend and I am sure his affected deference and respect was designed to lull you into thinking he was a good guy. 'Good afternoon, Mr Elleray, or may I call you David?' was his typical opening. This did not blind anyone to the physicality of his play which was frequently unacceptable. He tried hard to maintain his aplomb but it could slip, as I discovered when he reacted angrily after I booked him for a foul on a very hot May afternoon in 1991 in Wimbledon's final League match at Plough Lane. Perhaps fittingly, his booking was Wimbledon's last on the ground that had seen so much excitement as the 'Crazy Gang' rose to and then took on the First Division.

I refereed Fash's final match when he was playing for Aston Villa at Old Trafford. It turned out to be his last match because of an injury he sustained in the thirty-eighth minute. Those for whom he was a hate figure because of his combative style of play took perverse pleasure in his career being ended by a reckless tackle he made on an opponent. The challenge was so bad that I was debating whether or not to send him off. He was writhing in agony and I thought he was play-acting to avoid being booked or sent off but he was not and, to the unrestrained joy and derision of the Stretford End, Fashanu left the Premier League on a stretcher as I held the yellow card aloft.

Gary Mabbutt, in contrast, was a true gentlemen on and off the field. In my experience he was rivalled only by Gianfranco Zola. Players who believe that they can bully referees into finding in their favour could not be more wrong. It was always the players who were nice to me who got the benefit of the doubt, as Mabbutt discovered in a north London derby when I had to decide whether he had denied Arsenal an obvious goal-scoring opportunity. Mabbutt was disappointed to have been penalised in the first place and that, along with his outstanding reputation as a sportsman, probably persuaded me to give him only a yellow card.

What made Mabbutt and Zola stand out was their willingness to accept decisions and simply get on with the game. There might be the odd quizzical look but nothing more. They were sporting enough to compliment me if I got a tough decision right, even if the decision went against them. Zola accepted things with a smile and a shrug of the shoulders and always treated me with the utmost respect. He was much more interested in playing the game than trying to referee it. In terms of being spoken to politely, the best players were those, like Everton's David Weir, who came from the Scottish Premier League. Without fail and regardless of how angry they were, they always addressed me as 'Mr Elleray'.

Of current players, John Terry and Sol Campbell were two who I found simply got on with playing and rarely said anything. They accepted decisions and, aware that arguing would not change my decision, recognised that their priority was to get into position to defend. This made them easy players to referee as, even when they committed a bad foul, they usually accepted the consequences in a thoroughly professional manner.

I found Eric Cantona very silent but in a different way. His haughty demeanour could be offputting and his facial expressions, imperious gestures and looks of disbelief sometimes bordered on contempt and were used for all who upset him, not just referees. I always felt that he looked down on the rest of us but his supreme ability perhaps allowed him to. There was something thrilling about his flashes of genius but I sometimes sensed he was a volcano waiting to explode, as he did so outrageously at Selhurst Park. Refereeing his first game back after his lengthy suspension was eye-opening. He stood in the tunnel beforehand radiating majesty and calm, almost as if nothing

had happened and this was just another match. His professionalism when he took that penalty was incredible as was the
outpouring of joy when he celebrated.

Conversations with Cantona were rare and verbal exchanges
tended to be at his initiation and were usually inquisitorial.
'Why?' was his most frequent question, along with 'How could
you give that? I did nothing.' If you took action against him he
generally accepted it without comment. It was pointless asking
him his name as I found when I booked him at Wimbledon on
the afternoon of Beckham's wonder goal. As I scribbled on my
yellow card he just stood there, hands on hips, with an enigmatic
look on his face, almost as if his irritation was not the booking.
but the fact that the stoppage was holding up the physical
expression of his genius.

Unfortunately, some others in the 'genius' category were more
of a problem. Paul Gascoigne was an absolute nightmare
because you never knew what he was going to do next. I once
refereed him at White Hart Lane and he was great fun one
minute and a spluttering, red-faced 'Mr Angry' the next. He
was brought down by a sliding tackle which scooped up a long
chunk of turf. He picked it up, put it on my head and said,
'That's not a bad wig, David!' Everyone laughed but moments
later he was again fouled and turned and snarled at me, 'Aren't
you gonna f*****g do something?' At his best he was quite
brilliant and you never knew quite what example of genius
would come next. The problem was that when he lost his temper
all self-control went, as I experienced at half-time in Spurs v
Luton and again when my great friend Steve Lodge fell foul of
him as we walked off at half-time in a pre-season tournament.

As with rogues at school I felt a certain sympathy for Gazza,
especially towards the end when he really was a troubled soul. I
hated refereeing him then as he had lost his pace and touch and
quickly became frustrated and angry. I remember him coming on
as a substitute at Everton and after a couple of great one-touch
passes he made a few mistakes. His frustration was clear and for

the next five minutes he charged round the field glowering and threatening. He tried to kick several opponents but fortunately he was too slow and intent was not converted into action. Talking to him was pointless as it simply seemed to put me in the firing line.

I was mindful of his troubles on the opening day of season 1998/9 when, slightly overweight, he made his debut for Middlesbrough. The game seemed secondary to his running battle with the fiery Leeds midfielder Lee Bowyer. At one point Gazza caught Bowyer in the face with his elbow but I decided on a yellow rather than red card as he had used his arm to shrug off Bowyer's attentions rather than as a weapon. Both players were on a short fuse and I did my best to control them by constantly talking to them about challenges, decisions and the state of the game. The papers approved of my handling of the game and the *Sun*, under a headline 'Elleray Chats Up Gascoigne', commented, 'England's tormented soul can thank David Elleray ... The Harrow official has always been quick on the draw when it comes to reaching for the cards but the strict schoolmaster showed leniency, compassion, understanding and good old-fashioned common sense.'[43] Somehow the last thing I wanted to do was to send him off.

Another not dissimilar member of the mercurial gang was Ian Wright, whom I first clashed with when he was at Crystal Palace before we had a number of spectacular run-ins when he was with Arsenal. My major problem with Wright was that he could give it but not take it. He was adept at occasionally leaving his foot in the challenge and catching an opponent, but if he was caught late he would shout and scream and posture. He was easily aggrieved, as I found in a tough encounter with Leicester at Filbert Street in November 1994. Wright was at his most temperamental and I had no option but to book him for dissent just before half-time. The yellow card antagonised him and when the half-time whistle went he came looking for a major confrontation. Fortunately, he was bustled away down the tunnel where he proceeded to shout and swear and I had to send a message to the Arsenal dressing room that unless he calmed down he was unlikely to finish the game. He responded pretty well and satisfied himself with a series of gestures, glares and grunts. In his autobiography Wright mentions this match and uses it as an example of players being treated badly by referees. It is very easy for him to say such things but he was a nightmare to referee as he wanted to be your friend when it suited him, but on other occasions he was impossible to talk to.

He delighted in the 'theatre of the game' and if he could physically show his contempt he would; at times you had to take him on otherwise you would lose all credibility. With other players and the crowd watching intently he would deliberately walk away from you or turn his back in a manner that made it clear he had little respect for you or your decisions. You could ignore it, try and talk to him or give him the yellow card. As with all high-profile players, the way you dealt with him was always likely to be scrutinised by the media so you had to be very careful. A while later Wright was in trouble with the FA after he described me as 'a little Hitler', a comment which brought much amusement at Harrow, especially when one newspaper produced a photo of me in my refereeing kit with a tiny black moustache and swastika armband.

I saw Wright's dark side when I was reserve referee at West Ham and he trashed our dressing rooms after being sent off. Off the field, he was charming and great company. He is, of course, somewhat off-the-wall and I remember one Sunday morning I was on the telephone looking out of my study window when a large black limousine screeched to a halt and Wright got out, waved like mad, shouted a friendly greeting and then drove off. He had just picked up Mark Bright to go and do a radio show and Mark later told me that Ian had seen me at the window and had insisted on stopping to wave 'hello'. I met him a while later at an England game and he explained that it was not until he retired that he realised what a nightmare he had been to referee.

He said his outbursts all stemmed from the pressure he was under as he felt he had to perform exceptionally in every match; when he was below par his frustration quickly expressed itself in his antics. Referees like me were a very easy target and excuse for things going wrong.

Dealing with these characters was a great challenge because I knew that whenever I booked or sent them off there would be reams of analysis in the newspapers. It was a relief, therefore, that there were some players who were enjoyable, even fun, to referee. Dwight Yorke was one of them. He rarely argued and was always grinning broadly, often teasing me saying, in his lilting Caribbean drawl, 'What you doin' now, David?' Graeme Le Saux was also really enjoyable to referee as he was intelligent, if a little hot-headed. I could talk and reason with him and he listened and talked back. He loved telling me which referees he liked and which he did not like – his analysis was hard to argue with as he had an intense dislike of those who posed or gave the impression that they were more important than the players or the game.

Graeme was disarmingly honest about his temper and often used to ask me to keep talking to him to help him focus on not overstepping the mark. Another refreshingly honest player was Mark Bosnich. He once completely lost his cool at Elland Road when he was playing for Aston Villa and I sent him off. When I saw him the following season he told me that he had received 'the most almighty bollocking from [his] dad who had been watching the game on television in Australia'. We always used to joke about that and if ever he started to cause problems I'd remind him that if he forced me to card him he'd have his father to answer to as well!

Of all the rogues I refereed the two I most enjoyed being on the field with were Dennis Wise and Robbie Savage. They are always up to something but prepared to take the consequences when caught in a 'it's a fair cop, guv' sort of way. Whenever I think of Dennis I smile; indeed it was the good rapport I had with him and the rest of his Chelsea team-mates which made me look forward to the Cup Final with so much relish. In the end, I ruined his day with that second penalty. There are many photos of me waving away his pleading protests with one hand while the other is reaching for my back pocket and the yellow card. It stayed where it was, probably because I already knew it was a bad decision but just possibly, because I liked and respected him.

Dennis was totally unpredictable on and off the field, as I discovered with that pre-match kiss at Anfield. He always had an opinion on everything and many of our encounters became 'Den and Dave' conversations. He loved winding people up. Chelsea played Nottingham Forest in a League Cup tie and there was a scuffle between Lambourde and Rodgers. I decided that a lecture would suffice but no sooner had I started than Dennis butted in and said, 'Just send the f*****s off, David!' We all burst out laughing and he had done my job for me. A while later I noticed that he had a bruise on his nose and jokingly asked if someone had hit him. 'Yea, me old lady!' he joked back. There were times when I could cheerfully have given him a good smack but referees are not allowed to do that, at least not intentionally, although Robbie Savage was on the receiving end of referee Matt Messias's elbow at Newcastle in August 2003. Messias signalled for a free kick and caught Savage in the face and knocked him out. It was something many referees would love to have done and as Savage slowly recovered Alan Shearer jokingly showed Messias the red card.

When I first encountered Savage he was an embryonic Vinnie Jones, charging round the field with great energy, winding people up and following through with his body whenever he tackled. We had many battles but the turning point came in January 2002 when Arsenal visited Filbert Street and all-out war was expected between Vieira and Savage. I managed to get the two protagonists on my side early in the game. The press had been predicting that tough-tackling Savage would provoke Vieira but I was determined to snuff out any problems. For the first fifteen to twenty minutes I abandoned the traditional diagonal patrol path and stuck closely to both combatants. Whenever they looked as if they were going to do something rash I'd shout 'Steady, Robbie' or 'Careful, Patrick'. I talked to them both a great deal and I managed to keep Savage calm enough for him to channel his aggression into legitimate tackles. Midway through the half, Savage said to me, 'If we carry on chatting like this we're going to end up friends!' My plan worked and the match developed into a free-flowing game with scarcely a tackle out of place.

Thereafter, whenever I refereed Savage he seemed pleased to see me, not least in my final season when he was at Birmingham. I feared the worst when I refereed him in their Midlands derby with Aston Villa but he was great and we sparred verbally throughout the game which, I believe, helped him keep the lid on his emotions. He would occasionally snarl and I'd retort with, 'Look, Robbie, if I'd wanted a hard time tonight I'd have stayed at home!' He was not beyond taking liberties and when I awarded Birmingham a free kick close to the Villa penalty area he picked the ball up as if to place it for the free kick and then bounced it on my head. Having once been reprimanded by an assessor at Cardiff for not booking a player who jokingly squirted a water bottle at me during treatment for an injury, I wondered how to react but took it in good part.

Later that season, on Boxing Day, I received a highly enthusiastic welcome from Savage before the game. When I walked down the tunnel just before kickoff he smiled, said 'Hi, mate!' and enveloped me in a great bear hug! His warmth continued on the field and he was helpful and cooperative all afternoon. However, it is dangerous for a referee ever to think that the players are his friends. In the heat of battle they will do anything to gain an advantage. Even in this game Savage was still capable of a couple of meaty tackles and I had to make sure that I did not treat him too leniently just because he was being nice to me. After all, if the chips were down I would not be very high on his list of priorities.

If Savage and Wise were fun there were some who were quite the opposite because they were either continually moaning or just plain sour. Two of the most miserable in my experience were Denis Irwin and Nigel Winterburn: I found it was impossible to get a smile from them and they rarely spoke except to be negative and offensive. Their comments and haughty disdain were probably not evident to fans or television viewers and their silence contrasted with those who were never slow to make a comment. Close to the top of the Premier League of moaners would come Gary Neville and Peter Schmeichel. Schmeichel was never short of a word for me, his team-mates or his opponents. It was his way of deflecting any criticism that might be coming his way. He sometimes thought nothing of coming way out of his area as he did when he ran the length of the Anfield pitch to give us all the benefit of his wisdom. Gary Neville is a serial moaner on the field and his voluble comments when Rio Ferdinand was stopped from playing for England showed that he is the same off it as well. Never one to admit his own failings, let alone see another point of view, his face would contort with anger as he spat out his words of disagreement. It was somewhat ironic that he helped me make one of the biggest decisions of my career, sending Keane off after the tackle on Haaland. Given that Neville disputed almost every judgement which went against Manchester United, when he and Beckham shouted 'It's only yellow. It's only yellow' it convinced me that it was at least a red card!

However, Darren Anderton comes top of my moaners' Premier League. He was sour and unpleasant in virtually every game I refereed and I found it impossible to get even a neutral response from him. He would curl his upper lip and make some offensive remark which was usually best dealt with by ignoring it, although against Chelsea in 1999 when I was under great pressure after the Liverpool v Manchester United saga I nearly lost my self-control and swore back at him. For a while I thought that it was just me, but speaking to other referees, I found that others thought exactly the same. Refereeing Spurs became just that bit less enjoyable when Teddy Sheringham moved back there from United. While the Old Trafford team were perfectly capable of making their feelings felt, the Beckhams and Keanes were also willing to be pleasant and engage in some light-hearted banter. Not Sheringham – you either got silence or negativity, which may surprise many fans as he is not ostentatious in his disagreements.

The First Division of moaners would include Alan Shearer (in his early days), Ryan Giggs and Matt Le Tissier. They were not constantly at me but in some matches could be a real pain. Sometimes, Giggs would snap over the most insignificant decisions and if I asked him if he was in a bad mood he just glared. I noticed something of a connection between his moods and his stubble – the longer he went without shaving the more miserable he was. Le Tissier was similar. If he was on good form he was great fun, laughing, joking and really enjoying everything about the game. If he was out of sorts then he was miserable, surly and quick to react to any decision, good or bad.

Alan Shearer was a great moaner at the start of his career but I found he mellowed when he went to Newcastle. He was another example of an intelligent player from whom I could get a decent response if I explained what I was doing. He did not always agree and would sometimes offer me advice, but in the last few seasons we got on really well and beyond the occasional 'Come on, David!' and a shrug he allowed me to referee unhindered.

One of the nicest 'moans' of my career came from Gary Speed, a player I admired greatly. I gave a free kick against Newcastle at Villa Park and he came up and very politely said:

'David, I think you made a mistake. That was a dreadful decision.'

'Thank you, Gary!' I replied. The free kick came to nothing and the next time play was stopped I happened to be alongside Speed and said, 'Gary, that was the politest bollocking I have ever had!'

'Well, you always speak to us politely so I thought I would do the same.'

I got to know some players so well that they were almost like friends on the field and we would natter away throughout the game, breaking off our discussions for an attack and the occasional disagreement. Chris Marsden and Francis Benali of Southampton were always good to chat to, as was Jason Dodd, while Mark Viduka and I got on really well, especially after I refereed his hat-trick against Liverpool in November 2000. It was good to chat to the players but you had to be careful not to let this distract you or influence you too much. Occasionally, getting on with and liking a player could affect your judgement and there were several occasions when I should have booked Ian Harte of Leeds but did not because he was always so pleasant and so very plausible when he explained why he had committed a rash challenge.

Beyond these characters one of the great privileges and challenges was refereeing superstars like David Beckham and Thierry Henry. Henry is a class act and whenever I refereed him it was difficult not to marvel at his pace, skill and deftness of touch. He is much taller than he seems on television and moves with exceptional grace across the field. He expected to be protected but was not averse to the tough side of the game and was, in fact, the last Arsenal player I booked.

Beckham first came to my attention when I refereed that FA Youth Cup semi-final at White Hart Lane between Spurs and Manchester United in March 1992. My next encounter with him was at Blackburn in August 1995 but the most memorable of these early matches together was when Beckham imprinted himself on the nation's consciousness with 'that goal' in the closing moments at Wimbledon. I was impressed with the audacity of the strike and the way he coped with the press attention it brought. I first saw his volatile side at Old Trafford on New Year's Day 1997. Tempers flared on several occasions and there was an altercation between David Beckham and Villa's Savo Milošević in the forty-second minute which I put down to an overreaction from Beckham until afterwards, when TV and newspaper pictures suggested that the Villa player had spat at him.

I thought that he was extremely harshly dealt with after the Argentina game during World Cup 1998. Having been fouled, he lifted his leg in a minor retaliatory kick at Simeone but he hardly touched him. In the Premier League he would have received a yellow card. However, FIFA referees were expected to be extremely strict with anything resembling retaliation and Kim Milton Nielson produced the red card. I am sure that Beckham's stunned look was genuine; he would not have been expecting it. He had suffered partly because the Premier League had wanted a softer approach to on-field discipline, but they were doing the national team (and clubs competing in Europe) a disservice as European referees were stricter and English players had difficulty adjusting in the heat of the moment.

The vilification Beckham had to endure after the World Cup was beyond comprehension. He had been harshly sent off and, if anything, the country should have been sympathetic to his plight but we always need a scapegoat and he was the one. He was subjected to abuse of a level that probably no other player has endured for such a sustained period for many years, if ever. I remember refereeing him at Old Trafford when a section of away fans were provoking him with dreadful abuse. An incident occurred close to these fans and Beckham's body language told me he was close to giving back as good as he was getting. I sidled up and, trying to make a bit of a joke of it, I said, 'David, don't react and just think what a good job you're doing keeping them off my back!' Quick as a flash, he replied, 'Can't you give a couple of dodgy decisions and get them off my back?'

Beckham has never really taken on the haughty demeanour of some seasoned internationals and was generally communicative and respectful to me on and off the field. During the period when there was a strong feeling in the Manchester United dressing room that I had something against them, Beckham always remained courteous, if a little distant.

The magic associated with Beckham's free kicks is even more impressive when viewed from a few feet away. One of his classic free kick goals was at Anfield in December 1997. I awarded a free kick to the right of the Liverpool goal as Beckham looked at it – prime position for him. The wall was back a good ten yards and from the moment his foot made contact with the ball there was no doubt that it was destined for the back of the net. Knowing Beckham's speciality in this area of the field it was always important to be extra vigilant when Manchester United were attacking as they, quite understandably, sought free kicks in this zone. They would often position their bodies and the ball in such a manner so as to invite a clumsy tackle and, while not looking to cheat, they were always aware that if their path to goal was blocked being fouled was a very acceptable option.

Beckham's on-field conduct, rather like that off the field, is of a high level given the extraordinary physical and verbal provocation that he is subjected to. I believe it was an incredibly astute move to make him England captain and Alex Ferguson's endorsement of that decision demonstrated that it was part of a broader strategy to get the best out of him. Prior to the captaincy, Beckham had a propensity during tough games to get overinvolved as he became frustrated at his play, United's lack of progress or perceived injustices in treatment from opponents or the referee. You could sense him being galvanised by a constant adrenalin rush and he would charge round the field almost like the proverbial headless chicken. When players get like that the referee fears the worst and my tactic was always to try to give free kicks before the player exploded, to try to talk down his rage with a mixture of common sense and humour and, as a last resort, pray that when he started launching himself into challenges he would not make contact. In the famous final World Cup qualification game against Greece at Old Trafford, where Beckham sealed his hero status with the last-minute free-kick goal, he put in the work of three or four players. He seemed to be everywhere and it was this channelling of his energy in a positive manner which, for me, marked his arrival as a mature, focused, controlled player. Four years earlier and he would have been using the same energy to tackle players indiscriminately, sometimes wildly, and snarl at the referee. I remember watching the end of the game after refereeing a rugby match at Harrow and when he scored I, like thousands of others, leapt in the air with delight. He was everyone's hero that day.

Off the field Beckham, despite the Loos allegations, has been a great role model for young men and young fathers. His row with Ferguson when he did not turn up for training because Brooklyn was ill, and the frequency with which Brooklyn appeared on his shoulders to celebrate another Manchester United title or cup, publicly said that it is 'cool' to be a caring father. His influence in this respect is greater than any manual or advertising campaign. We may scoff at his hairstyle, his wearing his wife's underwear, and his sarongs, but he is never in the news for drinking, smoking or taking drugs, whilst Sam Taylor-Wood's video portrait has probably sealed his iconic status.

Beckham is not an academic but then that is not a fundamental requirement for success. He is a gifted athlete and he has the intelligence to surround himself with wise advisers and shrewd confidants. His 'corn row' plaits when he went to South Africa to play in a friendly and meet Nelson Mandela were not a gimmick or just another hairstyle, and were certainly not intended to poke fun at anyone. Indeed his gesture was quite the reverse. It was a very shrewd move, being seen in South Africa as a compliment as he was embracing African culture. It did a huge amount of good, as many South Africans remarked to me a few weeks later when I refereed there. Thousands appreciated what he had done as he had demonstrated an affinity with the people and it should be remembered that soccer is a predominantly black sport in South Africa, with cricket and rugby the traditional white sports.

However, without doubt, the player with whom I am most associated is Roy Keane. Keane could argue with some statistical justification that I had it in for him as he was the player who, according to my records, I disciplined more than any other. I first booked him when he was with Nottingham Forest in January 1993 and the last time was January 2001; coincidentally, Middlesbrough were the opponents on both occasions. In between these two yellow cards I sent him off four times and gave him another four yellow cards. One of the most difficult was in Cantona's comeback match at Old Trafford as I had only sent Keane off a few weeks earlier at Blackburn; when he chopped someone down I steeled myself for more abuse from the Manchester United faithful as I reached into my back pocket.

For a while Keane did his best to ignore me but he mellowed and we had a run of five matches without a booking. Fatally we joked about it before the City game as we waited in the tunnel. What happened next has already been recorded: we did make it six as far as yellow cards were concerned but Keane's horrendous tackle on Haaland ensured he saw my red card for the fourth time. Keane remarked, half jokingly, after that final booking at Middlesbrough, 'You couldn't wait to do that, could you?', but when I retired he was very sporting and when Premier League colleagues contacted Manchester United to ask if they could arrange a signed Roy Keane shirt for me he not only sent the shirt but also an amusing and generous letter.

One of the most exciting and interesting developments in the English game was the arrival in the Premier League of continental players, many of whom I had disciplined in Europe. Some continued to feature in my disciplinary records and seemed unable to escape my attention no matter what club they were at. Most notable was Emmanuel Petit, whom I first booked when he was playing for Monaco but who fell foul of me at Arsenal and then Chelsea. Similarly, the temperamental Gus Poyet first saw yellow for Real Zaragoza and then yellow again with Chelsea and finally red when at Spurs.

The benefit of so much Premier League football on television was brought home to me when I refereed Davor Suker's first

Premier League match at Highbury following his signing for Arsenal from Real Madrid. Before the kickoff he came up, shook hands and said, 'I am very pleased you are refereeing my first match. I have seen you many times on television in Spain.' We had an amusing exchange midway through the first half when he was fouled and rolled round on the floor as if in his death throes. I gestured that he should get up and said, 'Mr Suker, we do not behave like that in English football.' He apologised and we got on very well from that moment onwards. When he scored an absolutely stunning equaliser in first-half injury time I drifted past him and said, 'Fantastic goal!' After the game there was a knock on the dressing-room door and Suker came in and handed me his sweat-soaked shirt: 'I would like you to have this for treating me so well in my first match,' he said.

Some of the players I knew well in my early days as a League referee had become managers by the time my career was drawing to a close. In the year I refereed the Cup Final, Premier League Leeds were knocked out at home in the Fourth Round by Oxford United of Division Two. At the end a disgruntled Gordon Strachan, who was coming to the end of his playing days with Leeds, walked off with me bemoaning the lack of hunger among the young Leeds players: 'They get flashy cars, flashy homes and too much b****y money too young, if you ask me. They don't have the hunger that we had when I was a young player. It's all too easy for them and they don't have any fight in them.' His trenchant views were frequently heard when he managed Coventry and later Southampton. We did not get on particularly well and at half-time at Derby one Saturday he burst into my dressing room with a volley of questions and comments. He was like a human tornado and when he finished I was so irritated I leaned against the door and refused to let him out until I had had my say. He told the press afterwards that I locked him in! That set the seal on our relationship and when an assistant was injured at Leicester and I took over as fourth official, Strachan put his head in his hands and said, 'I didn't think it could get any worse but your f*****g appearance proves me wrong!'

The influx of foreign mangers radically changed the face of English club football and I have the greatest admiration for Gérard Houllier, Arsène Wenger and Claudio Ranieri for their technical skills and the professionalism they have brought to our national game. They were, however, very different characters.

The best insight I had into two of them was in my last season when I was reserve referee to Uriah Rennie on New Year's Day at Highbury. The Arsenal Manager (known by some referees as Arsène 'I did not see it' Wenger) was up and down like a yo-yo and his language belied the civilised, intellectual and sophisticated demeanour so evident on TV. In contrast, Claudio Ranieri was thoughtful, quiet and civilised. Midway through the second half Rennie gave a series of decisions which caused Wenger to leap to his feet and shout, 'F***! F***! F***!' He then turned to me and let loose a volley of abusive comments about Rennie. I simply stared at him and said nothing.

'What are you staring at?' Wenger enquired.

'I was wondering why you were swearing at me.'

'Well, the f*****g referee is dreadful.'

'When your players make a mistake or play badly, is it your fault?' I asked.

'Of course not!'

'So, don't take it out on me if you are unhappy with the ref. You can't control your players and I can't control the referee!'

Wenger turned away and a few moments later came back and apologised. I had no trouble from him after that and we warmly shook hands at the end of the game. Ranieri was very different. Late on in a pulsating game of seven goals, a tight offside decision went against Chelsea. When the incident appeared on the big screen it looked as if Chelsea had been unlucky. Ranieri shrugged and said, 'It is difficult to be a referee. I know because I sometimes blow the practice game and I make many mistakes. After all, you are only human!'

Two managers I really admire are Gérard Houllier and Sir Bobby Robson. Houllier is a true gentleman and I always looked forward to refereeing Liverpool after he took over the reins. What I liked most about Houllier was his honesty. If he thought you refereed well he would tell you, but he would also tell you if he was unhappy, as he once did at West Ham when he felt I had not been protecting his team. I explained that I had seen the fouls but had played the advantage which I thought helped Liverpool. He looked sceptical but later in the week he phoned me to say that he had studied the video and understood what I had been trying to do.

A powerful example of his integrity came after Robbie Fowler's infamous goal celebration in the Merseyside derby at Anfield. Fifteen minutes into the game Materazzi tripped Ince in the Everton penalty area. Fowler fired home the penalty and then ran to the Everton fans, got on his hands and knees and put his nose to the ground. Afterwards, the senior police officer came in and said he was unhappy that Fowler had mimed 'sniffing the line'. Apparently, Everton fans had been suggesting that he used cocaine and this was his response. Gérard Houllier came in and said he had spoken to Fowler whose actions had been misinterpreted. 'Robbie and Rigobert Song were mimicking cows eating grass. It is a traditional African celebration.' I thought Gérard was joking but he was deadly serious so I gave him a very old-fashioned look and thanked him for coming to explain.

Two days later I was Dermot Gallagher's reserve referee for Nottingham Forest v Liverpool. About an hour before kickoff Gérard Houllier asked to see me.

'David, I have been trying to contact you all weekend,' he said.

'I'm sorry, I've not been at home. Why?' I replied.

'Well, I wanted to apologise for misleading you on Saturday. When I told you about Robbie and Rigobert I genuinely believed they were telling me the truth, but they weren't. I wanted to apologise because, as a result, I was untruthful when I spoke to you.'

That he had felt so badly and had made a point of apologising personally was a measure of the man and whenever I heard Liverpool fans criticising him I felt sorry and angry that they doubt his abilities and commitment. He is one of the most honourable managers I have met and his attitude and observations helped me change my refereeing philosophy.

The Englishman who rivals Houllier for integrity and honesty is Sir Bobby Robson. I met the 'wise old man' of English football several times in Europe when I refereed Barcelona and PSV Eindhoven. His return to Newcastle brought hope to that sleeping giant and his analysis of players and referees always bears listening to. I took my fair share of criticism from him over the seasons but there was only one occasion, at Everton, where I felt his passion for Newcastle coloured his usual objectivity. It was a great pleasure for me that he was there for my final match. His kindness before and after the game was moving and his warmth and sincerity as he generously reflected on what I had achieved made that final day so much more special.

Given that most of my time at the top seemed inextricably linked with Manchester United, my final words must be about Sir Alex Ferguson. I have mentioned elsewhere his kindness before some games and the difficulties I had with him during and immediately after others, the worst being at Anfield in May 1999. However, I can only marvel at what he has achieved and how he has achieved it. He has been quite brilliant and, given that I am hugely competitive as a House Master, I admire the way he tries to turn every situation to his and United's advantage. His mind games are part of his brilliant strategy and while I have not always agreed with him and have, at times, suffered grievously because of what he has said about me, in the end I greatly admire how he has turned Manchester United into the best club in the world in the 1990s and the great players he has nurtured. My career would have been much the poorer had

Manchester United not been so successful as many of my best and most memorable English matches involved Ferguson's team. Perhaps the greatest compliments I received from him were the indirect ones, such as when he phoned the Premier League or the FA to complain about the referee appointed to a particularly tough United game. 'Why can't we have David Elleray? He never does us any favours but he always protects the players.'

# Chapter Fourteen

# *The Last Amateur*

*'When I was younger, I would be angered by his attitude.
He would not talk to us. Now, I have great respect for him.'*
NIALL QUINN[44]

My first game as the only 'amateur' among the newly created professional referees was live on Sky TV on Monday 20 August 2001 between Everton and Spurs. As I drove north that morning I did not feel ready for the start of the season and I had a sense of foreboding that things might not go well. I was confused about how I should referee. Over the years my own particular style had evolved but we were now being asked to referee in a very different way. Following Euro 2000, the 'in' way of officiating was 'safe refereeing', which meant penalising every foul, no matter how minor. The theory was that players would have more confidence in the referee because they would know that he was missing nothing. Moreover, some players and managers held that a free kick was better than keeping possession. People on the Continent are used to a more interventionist style of refereeing but I was not convinced it would suit the combative and free-flowing English game as players and spectators do not like constant whistling or a stop-start game.

The match started quietly enough and I gave free kicks for minor offences I would not normally have penalised. Whether it was this or I was just having a bad day I do not know, but I was certainly struggling. The first major error was when the ball was crossed from the Spurs left wing into the penalty area and I blew for the slightest of fouls by Everton's forward Alexandersson as he scored. As I blew I realised that the foul had actually been on Alexandersson rather than by him but I could not justify a penalty so I stuck with my original decision and gave a free kick to Spurs, mystifying everyone, not least the TV commentators. This completely unsettled me as it is rare that I have had cause to question my judgement so fundamentally. I seemed to have lost my mental equilibrium and what should have been straightforward decisions suddenly seemed difficult. It was very unsettling.

The game erupted just after the hour mark. I booked David Weir of Everton for a foul and two minutes later Spurs' Gary Doherty brought down Kevin Campbell. I controversially awarded a penalty and, almost as an afterthought, sent Doherty off for denying an opponent an obvious goal-scoring opportunity. This decision was greeted with mass protests from Spurs and the only way to calm things down was to book Teddy Sheringham and Christian Ziege for dissent. Duncan Ferguson converted the penalty to make it 1-1. Spurs were incensed and almost immediately Gus Poyet committed a dreadful tackle and I gave him a straight red card. The game was lurching out of control and, as is often the case, when things are going wrong no matter how hard you try they just seem to get progressively worse. I felt as if I was in the middle of a very bad dream and just wished I could wake up, but this was reality and I had to deal with it as best I could. I doubled my concentration and made sure I focused on every challenge and every decision. I reverted to the basics, taking one decision at a time, and I enjoyed some measure of success.

However, we then had an incident which caused much discussion and prevarication in the following days. Spurs' Taricco tackled Gravesen near the halfway line and the ball went out for an Everton throw. There was no reaction from either bench but Gravesen got up, stumbled a couple of paces and fell to the ground clutching his leg. I thought he was play-acting but he had a hole in his shin pad which went through into his leg. It was a bad injury and he had to leave the field. Never the most placid of players, he left complaining about an over-the-top tackle. I had no reason to doubt my original decision that it had been a fair challenge and restarted play with a throw-in. After this, the game settled down and there were no more incidents or cards.

As I blew for full time I needed no one to tell me that it was one of the worst refereeing performances of my career. I had not refereed so badly for a very long time and I was really low. Matters got worse when the assessor said he thought the Taricco challenge was bad and then he told me that Richard Scudamore had been in the Directors Box. More than anyone else, Scudamore had ensured that I was kept on the list when professional referees were introduced. What must he have been thinking now?

I was very depressed after the match and had an awful drive home. I knew that I had performed very badly and my mood was not helped by an e-mail from Daniel which simply said, 'What went wrong?' I wished that school had started as then I would have had something to make my mind off it. I could not believe that I had been so poor and what I found frustrating was that I could find no explanation for such poor judgement. My performance hung over me like a black cloud for days and I could never put it fully out of my mind. In the end, I decided to abandon 'safe refereeing' and go back to my old, tried and tested style of refereeing. I was also angry because it would be ammunition for Philip Don, now the Select Group manager, who resented having me as one of the twenty-four Select Group as the 'professional' referees were known. He phoned me the next morning to tell me I had had 'a nightmare'.

With other matches also having had controversial incidents it was a typically difficult start to the season for referees. Although I was unconvinced about the merits of professional referees, these early incidents showed that it was absolutely right that my twenty-three colleagues, on an annual retainer of some £30,000, were at last receiving a level of financial remuneration that began to equate to the demands being made of them, one of which was unlimited availability. As I did not receive this retainer, I could nominate days when School commitments meant I was not free to referee but I still had to achieve the same fitness levels and my performances were subject to the same scrutiny as the 'professionals'. The Select Group met fortnightly at Staverton Park from Wednesday evening to Friday lunch-time for training under the direction of an excellent fitness expert, Matt Weston, followed by discussion and video analysis of match incidents. I was told not to attend these meetings.

There were concerns that if I performed well it would undermine the system and clubs might question the need to spend so much money on professional referees if the 'amateur' was among the best performers. When I received my assessment for Southampton v Chelsea the marks in several sections had been changed and lower marks had been put in by Don, whose handwriting was easily recognisable. On several occasions assessors were asked about their report or my judgement of a particular incident but they stood by their original assessment and mark. Then, without explanation, I got no Premier League appointments for six weeks. More insidiously, debatable incidents from my matches were being shown at the fortnightly Select Group meeting. Several referees complained that it was unfair because, unlike the rest of the referees, I was not there to explain or defend myself. The referees were told that Don always discussed my matches with me afterwards and always talked through any incidents he was going to show. This was untrue.

One of my great frustrations was that I was not being told about decisions the Select Group referees were making at these meetings. I was concerned that I might go out on a Saturday and do something which was contrary to what had been agreed. This was brought home most starkly after Gerald Ashby died suddenly after assessing a game at Everton in December 2001. The weekend after his death I refereed the Saturday morning Midlands clash between Derby and Aston Villa, which was shown live on Sky. People often talk, somewhat tritely, about dedicating performances to lost family and friends but there is no doubt that I had a genuine determination (and I am sure my colleagues did) to referee extremely well in this game as a tribute to Gerald who was foremost in my pre-match and post-match prayers. I was devastated when someone phoned me that evening asking why I had not worn the green shirt with a black armband out of respect for Gerald as had been agreed at the Select Group meeting at Staverton.

As well as the number of games I received, the quality of my appointments also changed. Gone were the days when I would regularly feature in the high-profile matches. I was kept away from the top teams and given matches with teams in mid- or low-table positions. As the year progressed I saw Peter Jones, who was in his last season, treated in a similar fashion (three of his final matches were not even in the Premier League) which was dreadful for someone who had given so much to football and was so popular.

Despite all these difficulties I was determined to referee to the best of my ability to prove that I deserved to be in the Select Group and because I wanted to retire with my reputation as a top referee intact. My less confrontational style of refereeing continued to elicit a really good response from the players and I was enjoying refereeing as much as at any time in my career. I was firmly established as part of the Premier League and, as someone pointed out, I had the advantage of having been at the top level for over fifteen years, longer than most of the players. I found that the younger players were particularly respectful possibly because, for the likes of Beckham, Owen and Giggs, I had been a top referee since they first started watching, let alone playing, League football. I worked hard to consolidate my reputation by being more relaxed in my dealing with the players and I moved further away from the rigid, dictatorial style which had been the hallmark of my early career. It brought some really enjoyable matches and a real sense of fulfilment.

Such a match was Bolton v Sunderland and the assessor was Peter Willis, whom I admired greatly because he always spoke his mind and did not worry whom he upset. Beforehand he said how very unhappy he was with the new refereeing system which he thought was stifling the game by not allowing referees the freedom to use their personalities to control the game.

Everything went extremely well and Peter still talks about how I managed to have the players, managers and the crowd, in his words, 'eating out of my hand'. In the first half, a corner flag was knocked out of the ground. I held up play as a ball boy struggled to get it to stand up properly. He failed so I went across, pushed it back into the firm ground, and mimicked giving it a yellow card. The crowd roared with laughter so I gave them a small bow and we resumed play. Later on the ball went into the crowd and went missing. I signalled for a new one and two came on at the same time. I made a bit of play with the ball boys at being thrown two balls. They got their revenge when I blew the half-time whistle and, to the amusement of players and fans, every ball boy threw his spare ball to me! Peter Willis said I had had an outstanding game and had been thrilled by my interaction with the crowd over the corner flag incident and the balls at half-time. 'Never before have I seen a referee control the spectators as well as the players!' he remarked.

Evidence of my good rapport with the players came at The Valley when Middlesbrough were the visitors. The first foul did not occur until about the twelfth minute. It was a sliding, mis-timed tackle near the assistant. In a tougher match it might have merited a booking but as it was the first offence I satisfied myself with a lecture. The game proceeded for another ten minutes or so with hardly a foul and then Scott Parker of Charlton caught Paul Ince slightly late. I was reaching for the yellow card when Ince bounced up and I expected a major incident as he can be very volatile. However, he shook Parker's hand and said, 'Nothing to worry about. Let's get on with the game.' With both players happy there seemed no need for the yellow card as the game was fully under control. There were no goals and no controversy and everyone was happy, especially Keren Barratt, the assessor, who said that my man-management and level of involvement were exceptional. I was delighted and felt that I had finally got the Everton v Spurs nightmare out of my system. My decision to return to my former style of refereeing seemed fully vindicated.

Acceptance of my refereeing by the players made life so much easier as there was less dissent and they seemed happy to let me get on with refereeing the game while they focused on playing. This was particularly noticeable when I refereed Leeds v Manchester United on Easter Saturday 2002. It was a pulsating game which ebbed and flowed. Leeds took an early lead and then United blasted them with three goals before half-time. They were clearly on top but seemed to relax after half-time and Leeds fought back. By the end United were desperately hanging on to their 4-3 lead and were so rattled that, in the ninety-first minute, when David Beckham was caught offside he deliberately kicked the ball away to waste time. He happily accepted the yellow card and said, 'David, I had to do it!' I replied, 'I know, but I have to do you for it!' He smiled and a few minutes later there were warm handshakes all round at the end of what had been a quite awesomely entertaining match.

Soon after I was off to Old Trafford for the FA Cup semi-final between Arsenal and Middlesbrough. I always enjoy cup semi-finals and this was to be my eighth. I was mindful that the last time I refereed a semi at Old Trafford Middlesbrough had also been one of the teams and we had the great 'did it cross the line?' controversy. Jeff Winter rang me to remind me that I was

Middlesbrough's lucky semi-final referee as they had never lost one when I had been officiating.

The atmosphere was fantastic as we strode into the stadium. I was not sure how Middlesbrough would approach the game as Arsenal were the clear favourites, but their tactics soon became clear with several very hard tackles. They were obviously out to rattle their illustrious opponents. After three minutes I decided that I needed to put an end to the clear intimidation otherwise there would be a major reaction from the Arsenal players and I booked Dean Windass for his second late challenge on Patrick Vieira. This calmed things down and Arsenal soon took the lead. However, they were not playing at their best and there seemed every chance that Middlesbrough would equalise. I spent much of the afternoon carefully trying to man-manage the players. Vieira was particularly responsive, partly because we had established a good rapport at Leicester earlier in the season. As we came off at half-time he told me that a yellow card would put him out of the final and I used this to keep him calm and controlled throughout the second half. Ray Parlour was booked for a late challenge, as was Edu, but the conduct of both teams was excellent and it was a very good semi-final from the officials' point of view.

Before I knew what had happened my final season had started. I had trained harder in the close season than ever before. Indeed, my four compulsory treadmill fitness assessments in my last season were the best of my career, each one being slightly better than the last, so that I was actually at my fittest when I retired! Although I was still not getting many top matches the few I did get I got were memorable. My first major game of the season was newly promoted Birmingham City against Aston Villa, the first time these intense local rivals had met in a league match for sixteen years. There was much speculation about the battles that would be fought on and off the field, not least because Birmingham had signed the combative Robbie Savage from Leicester.

Arriving at St Andrews about two hours before kickoff, I could feel the tension everywhere. There was great concern about the volatile crowd and my confidence in the authorities was not enhanced by the police officer who briefed us. He read everything, including his own name and rank, word for word from a typed sheet. With a totally straight face he made two bald statements: 'This is a local derby' and 'The atmosphere is likely to be volatile'. I don't know if he thought we had just parachuted in from the planet Zog but my fears about security were confirmed later in the game when there were several pitch invasions. I officiated at Birmingham later in the season and the same man came and gave almost exactly the same briefing and still read his name and rank from a piece of paper!

Local derbies, full of tension, are a wonderful challenge for a referee and I was really looking forward to this match as it was one of the few in the Premier League in which I had not officiated. As the referee you are keen to reduce the tension and help the players funnel it into controlled aggression and passion. You do not want to kill the game stone dead but neither do you want it to get out of control. To use a culinary analogy, the best derbies are those which simmer, occasionally bubble but never boil over. I did not want an early yellow card and spent the first fifteen minutes buzzing round talking as much as I could, trying to open lines of communication and get the players on my wavelength. I had got on really well with Robbie Savage since the Arsenal game and I saw him as a key to my control. If I could stop him going overboard all would be well, I hoped.

In the end it was a great match for Birmingham which produced two talking points and an interesting exchange of words between Savage and Dion Dublin. In the fifty-seventh minute the ball was lobbed into the Birmingham penalty area and, because it looked as if the defender was going to head it clear, the assistant, Rob Lewis, kept his flag down. However, the defender headed it back towards his goal where it fell to Darius Vassell who scored as Rob belatedly but correctly raised his flag. Villa claimed he could not be offside as the ball had come from the defender but Vassell had been offside when the ball was initially lobbed in. As I gave the offside I could see that the Villa bench, and manager Graham Taylor in particular, were furious and the reserve referee, Clive Wilkes, was struggling to control them. I had walked up the tunnel with Graham Taylor at half-time and had always got on well with him so I went across and spoke to him and explained why I had given the offside. Being the gentleman he is he accepted my explanation. The first controversy was over but there was a bigger one to come.

Ten minutes later, Villa's Olof Mellberg took a throw-in deep in his own half and sent it firmly to his goalkeeper, Peter Enckelman. Like all goalkeepers, Enckelman was not allowed to handle a ball received from a throw-in from one of his team so he took an almightily swing at it to blast it upfield. Like a golfer on the tee he must have lifted his head at the vital moment because the ball went under his foot and into the goal. I was half watching and my immediate reaction was that it was a goal, but almost as quickly I remembered that if he had not touched it I had to award a corner kick as a team cannot score against itself directly from a throw-in. My instinct was that he had touched it and as Enckelman held his head in his hands I raced the width of the field to ask the assistant, Phil Barston, what he thought. He told me that Enckelman had definitely touched the ball with the underside of his foot and I awarded a goal. As with the first goal, the Birmingham fans rushed onto the field to celebrate and one of them stood in front of Enckelman, gesticulating in an obscene and provocative manner.

This incident raised the temperature and soon afterwards Robbie Savage and Dion Dublin squared up and then brought their heads forward as if they were going to butt each other. 'Time to take the heat out of the match by talking,' I thought. Dion stayed where he was but Robbie disappeared upfield so I whistled for him to return. As we waited Dion said to me, 'Don't worry, David, Robbie and I were youth players together at

Manchester United and we are great friends.' I told them both that I did not want any more nonsense. I added, 'We are on television and what you just did looked terrible.' 'What do you mean?' asked Dion. 'Well,' I said, 'it looked as if the two of you were going to kiss each other and seeing that on TV would have been really unpleasant!' They both roared with laughter and the sting was taken out of the clash. Interestingly, in the return match at Villa Park the two clashed again and Dublin was sent off for head-butting Savage.

The post-match analysis of the Enckelman incident demonstrated the impracticality of using video evidence to make decisions. Andy Gray used the television pictures to show I was wrong and that the keeper had not touched the ball, while ITV used exactly the same pictures to demonstrate that he had touched the ball and I was right!

I returned to St Andrews on Boxing Day for another memorable match. Everton were the visitors and it was a fierce encounter but the players responded well. The talking point came in the eighty-first minute when Wayne Rooney, who had only been on the field for sixteen minutes, launched into a nasty, two-footed jump tackle which caught Steve Vickers on the ankle. It was clearly serious foul play and I immediately showed him the red card. There was little reaction from the Everton fans who were at that end of the ground although Birmingham were incensed by the challenge as Vickers had to leave the field with blood coming from a gashed ankle, which required eight stitches. Within seconds I had to book Clinton Morrison for a wild tackle. The game finished as a draw and when we got back to the dressing room David Moyes asked to see me. The League Managers' Association had agreed a thirty-minute 'cooling off' period (to give their members time to calm down before talking to referees) so Moyes was asked to come back at 5.20 p.m. He brought a laptop with him and asked me to view footage of the Rooney tackle. I had never been confronted with this before but agreed. He showed me the tackle and it did not look too bad. I was puzzled as I drove home as I was sure it had been a really bad foul so I was quick to get to my video player and watch the tape the club had given me after the match. In 'real time' it looked a bad foul but then came the angle Moyes had shown me and it looked less bad. Then came another angle, which Moyes had conveniently not shown me, which confirmed what a dreadful tackle it really had been.

The incident drew a great deal of debate because, at seventeen, Rooney had become the youngest player ever to be sent off in the Premier League. Some said I should not have been so harsh on Rooney and should have taken account of his age. What rubbish! The logical extension of this is that before deciding whether a player is booked or sent off the referee has to ask his age. Were they really suggesting that if the player was under a certain age and committed a red card offence he should only get a yellow card? This would mean that two players could have a fight and one would be sent off because he was twenty-four but the other would stay on because he was sixteen!

Probably one of the most talked-about decisions I gave all season came at West Bromwich Albion in early February and involved the Bolton goalkeeper Jussi Jaaskelainen. Just before half-time he tried to throw the ball out and it hit Daniel Dichio on the back. Sensing danger, Jaaskelainen rushed out of his area and fouled Dichio. I blew for the free kick and as I hurried across to book Jaaskelainen Dichio, still with his back to the goal, took the free kick quickly, knocking it to Ronnie Wallwork who had a chance to shoot into an empty net. I was faced with a dilemma. Did I stop play for the booking or allow it to continue? I decided that the spirit of the Laws called for play to continue so I signalled advantage and Wallwork shot only for it to be blocked by Ivan Campo. Play broke upfield and it was a minute or more before the ball went out of play and, as luck would have it, it was in the opposition half so I showed Jaaskelainen the yellow card from about seventy yards!

There were two debates afterwards. Firstly, should

Jaaskelainen have been sent off? The WBA players and fans certainly thought so but the Laws define an obvious goal-scoring opportunity as existing only when a player is moving *towards* an opponent's goal and Dichio had his back to the goal, so it was only a booking. As far as playing the advantage was concerned I was convinced that, as at Wolves back in 1986, I had done the right thing. The wording of Law Five supported me as it says that when the referee has disciplinary action to take 'he is not obliged to take this action immediately but must do so when the ball next goes out of play'. This usually applies when a foul is committed and the referee allows play to continue but I believed that the 'spirit' of the Law applied to the WBA situation. Opinion was divided but the word from FIFA and those with an intimate knowledge of the Laws declared that I was right in both the spirit and the letter of the Law. The most interesting aspect, though, was that it reminded me how important a thorough knowledge of the Laws is and how very strange it is that senior referees in England are never tested on the Laws of the Game (unlike most other countries).

I quickly moved to the stage of the season where I was chalking up a series of 'lasts'. When Arsenal and Chelsea drew their Sixth Round match at Highbury I was appointed to the replay for what would be my last appearance in the FA Cup, almost twenty-seven years after my first FA match. To mark the occasion I invited Ken Ridden, who had been a wonderful mentor to me, to the match along with a couple of boys from Druries. It was a superb evening. Both teams played open, entertaining football and posed few challenges; it was a pleasure being on the field. I worked hard at my man-management and there was a final, classic example when Francis Jeffers and Emmanuel Petit clashed. I called them across and, without thinking, adopted my trademark 'I'm relaxed and not going to book anyone' pose and folded my arms. I'm told that colleagues like Keith Hackett roared with laughter when I did this as he often teased me about this relaxed form of body language which, he said, only I could get away with without it being seen as too casual. Of course some referees would have booked them both but I just said, 'Look, we are having a wonderful game here. I could easily book you or send you off but why don't you just get on and play and save me the hassle?' They responded very well. Arsenal dominated the game and won 3-1 despite having Pascal Cygan sent off in the sixty-seventh minute for deliberately bringing down Hasselbaink, who was breaking clear towards the Arsenal penalty area. It was a wonderful match with which to end my twenty-six and a half years' active association with the FA Cup.

It also turned out to be my last really big match as I was taken off what would have been the last top Premier League game of my career, Manchester United v Liverpool at Old Trafford. Apparently, Philip Don thought that I should have sent off Lucas Radebe at Elland Road a few weeks earlier even though my decision had been supported by the assessor, John Kirkby, who gave me a high mark. My coach told me that Don had pencilled me in for Old Trafford but switched me to Spurs v Birmingham. I had suspected something like this had happened as the assistants at Spurs were not part of the group I regularly worked with, whilst those on the United game were. I was saddened by what Tom Bune told me but there was nothing I could do.

During my career I had experienced a number of 'lasts' as far as grounds were concerned, including the final Premier League match at Filbert Street and Wimbledon's last League match at Plough Lane. There was thus a nice symmetry to my final Football League match being Wimbledon v Derby County, albeit at Selhurst Park. During the pre-match pitch inspection I had some good-natured banter with the Derby fans who were seated near the halfway line. Somebody shouted something rude at me in jest so I brought out my diary and held it aloft as if it was a red card. The fan got up from his seat and began walking out of the stand, taking his shirt off as he did. We all had a good laugh and there were some more exchanges so I promised I would send the smallest assistant, Roy Burton, across for them to abuse during the game as long as they promised not to shout at me!

The sprinkler system had been full on and with the afternoon being warm there was steam rising from the pitch as we strode out with the teams. In the tunnel beforehand I'd had a chat with the Derby captain Warren Barton and mentioned that on the radio on the way they had been talking about those amazing 4-3 games between Liverpool and Newcastle, the second of which we had both been involved in.

It was a very straightforward match and I did not give a foul until the eleventh minute. My next decision was to disallow a Ravanelli goal for a foul on the keeper, a decision he debated with me with utmost politeness. In the whole game I only gave sixteen fouls and did not speak to a player in anger until the ninety-third minute. Throughout the first half whenever Roy Burton flagged a Wimbledon player offside there were chants from our friends in the Derby crowd of 'We love Roy! We love Roy!' In the second half, whenever he flagged a Derby player offside they shouted, 'We hate Roy! We hate Roy!'

Midway through the first half I grinned at assistant referee Guy Beale when a hard clearance bounced off his knees and I implied that he should have controlled the ball rather better. Needless to say he had more than satisfactory revenge when, ten minutes later, jogging backwards after awarding a goal kick, I tripped over a Wimbledon player's boot (I'm sure it was accidental!) and fell flat on my back. This was just the latest of several falls I had (I can remember doing the same at Wembley in the First Division play-off final in 1991 and also being flattened by Nicky Butt in an FA Cup semi-final) and I did what I always tried to do and completed a backward roll and sprang to my feet. I would like to think that I bounced up athletically but I am sure I looked clumsy and ungainly. However, the crowd roared and I knew better than to look at either assistant who would be ready and waiting to take the mickey. The Derby fans made the most of my ungainly predicament so I turned and gave a small bow to them which brought me a cheer and we all smiled. Of course, Roger Wiseman, the referee assessor, announced post-match that it had been the highlight of the afternoon.

It is nice to have a rapport with the fans although some in authority would suggest that referees should not interact in case they lose concentration or appear undignified. I had come to believe that referees should try to be seen to be human and not aloof and if an opportunity presented itself I took full advantage of it. Everyone seemed happy at the end and the Wimbledon goalkeeper said that I was welcome to referee them every Saturday. We kept the match ball which everyone signed and several of the older stewards came in and kindly wished me luck in the future, reminding me of some of my past matches with Wimbledon, not least that final match at Plough Lane.

And then it was the last match of all – Newcastle v Birmingham. I wanted to share this game with those who had been a significant part of my refereeing career and requested Phil Sharp and Dave Babski as my assistants. I was delighted that Jeff Winter was the fourth official though saddened that Tom Bune, my coach and mentor, was told it was too expensive for him to travel from his home in Newbury to attend. He was sent to Blackburn instead.

I flew up to Newcastle the night before the game and had a relaxing dinner with Phil and Dave, reminiscing about overseas matches, especially trips to Saudi Arabia, Israel, Moscow and that final game in the icy wastes of Kiev. I slept really well and did not feel as if it was a momentous day. I was touched by the cards and telephone messages from friends and colleagues, particular Mark Halsey and Dermot Gallagher. Indeed, the overwhelming memory of the day was the kindness and generosity of so many people. I went for a walk in the hotel grounds to try to focus on what lay ahead and when I got back to my room there was a text message from Daniel saying that he had arrived safely at Heathrow and was with two young referees, Douglas and Nicholas Keen, who had become good friends. I went to the meeting room and laid out small mementoes for my colleagues – engraved silver salvers and a T-shirt with the match details and an amusing photograph of me on it. I felt very calm although my emotions came close to the surface when I did the pre-match instructions and said, 'I am delighted that the three of you are with me but we must remember that today is about Newcastle and Birmingham, and not me.'

Just before we left for the ground Steve Lodge and his son James arrived and then through the door walked Peter Jones. When we arrived at St James' Park my 'team' of my closest refereeing friends was completed as we were met by Daniel, Nicholas and Douglas, who carried our bags to the dressing room. The next half hour seemed to be a photo-fest for them and *The Times*, who were doing a feature on my last game and then we went upstairs for a cup of tea; Earl Grey, naturally.

About 1.30 p.m. I said goodbye to my friends and went down to the dressing room to start the preparations for the last time. A few minutes later Daniel appeared and presented me with a framed list of the South African FIFA referees and his first FIFA badge as a good luck token for the game. The time flew by and before I knew it I had given my instructions and my colleagues had gone to warm up. I was deep in thought with my head bowed for my regular pre-match prayer when the Premier League Chairman, Dave Richards, popped in to wish me luck. Then, with a final word to the assistants – 'Forget it is my last match until the final whistle!' – Phil rang the bell to summon the teams. Out of superstition I never rang the bell myself. Geoff Horsfield and Robbie Savage made kind comments as we waited in the tunnel and then the handshakes and photos were over and it was time to start. I felt remarkably calm and unemotional; all those years of developing professional focus were coming into play for my last match.

I blew my whistle and then blew it again. No, I had not had second thoughts. One of the Birmingham forwards had charged into the opposition half before the ball had been kicked so I insisted that the game restart – properly this time. I might be officially too old to referee but I was going to stay on my toes for one last game. I tried to forget it was my final match but it was not easy until the game started to heat up. In the thirty-sixth minute Dugarry went into a challenge with his arm raised for the third time and I booked him.

Five minutes later came the incident which ensured controversy followed me to the very end. Craig Bellamy was clear through on the Birmingham goal and was nudged to the ground by Matthew Upson. It was clearly a foul, but had it denied an obvious goal-scoring opportunity? On any other day I would not have hesitated and the red card would have come out straight-away but something stopped me. Should I send someone off in my last game? I was in turmoil yet, as I ran the incident back in my mind, I had no doubt it was a sending off. Inexplicably, I walked across to Dave Babski who confirmed my opinion and as I gave my red card its final flourish Upson trudged off. Hugo Viana curled in the free kick, the only goal of the game.

I was now under pressure from the Birmingham players and fans and at any moment expected to hear 'Thank God it's your last game' but it never came. I was despondent at half-time as I had wanted to avoid controversy but it had dogged me through-out my career and so why should my last game be any different? The players of both teams were fine when we restarted and it was nine minutes before I awarded a free kick, and also the final yellow card of my career to Bryan Hughes of Birmingham for a foul. I was then faced with a dilemma when Dugarry com-mitted yet another foul but I had had enough controversy for one day and did not send him off. The game continued quietly; the only excitement was a half-hearted Newcastle penalty appeal which I ignored. In fact, there were only nine fouls in the second half. The players were brilliant and Robbie Savage made a detour to come and shake my hand when he was substituted off towards the end. I had a great laugh with Stan Lazaridis when I refused to give him a free kick.

'That was a foul. Why didn't you give it?'

'Because you're Australian and you keep beating us at everything so I thought I'd get some revenge!' I replied. He roared with laughter.

The finality of it all did not hit me until I looked at my watch which showed that we had been playing for thirty-seven minutes. I had less than ten minutes left. I wanted them to pass slowly but also wanted them to pass without any trouble. I played two minutes additional time and then brought the whistle to my lips and blew time on my 2415th and final match. Geoff Horsfield and Jermaine Jenas were the first to come and shake hands.

Suddenly it was all over and I was back in the dressing room but not feeling emotional. Dave and Phil had organised a bottle of champagne and Phil, ever the perfectionist, had even bought five champagne glasses. I thanked my three colleagues for being with me and then Alan Wilkie, the match assessor, arrived and was very complimentary – he would not have dared be anything else! I toasted my friends and then the procession began. Dave Richards arrived with two magnificent bottles of champagne which he presented on behalf of the Premier League. Then Alan Shearer came to chat. He wished me well and presented me with one of his Newcastle shirts which he had signed and which had been framed. He was followed by Sir Bobby Robson who took me out into the reception area where he gave me a beautifully engraved silver salver and, true gentlemen that he is, said some very kind words about my career.

Everyone – stewards, security people, fans, ball boys, players, staff, the whole lot – was so generous. Birmingham brought in a bottle of their club champagne and Gary Speed dropped in to wish me luck. I showered, changed and went out onto the pitch and looked round at the empty stadium and felt hollow and sad. However, it was not a time for negative emotions. We went upstairs to a guest lounge to meet up with my friends. Dave and Phil had a framed and signed linesman's flag for me and then

John Elsom, the former Leicester City Chairman, telephoned to ask how the day had gone. Before I knew it, it was time to get to the airport. I was besieged by autograph hunters, the best an ample-bosomed lady who insisted I sign her shirt across her bust. 'I'll have to press hard!' I said. 'That's fine, my love!' she replied.

Back at the airport I was so busy being interviewed by Russell Kempson of *The Times* that I almost missed my flight. Daniel and I were sitting behind Nicholas and Douglas on the plane and sitting next to Douglas was the player who had given me trouble all afternoon – Dugarry! The irony was wonderful and it became even funnier when they both fell asleep and Douglas slumped sideways and slept with his head on Dugarry's shoulder. The flight was fun. I had a great chat with Chris Kamara of Sky TV but I did not mention that I had booked him a couple of times when he played for Swindon in the late 1980s. There were supporters of Arsenal, Birmingham and Carlisle on the plane and I quickly realised that it is only when you retire that people start thinking you are a good referee!

Douglas and Nicholas's mother Elaine picked us up at the airport and we all went back to Druries for a bite to eat and more champagne. I made presentations to them all and Daniel made a wonderfully moving speech telling Douglas and Nicholas of the impact I had had on his refereeing and his life. He said I had become like a father to him and that they were lucky to have me as a mentor and friend. It was touching but the most emotional part was when he said that it was now up to him, Douglas and Nicholas to take the torch from me and do even better than I had done.

The Keens left and Daniel gave me framed records of all my Premier League matches and all my major matches and international appointments. It was only then that I realised that my last Premier League game had also been my 200th. A couple of Drurieans popped in to see how the game had gone and also to tell me that they were disappointed that I had only sent one player off as it left me stranded four short of my 250th red card! I watched *Match of the Day* and was relieved that the coverage showed that I was right to have sent Upson off.

During *Match of the Day* I reflected on what a wonderful day it had been and how lucky I had been to have shared it with such special people. I thought of all the enjoyment and friendships refereeing had brought me and how insignificant the abuse was when viewed against the great moments and wonderful friends. Retirement seemed strange, a little like a death. It had happened but I was not really taking it in. I had trained myself not to get emotional and to block out everything, apart from the game, by almost operating on autopilot. I had been pretty controlled although tears had welled up when Jeff made a speech after the match and when Dave Richards made the Premier League presentation. I had cried when Daniel spoke so movingly.

As my thoughts swirled round I was brought back to reality when one of the boys came to report a blocked and overflowing urinal. A few moments later there I was, at 11.30 p.m., bailing out a bathroom in my shirtsleeves. For one last time Harrow had conspired to take my mind off my refereeing!

# *Epilogue*

When retirement came I was still enjoying refereeing immensely but I no longer craved the thrill and excitement. I looked forward to the matches but there were only one or two which made me nervous or set my pulse racing. I had been fortunate to have officiated in so many top matches that few held any fears for me, although there was always the danger that there would be a flashpoint and a game would explode.

I had thirty-six wonderful seasons as a referee and was privileged to have officiated at a time of great change and development within the game. In my early days as a Football League referee the national game was in something of a crisis, blighted by foul play and hooliganism blighting the sport. By the end of my career the Premier League had ensured that football was by far the country's most watched sport. Inevitably, but regrettably, referees have become more high profile but, reflecting society, respect for them and their decisions continues to diminish.

The introduction of professional referees has not yet raised the status or attraction of refereeing. Indeed, thus far there have been few tangible benefits, except an improvement in fitness, but this is party because the system was poorly thought out and badly managed. Keith Hackett's appointment as referee 'supremo' augurs well for the future and provides an opportunity to begin the work necessary for English referees to re-establish themselves as amongst the best in the world. Much will depend on how successful he is in instilling in the top referees a willingness to look at themselves critically. Only by admitting their shortcomings and trying to learn something from every game will their performances improve.

Apart from refereeing the occasional school match, my refereeing time is now spent looking for and developing the referees with potential to become the next generation of FIFA referees. Succession planning is vital and there is an urgent need to find, support and encourage young referees as they are integral to the game's future. I greatly enjoy my work with young referees in England, South Africa and New Zealand and this, along with running refereeing courses in Asia, Africa and for UEFA, helps me keep in touch with global refereeing issues. We must find incentives for referees at all levels of football and of all ages to continue officiating. Referees must be given more protection, especially on the local parks where the levels of abuse and violence are unacceptable. Football must never forget how important the 'local' referees are to the game's future and to the enjoyment of thousands of players.

There is also a great need for refereeing to communicate more effectively with the game's other stakeholders. For referees to be understood and even appreciated, players, managers and spectators need to know how hard they work, how much time they spend training and trying to improve their skills and even how and why they make certain decisions.

The future of refereeing is difficult to predict. The demands for technology to be involved in decision-making during the game will grow but must be resisted if the essential integrity of the game is to be preserved. Football is not about stoppages and video referees; it is about excitement and as close to non-stop action as possible. Refereeing will change, and we will see the growing influence of women; by the end of the present decade I hope to see a Premier League match controlled by a female referee.

I have many happy memories of my refereeing and my travels. To have officiated in more than thirty countries meant I had the privilege of visiting the great stadiums and going behind the scenes at some of the world's top clubs. I made a huge number of friends and have been touched that so many people have taken an interest in refereeing and my career. I was proud to have officiated in a major Cup Final on four continents and, although my quest for the World Cup Final was not successful, I was pleased to have got as close as I did. I feel a certain sense of sadness that my FA Cup Final and Euro '96 experiences were disappointing but games in South Africa, Brazil, Japan and Saudi Arabia compensated significantly.

I would never have achieved any of this had Harrow School not been so supportive. It has been fascinating to see the School change from an 'old-fashioned' public school into a vibrant establishment where the best traditions are maintained but where boys are treated as individuals and schoolmasters have to earn the boys' respect rather than beat it into them. The challenges of dealing with the young of today are made more difficult by the mobile phone and the 'blame culture', and these days we have to work that much harder to inculcate into the boys the importance of them taking responsibility for their actions. Nevertheless, teaching, and especially Housemastering, remains fantastically rewarding and enjoyable.

Looking back, I cannot imagine having been happier than I have been in the last thirty years and especially my time as a House Master of Druries and an international and Premier League referee. People often ask how I fitted it all in. I suppose it was by a mixture of limited sleep, ruthless efficiency with paperwork and a very limited social life, especially during term-time. But these were sacrifices well worth making.

It has been a real privilege to have been actively involved in English football for so long and at such an exciting time. I would not have missed any of it, even the darkest days, for the world. To have been there 'in the middle' when Blackburn won the Premier League title, when Beckham scored from his own half and Giggs scored that goal in the FA Cup semi-final was unbelievable. To have even been on the same pitch as the likes of Henry, Beckham and Ronaldo was incredible and even having on occasions to face my own demons when I got things wrong were experiences I would not forgo if I had my time again.

I have been very lucky.

# Statistics

## Match records:

| | |
|---|---|
| Refereed | 1780 |
| Lined | 600 |
| Reserve Referee | 35 |
| *Total* | *2415* |

## Cup Finals

| | |
|---|---|
| Refereed | 84 |
| Lined | 46 |
| Reserve Referee | 2 |
| *Total* | *132* |

## Highest attendance at Matches

100,000   Sao Paulo v Corinthians, Murumbi Stadium, Sao Paulo
3 May 1998

95,000   Red Star Belgrade v Real Madrid, Crvena Zvezda
4 March 1987

85,000   Russia v Ukraine, Luzhniki Stadium
9 October 1999

80,000*   South Africa v Brazil, FNB Stadium, Johannesburg
24 April 1996
(*official attendance but closer to 100,000 were in the
ground)

79,634   Chelsea v Manchester United, Wembley Stadium
14 May 1994

73,803   Leicester v Swindon, Wembley Stadium
31 May 1993

73,510   Liverpool v Birmingham, Millennium Stadium, Cardiff
25 February 2001

| 70,000 | Saudi Arabia v China, King Fahd Stadium, Riyadh 6 November 1997 |
| 68,000 | Real Madrid v Paris St. Germain, Bernabéu Stadium 2 March 1993 |
| 67,535 | Manchester United v Manchester City, Old Trafford 21 April 2001 |
| 65,000 | Barcelona v AIK Solna, Nou Camp 6 March 1997 |

## Teams refereed most

36 – Manchester United
32 – Aston Villa
28 – Leeds
27 – Liverpool, Southampton, Spurs
25 – Chelsea, Newcastle
24 – Arsenal, Everton

## Grounds at which I officiated most

20 – Villa Park
17 – Elland Road
16 – Highbury and Upton Park
15 – Stamford Bridge
14 – Wembley

## DISCIPLINE

Booked     2064          Sent off     246

## Fastest bookings

5 seconds – V Jones (Sheffield Utd) at Manchester City (19 January 1991) for a foul
25 seconds – S Wright (Sunderland) at Blackburn (17 August 2002) for a foul
80 seconds – P Johnson (Chelsea) at Wembley – (14 May 1994) for a foul

## Fastest sending off

15 minutes – M. Wallace (Stockport) at Wembley (29 May 1994) for spitting

## Time taken to reach disciplinary landmarks

1st 500 yellow cards – 19 years and 3 months
2nd 500 yellow cards – 6 years and 1 month
3rd 500 yellow cards – 4 years and 5 months
4th 500 yellow cards – 5 years and 10 months

1st 100 red cards – 17 years and 7 months
2nd 100 red cards – 12 years and 2 months

## Player most disciplined

Roy Keane (Nottingham Forest and Manchester United) – 4 red cards and 6 yellow cards

## Most booked player

Mick Harford (Luton, Derby, Sunderland, Wimbledon) – 8 yellow cards

## Teams most disciplined

| Red cards | | Yellow cards | |
|---|---|---|---|
| 6 | – Everton | 63 | – Leeds United |
| 5 | – Aston Villa, Manchester United, Tottenham Hotspur | 52 | – Manchester United |
| 4 | – Arsenal | 39 | – Arsenal, Aston Villa, Tottenham Hotspur |

## Worst fouls

Jorgen Kohler (Germany) v Brazil in Stuttgart on 25 March 1998
Roy Keane (Manchester United) v Manchester City at Old Trafford on 21 April 2001
Pat Van Den Hauwe (Tottenham Hotspur) v Luton Town at White Hart Lane on 15 December 1990

# Games with most cards

*Red cards*

3 – Spurs v Luton – Football League (1st division) – 15
     December 1990
   – Crystal Palace v Wimbledon – Football League (1st division)
     – 27 August 1991
   – Cambridge United v Cardiff City – Football League
     (2nd division) – 28 December 1999

*Yellow cards*

10– CSKA Sofia v Austria Memphis – UEFA European Champions
     Cup – 30 September 1992
   – Germany v Czech Republic – Euro '96 – 9 June 1996
9 – Portsmouth v Leeds United – Football League (2nd division)
     – 10 March 1987
   – Sparta Prague v Fiorentina – UEFA Cup Winners' Cup – 31
     October 1996
   – Derby County v Coventry City – Premier League – 22
     November 1997
   – Fiorentina v Widez Lodz – UEFA Champions League – 11
     August 1999
   – Namibia v Angola – COSAFA Cup Final – 2 October 1999

*Red and yellow cards combined*

   2 red cards and 9 yellow cards
   – Tottenham Hotspur v Arsenal – Premier League – 7 November
     1999
   – FC Metz v MSK Zilina – Inter-Toto semi-final – 11 July 1999

   2 red cards and 8 yellow cards
   – Newcastle United v Everton – Premier League – 1 February 1995

# Becoming softer in England but strict abroad

|                               | *Season* *1986–7* | *Season* *2002–3* | *International* |
| ----------------------------- | ----------------- | ----------------- | --------------- |
| Average bookings per match    | 3.78              | 2.73              | 4.98            |
| Average sendings off per match| 0.39              | 0.19              | 0.54            |

## Players booked or sent off abroad and then in the Premier League

Tomas Dahlin – Sweden then Blackburn
Marcel Desailly – AC Milan then Chelsea
Jesper Gronkjaer – Denmark then Chelsea
Jürgen Klinsmann – Monaco then Spurs
Guy Poyet – Real Zaragoza then Chelsea then Spurs
Emmanuel Petit – Monaco then Arsenal then Chelsea
Lucas Radebe – South Africa then Leeds
Tomas Repka – Sparta Prague then Fiorentina then West Ham
Stefan Schwartz – Fiorentina then Sunderland
Christian Ziege – Germany then Liverpool then Spurs

# Landmarks in Refereeing and the Laws

When football first started there were many different sets of 'rules' based largely on the practice and customs of the different versions of the game at different schools. Over time they became a single set of 'Laws' which now apply to all levels of football throughout the world. The Laws continue to evolve and change to improve the game. Since 1885 Law changes have been the prerogative of the International FA Board. Changes come into effect on 1 July each year (if that date falls in the middle of a competition such as Euro 2004 the changes do not affect that competition). There have been many changes in the last 140 years or more and many were highly controversial at the time they were introduced.

1863 – First set of FA Laws (fourteen in total) produced, but they are not used universally. Tripping, kicking, holding, and pushing an opponent are banned

1865 – The two posts which constitute the goal are required to have a 'tape' 8 feet from the ground under which the ball has to pass for a goal to be scored

1866 – 31 March – C W Alcock becomes the first player caught offside in an official FA match

1873 – Offside penalised only when the ball is passed

1874 – Use of shinguards becomes widespread

1875 – Solid crossbars start to replace the 'tape'

1877 – The FA and the Sheffield Association agree on a single set of Laws of the Game

1878 – Referee's whistle used for the first time in an FA cup match between Nottingham Forest and Sheffield

1880 – Throw-in can now be in any direction (previously the ball had to be thrown in at right angles to the touchline)

1881 – Players no longer offside at corners

1883 – Crossbars become compulsory

1885 – Creation of the International Football Association Board as the single authority on the Laws. The FA issues the first attempt to give advice to match officials on the 'Laws' and the control of the game.

1891 – Penalty kick introduced; goal nets used for the first time in January
The two umpires are moved to the touchline and are replaced by a Referee on the field (the referee had been on the pitch side and made a decision only if the two umpires could not agree)

1892 – Two-handed throw-in becomes legal

1895 – Dimensions of the goal standardised

1896 – FA publishes first 'Referees' Chart' (now known as the Laws of Association Football); usually published annually

1897 – Laws specify for the first time that matches will be 90 minutes long; until now 90 minutes had only been the agreed custom

1898 – Laws reach 17 in number and have remained at this number ever since

1902 – Penalty area and halfway line introduced

1904 – FIFA formed

1905 – Goalkeeper required to stay on his goal-line until the penalty kick is taken

1907 – Players can now only be offside in opponents' half (previously they could be offside anywhere on the field)

1909 – Goalkeeper required to wear a distinctive jersey colour; colours allowed: scarlet, white or royal blue

1912 – Goalkeeper restricted to handling the ball in his penalty area (previously he could handle it anywhere in his own half)

1913 – Distance opponents must retire at free kicks changes from 6 yards to 10 yards

1920 – Players no longer offside at throw-in

1921 – Goalkeeper in international matches must wear a deep yellow jersey

1923 – Laws state for the first time that matches are 11-a-side; previously the captains had agreed the numbers on each side although the FA Cup always required 11-a-side

1924 – Concept of 'interfering with play' introduced to the offside Law

Goal may be scored directly from a corner kick

1925 – Player not offside if two (instead of three) opponents are nearer their goal line

1929 – Goalkeeper must stay on goal-line *and not move feet* until penalty kick taken

1937 – The penalty arc of a radius of 10 yards from the penalty-mark introduced

1958 – Substitutes for an injured goalkeeper and one other injured player permitted

1967 – Requirement for a player to be injured before being substituted removed

1970 – Red and yellow cards introduced for the World Cup in Mexico

1990 – Shinguards made compulsory. A player who is '*level*' with the second last defender no longer offside

1992 – Goalkeeper banned from handling the ball if deliberately kicked to him by a team mate

1993 – Red and yellow cards mandatory for all levels of football. Coaches allowed to convey instructions to their teams during the game

1995 – Linesmen re-named Assistant Referees to reflect their role more clearly and to recognise the growing number of women officials in the game

Offside Law clarified to distinguish between an offside 'position' and an offside 'offence' by introduction of concept of 'active play'

1996 – Referees no longer required to judge the 'intent' of a player when challenging for the ball

1997 –   Goal may be scored direct from the kickoff, corner kick
          and goal kick. Yellow card offences of 'ungentlemanly
          conduct' to be called 'unsporting behaviour'.
          Official spelling of off-side changes to offside (hyphen
          goes)
2005      International Football Association Board give approval for
          goal-line technology experimentation using a chip inside
          the ball.

# Notes

1. *Dover Express* – 23 May 1969
2. *East Anglian Daily Times* – 13 September 1986
3. *Brighton Evening Argus* – 27 December 1986
4. *Sun* – 27 December 1986
5. *Brighton Evening Argus* – 27 December 1986
6. *The News* – 11 March 1987
7. *Sun* – 23 November 1987
8. *Sun* – 23 November 1987
9. *News of the World* – 22 November 1987
10. *Liverpool Echo* – 23 November 1987
11. *Daily Mail* – 16 March 1989
12. *Guardian* – 17 March 1989
13. *Observer* – 19 August 1991
14. *Sunday Telegraph* – 23 December 1990
15. *Daily Express* – 24 December 1990
16. *Guardian* – 24 December 1990
17. *Observer* –24 December 1990
18. *Observer* – 22 December 1991
19. *Daily Express* – 19 August 1991
20. *Manchester Evening News* – 19 August 1991
21. *Daily Express* – 28 August 1991
22. *Daily Express* – 28 August 1991
23. *Guardian* – 28 August 1991
24. *Today* – 29 September 1995
25. *FourFourTwo* magazine – December 1995

26. *Today* – 30 September 1995
27. *Daily Express* – 2 October 1995
28. *The Times* – 29 August 1995
29. *Sun* – 29 August 1995
30. *Daily Express* – 30 August 1995
31. *Sporting Life* – 31 August 1995
32. *Guardian* – 10 June 1996
33. *Daily Telegraph* – 19 January 1998
34. *Mail on Sunday* – 4 August 1996
35. *Daily Mail* – 6 October 1997
36. *Daily Telegraph* – 19 January 1998
37. *Derby Post and Herald* – 13 November 1991
38. *Daily Telegraph* – 6 May 1999
39. *Mail on Sunday* – 9 May 1999
40. *Daily Telegraph* – 8 November 2000
41. *Daily Mail* – 24 August 2000
42. *Keane: The Autobiography* by Roy Keane with Eamon Dunphy (Michael Joseph, 2002)
43. *Sun* – 17 August 1998
44. *The Times* – 5 May 2003

# Index

# GREAVSIE

## *Jimmy Greaves*

A goalscoring legend. One of the game's great characters. A man who faced down the demons. Top television pundit and columnist. This is the story of 'Jimmy' Greaves, one of the all-time greats of English football.

'As a goalscorer and human being, Jimmy Greaves has few equals' *Daily Telegraph*

'Greaves could fill a library with his stories' *Independent*

# LEEDS UNITED ON TRIAL

## *David O'Leary*

David O'Leary is arguably the most charismatic football manager in Britain today. But nothing could have prepared him for the astonishing events that were about to engulf him and his young Leeds side at the start of the 2000–2001 season.

*Leeds United on Trial* is the explosive inside account of the season that transformed a youthful, inexperienced side into one of the most feared in Europe, against the background of a high-profile court case that was never out of the headlines. O'Leary talks frankly about how he had to juggle the task of conquering Europe with the trauma and collapse of a major court trial; the £18 million signing of Rio Ferdinand that broke the British transfer record – and how a season that began with a Rivaldo masterclass at the Nou Camp ended with a high tension Premiership duel with Liverpool and a battle with Valencia for a place in the Champions League final.

'O'Leary's honesty and willingness to confront the issues . . . make this an absorbing and illuminating read'
*Sunday Express*

# SERIOUS

## *John McEnroe*

John McEnroe made waves from his very first Wimbledon in 1977. An eighteen-year-old qualifier from Queens, New York, he stunned the tennis world by reaching the semi-finals, and shocked it with his on-court behaviour. What followed was a double act of technique and temperament that set the sport alight: Supermac, the sublime, unorthodox genius, who won seven Grand Slams and seventy-seven singles titles; Superbrat, the foul-mouthed fireball, furiously yelling at officials, fans, players and himself alike.

John McEnroe can be serious. He can also be humorous, impassioned, controversial and painfully honest. This is his autobiography, a book as enthralling and as straight-talking as the great man himself.

'McEnroe emerges as a funny, wise and articulate raconteur, acutely aware of his foibles . . . *Serious* is an antidote to the anodyne dross contained in most sporting autobiographies'
*The Times*

'Frank and engrossing' *Daily Telegraph*

'An ace' *Sunday Telegraph*

# MICHAEL WATSON'S STORY:
# THE BIGGEST FIGHT

## *Michael Watson*

A portrayal of a man whose determination and strength of spirit helped him win the biggest fight of all – the fight for his life.

Michael Watson, the former Commonwealth Middleweight Champion, had his career tragically cut short after a controversial world title fight with Chris Eubank in 1991. The subsequent rematch saw Watson collapse in the twelfth round as a result of the head injuries he had received, and serious brain damage left him paralysed.

Against appalling odds, the twenty-six-year-old boxer made an extraordinary recovery. For a man not expected to live, let alone walk again, completing the London Marathon in 2003 was nothing short of a miracle.

*The Biggest Fight* is a testament to why Michael Watson was, is and always will be 'the people's champion'.

'An inspirational text that celebrates his recovery'
*Guardian*

'One of the most moving books you will read' *Pride*

**Other bestselling Time Warner Books titles available by mail:**

| | | |
|---|---|---|
| ☐ Greavsie | Jimmy Greaves | £6.99 |
| ☐ Leeds United on Trial | David O'Leary | £6.99 |
| ☐ Serious | John McEnroe | £6.99 |
| ☐ Michael Watson's Story: | | |
| The Biggest Fight | Michael Watson | £7.99 |

*The prices shown above are correct at time of going to press. However, the publishers reserve the right to increase prices on covers from those previously advertised without further notice.*

TIME WARNER
BOOKS

**TIME WARNER BOOKS**
**PO Box 121, Kettering, Northants NN14 4ZQ**
**Tel: 01832 737525, Fax: 01832 733076**
**Email: aspenhouse@FSBDial.co.uk**

**POST AND PACKING:**
Payments can be made as follows: cheque, postal order (payable to Time Warner Books), credit card or Switch Card. Do not send cash or currency.

| All UK Orders | **FREE OF CHARGE** |
|---|---|
| EC & Overseas | 25% of order value |

Name (BLOCK LETTERS) ...............................................

Address ...............................................

...............................................

Post/zip code: ...............................................

☐ Please keep me in touch with future Time Warner publications

☐ I enclose my remittance £ .........

☐ I wish to pay by Visa/Access/Mastercard/Eurocard/Switch Card

| | | | | | | | | | | | | | | | | |
|---|---|---|---|---|---|---|---|---|---|---|---|---|---|---|---|---|

Card Expiry Date | | | | |     Switch Issue No. | | |